HOT CARS OF THE
60s

THE BEST CARS OF THE DECADE

HOT CARS OF THE
60s

THE BEST CARS OF THE DECADE

GENERAL EDITOR: CRAIG CHEETHAM

Grange BOOKS

First published in 2004 for Grange Books
An imprint of Grange Books plc
The Grange
Kingsnorth Industrial Estate
Hoo, Nr Rochester
Kent ME3 9ND
www.grangebooks.co.uk

A catalogue record for this book is available from the British Library.

ISBN 1-84013-637-5

Produced by
Amber Books Ltd
Bradley's Close
74–77 White Lion Street
London N1 9PF
www.amberbooks.co.uk

Printed in Singapore

Contents

Introduction

Hot Cars of the '60s celebrates in metal form one of the most significant decades of the 20th century, where people's opinions, lives, and futures were revolutionized. A new world order was born, style and image grew more important than ever, and the automobile became an integral part of everyday life for most people.

Over the course of the decade, the car would advance in appearance, reduce in size, and become a showpiece for modern technology. It would also become an icon of an era that many still regard as one of the most exciting periods in modern history.

The 1960s was a decade of technical innovation and social revolution. It was in 1960 that NASA launched its first space mission—and nine years later, in the same decade, Neil Armstrong became the first man to walk on the moon. In 1962 Telstar 1 became the world's first orbital satellite and Martin Luther King left millions spellbound with a speech that would do wonders for racial harmony in the United States. Technology was moving on

apace, and that meant significant developments across the car industry, with innovations such as electric windows, power steering and radio-cassette players making their debuts on top of the range models. Other inventions of the 1960s included the miniskirt, Doc Martens boots, the push-button telephone, FM radio, the electric typewriter, and the first-ever supersonic airliner—the Concorde, co-developed by British Airways and Air France, so it's no surprise that new and innovative technologies were quickly applied to the automobile as well.

In cinemas, crowds flocked to see the James Bond films, which saw Sean Connery debut as 007 in *Dr No*, followed by the box office smash *Goldfinger*. Other cult movies of the decade included *The Italian Job* and *The Graduate*. All of

A classic in the British mould, the Aston Martin DB6 was more aerodynamic than earlier Aston Martins because of its cut-off style tail.

these movies had a common theme aside from their cultural significance, as each featured a car that was as prominent as its lead actors—James Bond's Aston Martin DB5, Mrs Robinson's Alfa Romeo Duetto and the fleet of red, white, and blue Mini Coopers made these movies. The car had become a cultural icon.

But it was the music for which the 1960s will be best remembered. In the United States, Elvis Presley was the undisputed king of rock 'n' roll and spent the decade at the peak of his career, while the Beach Boys sang the hymns of a surfer generation. For those with more of a social conscience, a young folk singer called Robert Zimmerman made his stage debut in 1961. Known

The Citroën DS was a revolutionary sedan for its time, bristling with technical innovations, such as hydraulically-operated self-levelling suspension and brakes.

as Bob Dylan, by the end of the decade he would be seen as the spokesman of a generation. To each and every one of them, cars were recognized as a theme of their music. Be it a "Little Deuce Coupe" or a "Pink Cadillac," each artist used evocative images of cars to convey their message. Over the other side of the Atlantic, the biggest boy band in history made waves. John Lennon, Paul McCartney, George Harrison, and Ringo Starr became household names as the Beatles drove around in John Lennon's psychedelically-painted Rolls-Royce.

The GT40 was Ford's first foray into motor racing. It spectacularly won the Le Mans 24-hour race in 1966, with three Mk IIs crossing the line in an historic first win.

The 1960s was also a period of war and social upheaval. In 1962 Nuclear War almost broke out following the Cuban Missile crisis, while a year later President John F Kennedy was shot dead as his motorcade drove through Dallas. His Lincoln Continental will always be remembered as the vehicle in which he was assassinated.

AN ERA OF SPEED AND MUSCLE

With so much going on in the world, it is little wonder that the car industry moved on so quickly. In the United States, 1950s excesses gave way to blunt yet effective style—and in *Hot Cars of the '60s* you will find all the classics. In 1964, the Pony Car was born. The Ford Mustang, rightly remembered here in our wonderful studio photographs, became the fastest selling car of all time with over a million finding new homes in the first year of production. The Ford Galaxie proved that big and beautiful could be intrinsically matched, while the Chevrolet Impala became America's favorite family car and the Oldsmobile Toronado proved that not all Detroit performance cars had to have conventional rear-wheel drive.

Later in the decade, the Muscle Car era began. Who could forget the fast and mean street racers of the era, such as the Pontiac GTO, Plymouth Roadrunner, Chevrolet Camaro Z28, Chevrolet

Corvette Sting Ray, Pontiac Trans Am, Oldsmobile 4-4-2, and Shelby GT500?

Then there was the AC Cobra. Born in Britain and developed in the United States by Texan Carroll Shelby, the Cobra was—and remains—one of the most brutal and feared cars ever. Notoriously tricky to drive, yet alluringly beautiful to look at, the Cobra still seduces car enthusiasts around the world.

If you remember these classics fondly, or want to find out more about the ultimate cars of the wildest decade of the 20th century, *Hot Cars of the '60s* brings them closer to you. With expert analyses, detailed driving impressions, and comprehensive technical specifications, this book brings these superb and stylish machines to life once again. Read our descriptions, close your eyes, and imagine a two-lane blacktop opening up in front of you as you pilot the finest of Detroit iron across fast interstate highways.

In the 1960s, American cars were truly unique. Over in Europe, the focus was on changing technologies. Gone were the Detroit-influenced classics such as the Ford Consul and Zodiac, to be replaced by a new era of compact yet fascinating machinery that would bring the industry forward to a level of refinement, luxury, and value for money never before experienced. These developments made the car affordable for all.

Britain's thriving car industry continued to sell millions of motors. At the top end of the market, buyers could choose from the likes of the intricate yet agile Jaguar Mk 2—which rightly claimed to offer "grace, pace, and space"—the effortlessly elegant Rover P5B, or the technically fascinating Rover P6, with its panels bolted onto an unique metal skeleton. On a smaller scale, who could forget the wonderful Mini Cooper—with a wheel at each corner and four full seats, it was a masterpiece of packaging that has become an all-time classic.

FROM THE SPORTY TO THE ECCENTRIC

Sports cars continued to grow in popularity, too. 1961 saw the birth of what many enthusiasts regard as the most beautiful car ever built—the Jaguar E-Type. Capable of 150 mph, yet as affordable as a mid-size luxury saloon, the E-Type had one of the most stunning silhouettes of any car ever created, yet had the performance and handling to match. Other sports car classics included the Aston Martin DB6, made famous by the James Bond movies; the Jensen Interceptor, which used a 6.3-liter American-built Chrysler engine; the Austin Healey 3000, a performance car in its most muscular form; the Lotus Elan, with gorgeous lines and lithe handling; and the Triumph Spitfire, which offered E-Type looks and performance in a package well within the financial reach of the average motorist. Each one of them is featured here in glorious detail.

We've also thrown in a vast selection of other European classics. The wonderfully eccentric Citroën DS is regarded as one of the most original cars ever built, with features such as self-levelling suspension, headlamps that turn with the steering wheel, and class-leading aerodynamics that do not even feature on many of today's executive models. Other famous European classics gathered here include the beautiful VW Karmann Ghia—who would have thought it was a VW Bug underneath? Also featured are the sturdy yet sporty Volvo 120 Amazon, the rally-winning Saab 96, the oddball NSU Wankel Spider, and the opulent Mercedes 600. *Hot Cars of the '60s* also features the original Porsche 911—a classic, stylish sports car still produced in updated form today, 35 years after the original machine hit the streets.

Then there are the true exotics. We could not leave out the seductive Lamborghini Miura, stunning Ferrari 330GT, or characterful Maserati Mistral, could we?

The criteria for selecting the vehicles that feature in this book is simple: they are either cars that were on the roads in the 1960s, or were produced in that revolutionary decade. They are all here—and if they have fired up your engine, then why not check out the other two books in this series. *Hot Cars of the '50s* and *Hot Cars of the '70s* will offer you an encyclopedic knowledge of classic cars covering three decades of fascinating automobile design.

With its sleek profile, sensuous curves, and devastating speed, the Jaguar E-type remains one of the most sought-after sports cars of all time.

UK • US 1963-1965

AC **COBRA 289**

Carroll Shelby had the brilliant idea to crossbreed an AC Ace body and chassis with a Ford V8 engine and the immortal Cobra was born. AC built its chassis in Britain, then shipped it out to California for engine fitting.

"...simply shattering."

"One look at the performance figures for the 289 Cobra tells the story. No other road car in the early 1960s could reach 60 mph so quickly. In a straight line, it is simply shattering, but you have to watch your speed because the Cobra's chassis is hardly sophisticated. Living up to its name, it will snake through bends but it requires the utmost respect and takes skill to pilot properly. The controls are pretty heavy, except for the delightful short-throw gearshift."

Standard interior features include a tachometer and leather bucket seats.

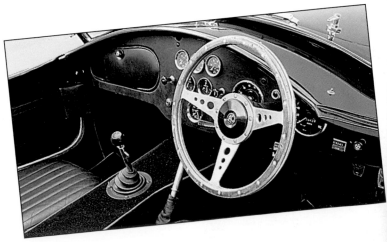

Milestones

1961 Carroll Shelby approaches the Hurlock brothers at AC with the idea to install a V8 engine into their Ace. They jump at the chance.

The AC Ace has more subtle lines than its muscular-looking Cobra offspring.

1962 Production begins at Thames Ditton and Shelby installs 260-cubic inch Ford engines in the U.S.

1963 A larger 289-cubic inch V8 is installed and rack-and-pinion steering replaces worm-and-sector system.

A small number of homologation Cobra 289s were built to qualify the car for sports car racing.

1965 As the monster MKIII Cobra 427 is launched, the 289 model continues into its last year.

1968 Cobra production comes to an end.

UNDER THE SKIN

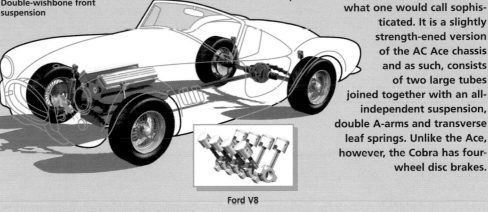

Disc brakes front and rear

Leaf-sprung rear suspension

Double-wishbone front suspension

Ford V8

Tubular chassis

The Cobra's chassis is hardly what one would call sophisticated. It is a slightly strength-ened version of the AC Ace chassis and as such, consists of two large tubes joined together with an all-independent suspension, double A-arms and transverse leaf springs. Unlike the Ace, however, the Cobra has four-wheel disc brakes.

THE POWER PACK

Small-block, big bang

The whole point about the Cobra is its engine—an outsized but lightweight Ford V8 shoehorned into a featherweight home. Carroll Shelby had the idea and completed the engine installation in Venice, California. He chose the Ford small-block V8 engine, as Ford was committing itself to a new Total Performance program and was happy to supply engines. Initially the 260-cubic inch V8 was fitted, but only the first 75 cars had this unit. Then Shelby went up to the 289-cubic inch V8 that had a nominal output of 271 bhp, but many were tuned to make more than 300 bhp. It didn't end there, as the Cobra later got Ford's 427 and 428 units.

289 Cobra

While the later wide-bodied 427 steals the limelight with its superior power, in many ways the narrow-arch 289 is purer to Shelby's concept. It is still outrageously fast and there is something fascinating about a beast that can barely be tamed.

The evocative lines of the 289 Cobra continues to draw gasps of admiration.

AC **COBRA 289**

The AC Cobra is the most legendary U.S. sports car ever manufactured. American muscle combined with a lightweight British sports car body to produced a fast machine. On the track it was almost unbeatable.

Ford V8
Ford agreed to supply Carroll Shelby with its V8 engines for use in the Cobra. Cast into the aluminum valve covers were 'Cobra' and 'Powered by Ford.' The 289 small-block engine produced a very healthy 271 bhp but was light enough not to upset the handling.

Manual transmission
Mated to the Ford V8 engine was a Borg-Warner four-speed manual transmission. A Salisbury final drive and limited-slip differential were also standard.

Sports body
The only body option offered for the Cobra was an open sports style shell with a removable soft-top. The coupe option of the earlier Aceca was not carried over.

AC chassis

John Tojeiro and John Cooper had built various racing chassis in the early 1950s and the design was adapted to sit under the AC Ace. With surprisingly little modification, this large-diameter twin-tube ladder frame was carried over for the Cobra.

Disc brakes

While the old Ace was equipped with drum brakes, the extra performance of the V8 engine led to the sensible fitment of four-wheel disc brakes.

Wire wheels

72-spoke wire wheels with knock off hubs were standard on all 289 Cobras.

Specifications

1963 Shelby Cobra 289

ENGINE

Type: V8

Construction: Cast-iron cylinder block and cylinder heads

Valve gear: Two valves per cylinder operated by single camshaft with pushrods and rockers

Bore and stroke: 4.00 in. x 2.87 in.

Displacement: 289 c.i.

Compression ratio: 10.5:1

Induction system: Single Holley four-barrel carburetor

Maximum power: 271 bhp at 5,750 rpm

Max torque: 285 lb-ft at 4,500 rpm

Top speed: 145 mph

0-60 mph: 5.5 sec.

TRANSMISSION

Four-speed close ratio manual

BODY/CHASSIS

Separate chassis with two-door body in aluminum

SPECIAL FEATURES

The soft-top has a slightly clumsy look to it when up.

The discrete badge just above the cooling vent is the only real clue to the Ford engine.

RUNNING GEAR

Steering: Rack-and-pinion

Front suspension: Wishbones with transverse leaf spring and shocks

Rear suspension: Wishbones with transverse leaf spring and shocks

Brakes: Discs (front and rear)

Wheels: Wire 15-in. dia.

Tires: 6.5 x 15 or 6.7 x 15

DIMENSIONS

Length: 151.5 in.   **Width:** 63.0 in.

Height: 48.0 in.   **Wheelbase:** 90.0 in.

Track: 51.5 in. (front), 52.5 in. (rear)

Weight: 2,020 lbs.

Alfa Romeo SPIDER 1750

One of Alfa Romeo's most successful and best-known models, the Spider remained in production for an incredible 26 years. However, the early boat-tailed 1750-engined cars are probably the most beautiful and exciting to drive.

"...truly delightful."

"Early Spiders, with their painted metal dashboards and deeply set instruments, are truly delightful. On the road, the little car is great to drive. The free-revving 1750 engine has a flat torque curve and offers plenty of grunt at low speeds. The five-speed transmission is extremely slick with short throw. Its all-independent suspension and quick-responding disc brakes enable the Spider to tackle twisty roads with ease."

The simple and uncluttered dashboard is particularly elegant.

Milestones

1966 A new 1600 Spider, with swoopy boat-tail styling by Pininfarina, is launched.

The 2000 Spider was launched in 1971 and supplanted the 1750.

1967 A larger 1750-engined model makes its debut. It is aimed primarily at the U.S. sports car market and is offered with mechanical Spica injection and a five-speed transmission.

The final version of the Spider was the 2000 Quadrifoglio.

1971 The Spider 2000 is introduced. It has revised equipment and a new squared-off tail end.

1986 This year sees the launch of the Spider 2000 Quadrifoglio. New front and rear spoilers and revised body panels give the ageing Spider a more modern look, and the seats are improved for better support. This version is produced with few changes until 1990.

UNDER THE SKIN

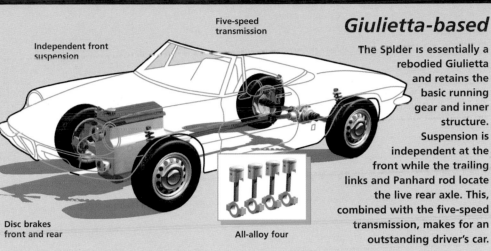

Five-speed transmission

Independent front suspension

Disc brakes front and rear

All-alloy four

Giulietta-based

The Spider is essentially a rebodied Giulietta and retains the basic running gear and inner structure. Suspension is independent at the front while the trailing links and Panhard rod locate the live rear axle. This, combined with the five-speed transmission, makes for an outstanding driver's car.

THE POWER PACK

Classic Alfa four

The 1750 is the classic Alfa twin-cam, regarded by many as the finest four-cylinder engine that Alfa Romeo has produced. Constructed from light alloy, with a bore and stroke of 3.15 inches x 3.48 inches, the engine produces an impressive power output and has a flat torque curve, resulting in a favorable power to weight ratio. All U.S. cars are equipped with a Spica mechanical fuel injection system, which reduces emissions and improves low-speed driveability.

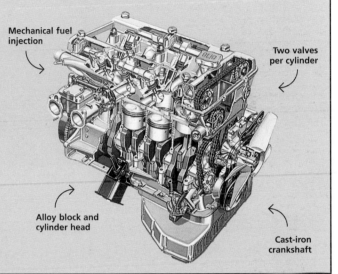

Mechanical fuel injection

Two valves per cylinder

Alloy block and cylinder head

Cast-iron crankshaft

Pure and rare

With the 1750 injection engine, the Duetto was the most exciting Spider to drive. In the eyes of many enthusiasts, it is also the prettiest with its boat-tail rear deck and faired in headlights. It is also rare compared to the later and long running Spider 2000.

The 1750 models are among the rarest of all Spiders.

Alfa Romeo SPIDER 1750

The Spider 1750, nicknamed the Duetto, is one of the all-time classic Alfa Romeos. It was immortalized as Dustin Hoffman's car in the movie *The Graduate*.

Faired-in headlights

Like the Kamm-tailed 2000, the 1750 had faired in headlights. These were aimed at improving the aerodynamics of the car, but weren't fitted to U.S. models.

Improved transmission

The five-speed transmission in the 1750 Spider is an improvement of that in the older Giulia Spider, with the addition of synchromesh on all gears. It is renowned for its quick and smooth shifts and very direct selection.

Steel wheels

Spiders are fitted with steel rims shod with 165/70 SR14 tires. Stopping power is provided by four-wheel discs with single piston calipers.

Conventional suspension

For the time the suspension was rather conventional. At the front are wishbones, coil springs, shock absorbers and an anti-roll bar. The live rear axle is located by trailing arms and a Panhard rod, giving the Spider its exceptional roadholding ability.

Spider hard top

A removable hard top was available as a factory option throughout the range. However, this was not popular and spoiled the classic styling.

Specifications

1967 Alfa Romeo Spider 1750

ENGINE

Type: In-line four-cylinder

Construction: Alloy block and head

Valve gear: Two valves per cylinder operated by twin overhead camshafts

Bore and stroke: 3.15 in. x 3.48 in.

Displacement: 1,779 cc

Compression ratio: 9.0:1

Induction system: Spica mechanical fuel injection

Maximum power: 135 bhp at 5,500 rpm

Maximum torque: 137 lb-ft at 2,900 rpm

Top speed: 118 mph

0-60 mph: 10.0 sec.

TRANSMISSION

Five-speed manual

BODY/CHASSIS

Steel monocoque with two-door convertible body

SPECIAL FEATURES

The 1967 Spider 1750 Veloce is fitted with the traditional Alfa grill.

Faired-in headlights are unique to early models of the Spider.

RUNNING GEAR

Steering: Recirculating ball

Front suspension: Upper and lower wishbones with coil springs, telescopic shock absorbers and anti-roll bar.

Rear suspension: Live axle with trailing arms, Panhard rod, coil springs, anti-roll bar and telescopic shock absorbers

Brakes: Discs (front and rear)

Wheels: Steel disc, 14-in. dia.

Tires: 165/70 SR14

DIMENSIONS

Length: 161.23 in.   **Width:** 64.1 in.

Height: 50.8 in.   **Wheelbase:** 88.6 in.

Track: 52.2 in. (front), 50.2 in. (rear)

Weight: 2,315 lbs.

Aston **MARTIN DB6**

Few cars are so quintessentially British as the Aston Martin DB6. Elegance, hand-built craftsmanship, power, ruggedness, and charm combine to produce a wonderful expression of classic Gran Turismo qualities.

"...a magical drive."

"Step inside the DB6 and the smell of the leather upholstery, the feel of the wood-rimmed steering wheel, and the cluster of gauges tell you that this is going to be a magical drive. There is a lot of power under your right foot, and despite its bulk, the DB6 is surprisingly quick off the line. The handling is old fashioned but faithful. It is fast through the gears and stops quickly and very straight.

The DB6 has one of the greatest interiors of all British classic cars. Dashboard, carpets and trim all exude quality.

Milestones

1965 The new DB6 is launched
to replace the DB5. Unlike the DB5, it uses a more modern monocoque construction. Its cut-off tail improves aerodynamics, increasing top speed despite the extra weight.

The open-top Volante is the most valuable DB6 model.

1969 A DB6 Mk 2 is introduced.
It has DBS-style wider wheels and flared arches, as well as power steering and the option of fuel injection.

Aston Martin revived the famous DB line with the DB7, which was launched in 1994.

1970 Production draws
to a close and the DB6 retires as the most popular Aston Martin yet made. Its replacement, the DBS, has been in production since 1967. The DBS V8 is the last of the DB line until the arrival of the DB7 in 1994.

UNDER THE SKIN

Live rear axle

Limited-slip differential

Aluminum body panels

4.0-liter in-line six

Traditional qualities

Unlike its predecessors, the DB6 has a more traditional construction of box-section steel inner panels over the steel floorpan with aluminum bodywork. The DB6 has a 3.7-inch longer wheelbase than the DB5, but retains the basic suspension layout of double wishbones and coil springs up front, with a live rear axle with Watt linkage, radius arms, and coil springs at the rear.

THE POWER PACK

A well proven six

By the time it went into the DB6, the Tadek-Marek-designed straight-six had grown to 4.0 liters. Of all-alloy lightweight construction, the engine features double overhead camshafts, seven main bearings, and solid valve lifters. In standard tune, it is fitted with three SU carburetors and develops 282 bhp. The very popular Vantage engine option has triple twin-choke Weber 45DCOE carburetors and pumps out 325 bhp at 5,750 rpm.

Two chain-driven overhead camshafts

Two valves per cylinder

Seven main bearings

All-alloy construction

Best choice

The Vantage engine, with its extra power and performance, is the obvious power unit to choose. Although the coupe is graceful, the Volante convertible is a timeless design. Its electric roof folds neatly away at the touch of a button.

The cut-off tail with lip spoiler is a DB6 trademark.

Aston MARTIN DB6

With its graceful lines, elegant interior, and sophisticated mechanicals, the DB6 lived up to the Aston Martin reputation of providing expensive upper-class Grand Touring cars.

Alloy engine

The Tadek-Marek-designed straight-six is made of light alloy. It features removable wet liners and wet sump lubrication. All engines have triple carburetors except for the Vantage powerplant which has twin-choke Webers.

Four-wheel disc brakes

To stop more than 3,000 lbs. from speeds approaching 150 mph, disc brakes are necessary. They are substantial and are clearly visible through the chromed wire wheels.

Kamm tail

While the DB6's rear end styling may lack the purity of line of the original DB4/DB5 design by Touring of Milan, it certainly helps aerodynamics. The raised rear lip forms a spoiler and halves the aerodynamic lift on the rear end, thereby boosting high-speed stability.

Choice of body styles

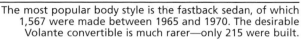

The most popular body style is the fastback sedan, of which 1,567 were made between 1965 and 1970. The desirable Volante convertible is much rarer—only 215 were built.

Luxurious interior

The interior is of the highest quality. Wall-to-wall carpeting, rich leather upholstery, multiple gauges and a racing-style wood/metal sandwich steering wheel are just some of its features.

1965 Aston Martin DB6 Vantage

ENGINE

Type: In-line six-cylinder

Construction: Aluminum block and head

Valve gear: Two valves per cylinder operated by double overhead camshafts

Bore and stroke: 3.77 in. x 3.62 in.

Displacement: 3,995 cc

Compression ratio: 8.9:1

Induction system: Three twin-choke Weber carburetors

Maximum power: 325 bhp at 5,750 rpm

Maximum torque: 290 lb-ft at 4,500rpm

Top speed: 150 mph

0-60 mph: 6.7 sec.

TRANSMISSION
Five-speed manual or three-speed automatic

BODY/CHASSIS
Integral steel chassis with two-door aluminum coupe or convertible body

SPECIAL FEATURES

The wire wheels are held on by central spinners which have to be knocked off using a special mallet.

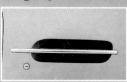

The vents in the front fenders are still a current feature on new Aston Martins.

RUNNING GEAR

Steering: Rack-and-pinion

Front suspension: Double wishbones with coil springs, telescopic shocks and anti-roll bar

Rear suspension: Live axle with radius arms, Watt linkage, telescopic shocks and coil springs

Brakes: Discs (front and rear)

Wheels: Spoked, 15-in. dia.

Tires: 6.70 x 15 in.

DIMENSIONS

Length: 182 in.   **Width:** 66 in.

Height: 52 in.   **Wheelbase:** 101.8 in.

Track: 54 in. (front), 53.5 in. (rear)

Weight: 3,418 lbs.

Austin HEALEY 3000

The combination of Austin's 3-liter engine and Donald Healey's sports car produced a rugged classic with enormous character and an impressive competition record.

"...it needs a firm hand."

"Healeys are not the easiest of cars to drive, as the 'works' rally drivers would testify. Steering is heavy and shifting is awkward (although flicking a switch in and out of overdrive is delightfully easy). The Healey's basic tendency is to go straight at corners, so it needs a firm hand. Bumpy roads will throw the stiffly sprung back axle off line, make the scuttle shake and the steering wheel kick. Apply too much power in corners and you easily trade understeer for oversteer, though that's just an accepted part of the car's character."

MkIII Austin-Healey 3000 has improved interior with a wooden dashboard.

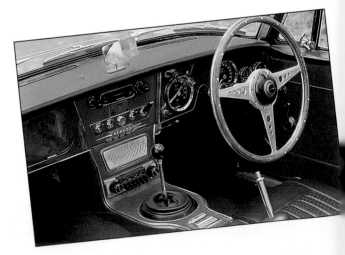

Milestones

1952 Healey 100 is completed in time for the British Motor Show. It has a four cylinder, 90-bhp Austin A90 engine. The design is built by BMC as an Austin-Healey.

1956 100 turns into the 100/6 when equipped with Austin's 2.6-liter, six-cylinder engine.

The 3000 was a great rally car. The fiercest of all 'works' cars were Mark IIIs with 210 bhp.

1959 3000 introduced with power up to 124 bhp.

1960 Proving what a great rally car the 3000 is, Pat Moss wins the Liège-Rome-Liège Rally.

1961 Power increases to 132 bhp producing the 3000 MkII. A restyle takes place in the following year.

Austin-Healey experimented with a closed version of the 3000, but it never reached production.

1964 Definitive 3000, the MkIII appears. Rauno Aaltonen/Tony Ambrose win the Spa-Sofia-Liège rally in one.

UNDER THE SKIN

Fold-away soft-top in 1962

2+2 seating

Front disc brakes

Double-wishbone front suspension

Underslung chassis

Straight-six

Limited travel

A traditional ladder-frame chassis is used with a cruciform brace, but where such chassis usually kick up at the rear to clear the axle, the Healey's chassis rails run below, limiting suspension travel. Front suspension is a modified form of that used on the A90 sedan, while cam-and-peg steering is used. Earlier Healeys have brake drums all around but the 3000 uses discs at the front.

THE POWER PACK

C-Series improved

Healey modified the Austin C-Series engine built for sedans like the Austin A90. It has a cast-iron block and cylinder head with a single block-mounted camshaft and conventional rocker-driven overhead valves. The camshaft profile is modified and the cylinder head is improved to increase power, which ranges from the 124 bhp of the Austin-Healey 100/6 to the 148 bhp of the final 3000 variant, which could also boast 165 lb-ft of torque. With triple Weber carburetors for competition, 210 bhp is possible.

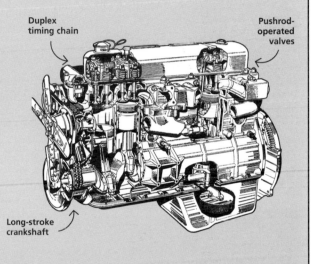

Duplex timing chain

Pushrod-operated valves

Long-stroke crankshaft

Ultimate mark

The last, the best, and definitely the fastest of the 3000 line is the MkIII. It has an improved interior, wooden dashboard, power up from 131 bhp to 148 bhp, plus a revised chassis which improves the rear suspension and better locates the back axle.

Best interior and most power make the MkIII the one to have.

Austin **HEALEY 3000**

This hybrid designed by Donald Healey and incorporating Austin running gear helped make the 3000 one of the greatest British sports cars ever assembled.

Knock-on wire wheels

Traditional knock-on center-lock wire wheels are the usual fitment on the Austin-Healey, although bolt-on steel disc wheels were available.

Austin engine

All the 'Big Healeys', as they were commonly known, use modified cast-iron Austin engines. They are uncomplicated overhead-valve designs, but are tuneable and very strong.

Front disc brakes

Early Austin-Healeys were drum braked but from 1959 more effective servo-assisted discs were fitted at the front.

In-house styling

Donald Healey relied on his own company to style the original Healey 100, and much of that style lived on in the 3000.

Poor ground clearance

Austin-Healeys are notorious for their poor ground clearance and the exhaust system is particularly vulnerable. This was a great problem for the rally cars and one reason why clearance was improved in 1964.

Two-seaters and 2+2s

From 1962 the two-seater option was deleted and all the 3000 MkII and MkIII models were 2+2s, so occasional passengers could be squeezed in.

Live rear axle

Donald Healey did not want the expense and complication of independent rear suspension and used a live axle. At one time there was a Panhard rod but that was discarded after 1964 and radius arms were fitted.

Cam-and-peg steering

Although the smaller Austin-Healey Sprite uses rack-and-pinion steering, the 3000 has a less precise cam-and-peg system because it was easier to accommodate with the big six-cylinder engine.

Underslung chassis

The chassis was designed for a low, sleek look with the rear axle mounted above the chassis rails.

Specifications

1964 Austin-Healey 3000 MkIII

ENGINE
Type: In-line six cylinder

Construction: Cast-iron block and head

Valve gear: Two in-line valves per cylinder operated by single block-mounted camshaft, pushrods and rockers

Bore and stroke: 3.26 in. x 3.50 in.

Displacement: 2,912 cc

Compression ratio: 9.0:1

Induction system: Two SU carburetors

Maximum power: 148 bhp at 5,250 rpm

Maximum torque: 165 lb-ft at 3,500 rpm

Top speed: 121 mph

0-60 mph: 10.1 sec.

TRANSMISSION
Four-speed manual with overdrive on third and fourth gear

BODY/CHASSIS
X-braced ladder-frame chassis with steel 2+2 convertible body

SPECIAL FEATURES

The left-exiting exhaust on this car indicates that this is a left-hand-drive model. Around 90 percent of 3000s were exported.

The big six-cylinder engine generates a lot of heat and the competition cars have large vents behind the front wheels to help cooling.

RUNNING GEAR
Steering: Cam-and-peg

Front suspension: Double wishbones, coil springs, lever arm shocks and anti-roll bar

Rear suspension: Live axle with semi-elliptic leaf springs, lever arm shocks and radius arms

Brakes: Discs (front), drums (rear)

Wheels: Knock-on center-lock wire spoke 4.5 in. x 15 in.

Tires: Crossply 5.9 in. x 15 in.

DIMENSIONS
Length: 157.5 in. **Width:** 60.5 in.

Height: 50 in. **Wheelbase:** 92 in.

Track: 48.8 in. (front), 50 in. (rear)

Weight: 2,549 lbs.

BMW 2000 CS

Before BMW's great six-cylinder coupes like the 3.0 CS and CSL or the 635 CSi, the company built the striking 2000 CS. This relied on a 135-bhp four-cylinder engine to give it its 115-mph top speed.

"...a pleasure to drive."

"The 2000 CS just radiates class, style and high-quality construction. This distinctive-looking coupe is very comfortable and a pleasure to drive, too. Its suspension combines enough travel for a comfortable ride, with good enough location to give impressive handling. There is a fair amount of roll upon hard cornering. These characteristics make the car easy to live with, even if the performance from the 2.0-liter engine is anything but outstanding."

Even 30 years later, the BMW's tidy dashboard has an air of refined distinction.

Milestones

1962 BMW builds

what proves to be one of its most important models, the now almost-forgotten 1500 sedan. It starts BMW on the road to true mass production and is progressively given bigger engines to form the 1800 and then 2000 sedans.

The 2000 CS took its styling cues from the upmarket 3200 CS.

1965 BMW chooses

its home Motor Show at Frankfurt to unveil the new 2000 CS coupe. It is based on the 1800 sedan but has an enlarged 2.0-liter engine and more power. The styling is inspired by the exclusive 3200 CS model, and the bodies are made by Karmann.

Sleek and fast, the 3.0 CSL is the ultimate evolution of the theme.

1969 2000 CS

production comes to an end after just over 8,800 have been made. It is replaced by the 2800 CS, as BMW decides its coupes should be more desirable six-cylinder designs.

UNDER THE SKIN

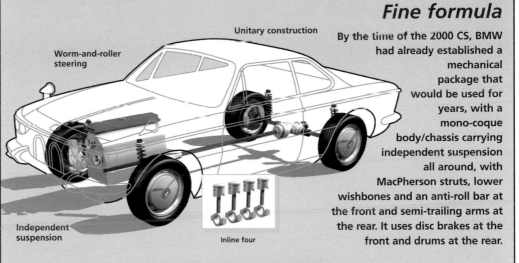

Worm-and-roller steering

Unitary construction

Independent suspension

Inline four

Fine formula

By the time of the 2000 CS, BMW had already established a mechanical package that would be used for years, with a mono-coque body/chassis carrying independent suspension all around, with MacPherson struts, lower wishbones and an anti-roll bar at the front and semi-trailing arms at the rear. It uses disc brakes at the front and drums at the rear.

THE POWER PACK

Growth process

To give the CS coupe the extra power it greatly needed, BMW enlarged its existing 1.8-liter, four-cylinder engine to 1,990 cc by boring the cylinders out to 3.50 inches (making it very oversquare). It is the same engine as fitted in the more famous BMW 2002. The cast-iron block is topped by a free-flowing, alloy cylinder head with hemispherical combustion chambers and two valves per cylinder opened by a single chain-driven overhead camshaft. With a 9.3:1 compression ratio and two twin-choke Solex sidedraft carburetors, power is very respectable at 135 bhp in U.S. ratings.

Good looker

These days, the 2000 CS is bought exclusively for its distinctive style rather than its performance, as it can easily be out-performed by the later 2002 models such as the Ti, which are shorter, narrower, lighter and therefore faster.

Its well-proportioned lines helped the 2000 CS establish a name for itself.

BMW 2000 CS

Although it was obviously inspired by the look of the bigger Bertone-designed, V8-powered 3200 CS coupe, the 2000 CS was designed independently by BMW and was easily just as stylish and attractive.

Four-cylinder engine

The inline, single overhead-cam, 2.0-liter, four-cylinder engine developed for the 2000 was an excellent and extremely strong design, which was used more effectively in the lighter 2002 models.

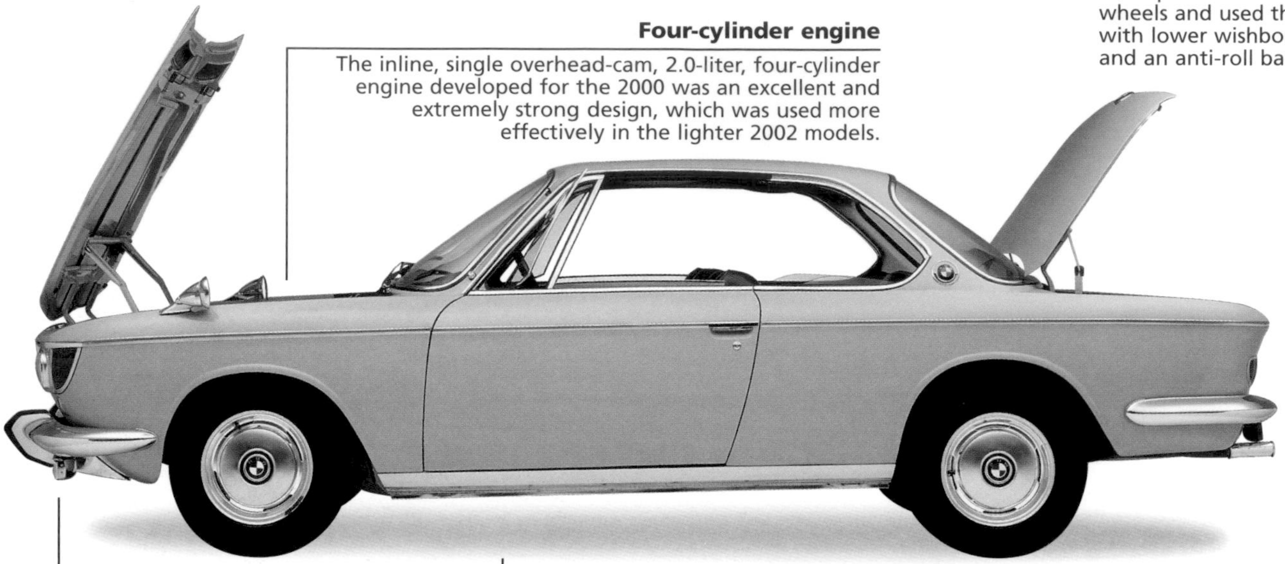

MacPherson struts

In the 1960s, BMW decided MacPherson struts were the ideal way to suspend the front wheels and used them with lower wishbones and an anti-roll bar.

Pillarless design

One of the keys to the 2000 CS's good looks is the absence of a central door pillar. This helps give a longer, sleeker look.

Covered lights

In Europe, the 2000 CS was sold with its original headlight design of one round and one square light behind curved glass covers. But this arrangement was illegal in the U.S., where the car had two small headlights without glass coverings.

Specifications

1966 BMW 2000 CS

ENGINE

Type: Inline four-cylinder

Construction: Cast-iron block and alloy cylinder head

Valve gear: Two valves per cylinder operated by an overhead camshaft

Bore and stroke: 3.50 in. x 3.15 in.

Displacement: 1,990 cc

Compression ratio: 9.3:1

Induction system: Two Solex 40 PHH sidedraft carburetors

Maximum power: 135 bhp at 5,800 rpm

Maximum torque: 123 lb-ft at 3,600 rpm

Top speed: 115 mph

0-60 mph: 11.3 sec

TRANSMISSION
Four-speed manual

BODY/CHASSIS
Unitary monocoque construction with steel two-door coupe body

SPECIAL FEATURES

U.S.-market cars have exposed quad headlights with no glass covering.

The 2000 CS came with these standard steel wheels which suit the car's uncluttered and simple lines.

RUNNING GEAR

Steering: Worm-and-roller

Front suspension: MacPherson struts with lower wishbones, telescopic shock absorbers and anti-roll bar

Rear suspension: Semi-trailing arms with coil springs and telescopic shock absorbers

Brakes: Discs, 10.8-in. dia. (front), drums, 9.8-in. dia. (rear)

Wheels: Pressed steel discs, 14-in. dia.

Tires: 6.95 x 14

DIMENSIONS

Length: 178.3 in.   **Width:** 65.9 in.

Height: 53.5 in.   **Wheelbase:** 100.4 in.

Track: 52.4 in. (front), 54.3 in. (rear)

Weight: 2,630 lbs.

Four-speed transmission

With the four-speed manual, BMW had top gear as the conventional 1:1 ratio and geared the final-drive ratio to give 19.8 mph per thousand revs as the best compromise between outright performance and acceptable top-gear cruising. Buyers could opt for a ZF three-speed automatic instead.

Chevrolet CORVETTE STING RAY

When Chevrolet® introduced the Corvette Sting Ray in 1963, it was the quickest roadster Detroit had ever made. Its 327-cubic inch V8 gave the new Corvette serious muscle, and for the first time, an American sports car could out-gun its European rivals.

"America's favorite sports car."

"Off the line, this Vette™ has the kind of low-end grunt that will leave most modern sports cars in a cloud of dust and burning rubber. First you hear the throaty rumble of the big-shouldered 427 V8, then the three two-barrel carbs snarl to life and you can feel the power throb through the chrome shifter. Both the steering and clutch are heavy, while the handling and brakes are crude by today's standards. But that snap-your-head-back lunge of power still makes the Sting Ray America's favorite sports car."

The cockpit is spartan and functional with a classic hot rod feel often imitated but never quite equaled.

Milestones

1953 The first Motorama Corvette
show car enters production with a six-cylinder engine.

1955 Zora Arkus-Duntov, father of the Sting Ray, becomes head of the Corvette program, a position he held until retirement in 1982. Under him, manual transmission and the V8 engine are offered as options (1955) and fuel injection becomes available (1957).

1957 The Vette is the fastest real production car in the world, showing what can be done when conventional engineering is applied well.

The 1963 convertible. Soft top is stored under a panel behind the seats.

1963 The first Sting Ray production car is built, with all-independent suspension and the first coupe body. Its styling is based on a racing car design originally developed in 1958 by Bill Mitchell.

1965 Big-block engine and disc brakes are available. The 396-cubic inch V8 with a solid cam is introduced with 425 bhp.

1967 Pinnacle of performance is the L88 427-cubic inch V8. This also marks the last year of this body style.

UNDER THE SKIN

Steel ladder frame

Independent rear suspension sprung by a transverse leaf spring

All-around disc brakes replaced drums in 1965

Fiberglass body

Optional knock-off aluminum wheels

Traditional American V8

Technical advances

The 1963 Sting Ray was the first Corvette to have independent suspension. Earlier cars had used obsolete 1953 Chevy sedan suspension. The 1965 was the first Corvette with disc brakes. The V8 engine drives the rear wheels through a four-speed manual or a three-speed automatic transmission.

THE POWER PACK

Chevy® V8s

The Sting Ray started out with Chevrolet's famous small-block V8. This 327 engine made from 250 bhp up to 375 bhp with fuel injection. In 1965, the Corvette gained the new Mark IV big-block engine. Power increased to 425 bhp from its 396 V8. In 1966, the engine was enlarged again to 427-cubic inches and made up to 425 bhp. The 435 bhp 427 L88 was offered the very next year.

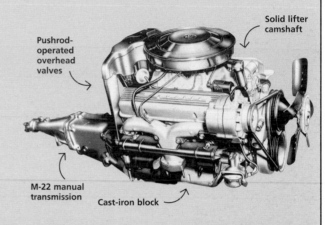

Solid lifter camshaft

Pushrod-operated overhead valves

M-22 manual transmission

Cast-iron block

Split rear window

The most sought-after Sting Ray is the 1963 split rear window coupe model. The designer, Bill Mitchell, intended it to form a visual connection with the central raised sections on the hood. The feature was dropped because it spoiled rear vision. Some later cars have been retro-fitted with the center pillar in an attempt to raise their values.

The split rear window coupe was only available in 1963.

Chevrolet CORVETTE STING RAY

The Sting Ray was introduced in 1963, 10 years after the Corvette's first appearance. The engine is set well back in the frame, giving nearly 50/50 weight distribution and excellent handling for the day.

Fiberglass body

Like all Corvettes, the Sting Ray has a body made from a number of fiberglass panels mounted on a traditional separate frame.

Disc brakes all around

Vented discs with dual-pot calipers on each wheel were fitted from 1965. While old stocks lasted, buyers could opt for the discontinued drums to save money.

V8 engine

Apart from the very early models, all Corvettes are powered by V8 engines. There is a wide variety of displacements and states of tune. The 327-cubic inch engine in 350-bhp tune is typical.

Optional side exhausts

The Sting Ray's enormous options list included the Side Mount Exhaust System. The side pipes are covered with a perforated shield to prevent the driver or passengers from burning themselves. Side exhausts were chosen mainly for visual effect.

No trunk lid

To preserve the contour of the car, there is no trunk lid and access to the luggage compartment is from behind the seats.

Foldaway top

The Corvette's convertible top folds away completely when not in use and is stored beneath a flush-fitting fiberglass panel behind the driver. Optional hard top cost $231.75 in 1966.

Alloy gearbox and clutch housing

To save weight, the Sting Ray was given an alloy clutch housing and an alloy-cased gearbox. This also improved weight distribution.

32

Flip-up headlights

The headlights are rotated by two reversible vacuum operated motors—a postwar first for an American car.

Triple side vents

Side vent arrangement, like many minor details, changed over the years. The 1965 and '66 models like this one have three vents.

Independent rear suspension

Another Corvette first, the Sting Ray has a crude but effective system with a transverse leaf spring mounted behind the differential.

Specifications
1966 Chevrolet Corvette Sting Ray

ENGINE
Type: V8, 90°

Construction: Cast-iron block and heads; Single cam, pushrods

Bore and stroke: 4.0 in. x 3.25 in.

Displacement: 327 c.i.

Compression ratio: 11:1

Induction system: Rochester fuel injection or one/two Carter four-barrel carbs

Maximum power: 375 bhp at 6,200 rpm

Maximum torque: 350 lb-ft at 4,000 rpm

Top speed: 135 mph

0-60 mph: 5.6 sec.

TRANSMISSION
Three-speed automatic (optional four-speed manual)

BODY/CHASSIS
Steel ladder frame with two-door convertible or coupe fiberglass body

SPECIAL FEATURES

Innovative retractable headlights.

Soft top folds away neatly into compartment behind seats, with luggage space below.

RUNNING GEAR
Front suspension: Double wishbone, coil springs, anti-roll bar

Rear suspension: Semi-trailing arms, half-shafts and transverse links with transverse leaf spring

Brakes: Vented discs with four-pot calipers (optional cast-iron drums)

Wheels: Five-bolt steel (knock off aluminum optional) 6 in. x 15 in.

Tires: 6.7 in. x 15 in. Firestone Super Sport 170

DIMENSIONS

Length: 175.3 in.	**Width:** 69.6 in.
Height: 49.8 in.	**Wheelbase:** 98 in.

Track: 56.3 in. (front), 57 in. (rear)

Weight: 3,150 lbs.

USA 1966

Chevrolet SUBURBAN

Launched in 1935, the Suburban is one of Chevy's best-loved and longest-lasting nameplates. With examples like this outstanding high-riding 1966 model, it is easy to see why.

"...a perfect match."

"If there was ever a near-perfect match between classic looks and modern levels of comfort and dependability, this is it. The seats are supportive and the cabin is light-years away from a stock 1966 Suburban. Performance is better, especially with a 300-bhp small-block under the hood. This rig can hold its own on the highway and gobbles up the miles with ease, but with its big, grippy tires and strong 4-WD driveline, it makes light work of rock crawling, too."

Digital gauges and modern seats are a tasteful and practical addition.

Milestones

1935 The Model EB Suburban, a steel-bodied station wagon built off the Master Series Truck, arrives on the scene. It can seat eight people and is offered with a number of different door configurations.

The shorter C/K-5 Blazer supplemented the Suburban from 1969.

1960 Like the rest of Chevy's C10 series, the Suburban gets new angular sheetmetal, yet is still available with rear doors or a tailgate, plus six cylinder or V8 power.

Suburbans are still built off the full-size pickup platform.

1962 The full-size trucks revert to single headlamps and front-end styling, and model designations are simplified.

1966 A revamped C10 arrives.

Complete Jimmy driveline

Power front disc brakes

Separate steel chassis

Worked small-block V8

Four by far

In 1966, the Suburban was built off the short-wheelbase C-14 pickup, which meant a separate, ladder-type chassis and a choice of two-wheel or four-wheel drive configurations. With four-wheeling in mind, the owner of this rig decided to upgrade his vehicle. It now rides on front and rear axles and wheels from a 1980 Jimmy, which also donated its power front disc brakes. Airlift shocks mean the ride height can be raised or lowered depending on changes in terrain.

THE POWER PACK

Better than stock

The base powerplant for the 1966 Suburban was the ancient Thriftmaster six, which, with its 140 bhp and single one-barrel Rochester carburetor, was not very sporty. Bigger 250 and 292 sixes, plus 283- and 327-cubic inch small-block V8s, were available for those who wanted more grunt; but for the owner of this truck, even these were not enough. Sitting between the light blue fenderwells is a 1970-vintage 350-cubic inch motor. With an 8.5:1 compression ratio, Edelbrock Performer intake manifold, and four-barrel carburetor, it packs a whopping 300 bhp and 380 lb-ft of torque.

Sixties simplicity

Back in the 1960s, the Suburban was far from the luxury wagon it is today. Most were still purchased for commercial duties, which explains why only 12,051 were built for 1966. Nevertheless, these old trucks possess plenty of character and simple, robust mechanicals, making them ideal candidates for resto-mod duty.

With only a few modifications, this 1966 Suburban really turns heads.

Chevrolet SUBURBAN

Amazingly, the turquoise paintwork of this 1966 Suburban is the original factory color. Subtle graphics and stock 8 x 15-inch color-coded wheels lend it a thoroughly modern look, however.

Jimmy suspension

With greater ground clearance than a stock K-14 Suburban, this vehicle owes its increased ride height to a 1980-vintage GMC Jimmy. The modern sport utility also donated its front and rear axles, plus the center differential. With less weight than a stock 1980 Jimmy, this Suburban can tackle all but the roughest terrain with considerable ease.

Final year styling

The 1966 full-size trucks were final iteration of the 1960 de Over the seasons, the appear of these rigs was cleaned up satisfy buyer tastes. The grill hood brightwork were simpli for 1962, and single headlam returned for the first time. T 1967 line was even cleaner.

Rear tailgate

In 1966, as today, the Suburban could be ordered with either twin rear hinging doors or a drop-down tailgate. This one has the latter and it opens in two sections making the truck easier to load and unload.

Original and modern

One of the most appealing aspects of this truck is the interior. The stock dash is kept, but the instruments have been replaced. The old seats have been replaced by late-model buckets, which offer more support for the driver and passengers.

Hi-po small-block

A torquey 350-cubic inch V8 is just the ticket for towing and off-road excursions. With 380 lb-ft, it can power the Suburban to 60 mph in 10.4 seconds.

Specifications
1966 Chevrolet Suburban

ENGINE
Type: V8
Construction: Cast-iron block and heads
Valve gear: Two valves per cylinder operated by a single V-mounted camshaft with pushrods and rockers
Bore and stroke: 4.00 in. x 3.48 in.
Displacement: 350 c.i.
Compression ratio: 8.5:1
Induction system: Edelbrock Performer four-barrel carburetor
Maximum power: 300 bhp at 4,800 rpm
Maximum torque: 380 lb-ft at 3,200 rpm
Top speed: 114 mph
0-60 mph: 10.4 sec.

TRANSMISSION
700RS four-speed automatic

BODY/CHASSIS
Separate steel chassis with two-door station wagon body

SPECIAL FEATURES

The embroidered bowtie logo on the headrest is just one of several subtle touches.

These wheels are stock items on 1980 Blazers and Jimmys.

RUNNING GEAR
Steering: Recirculating-ball
Front suspension: Live axle with semi-elliptic leaf springs and telescopic shock absorbers
Rear suspension: Live axle with semi-elliptic leaf springs and telescopic shock absorbers
Brakes: Discs (front), drums (rear)
Wheels: Pressed steel, 8 x 15 in.
Tires: BF Goodrich All Terrain

DIMENSIONS
Length: 193.19 in.   **Width:** 86.8 in.
Height: 81.6 in.   **Wheelbase:** 115.0 in.
Track: 74.9 in. (front), 66.7 in. (rear)
Weight: 3,850 lbs.

Chevy IMPALA SS 427

When Chevrolet put the engine used in the Corvette® in very nearly the same tune into the big Impala SS™, the car's sheer size meant the result wasn't quite as dramatic. It did, however, produce a high-speed cruiser with plenty of power to spare.

"...full-size muscle monster."

"For some, bigger is better, and this is certainly true of the SS 427. The front bucket seats are huge. The monster 427-cubic inch V8 has enough torque to move mountains and motivates the tremendous bulk of the Impala down the road at maximum velocity. It would be natural to think that the SS 427 would plow through corners, but a wide track and well-located rear end ensure this is one of the better behaved full-size muscle monsters of the late 1960s.

The Impala SS has full instrumentation and tremendous interior space.

Milestones

1965 Impalas are redesigned

with smoother, more modern contours and a new perimeter chassis, plus revised suspension. The Impala SS returns with available bucket seats and a new optional Mark IV 396-cubic inch V8 engine. The 409 will be dropped at the end of the year.

The last year for the boxy, square Impala SS was 1964.

1966 Externally, few changes mark

this year's full-size Chevys®. The big news is under the hood. The 396 engine is joined by a larger 427-cubic inch unit available in 390-bhp and 425-bhp versions.

1965 Impala SS models came standard with an in-line six.

1967 A new fastback

roof is grafted to the Impala Sport Coupe.

1969 Having reverted

to an option package in 1968, the Impala SS is retired this year.

UNDER THE SKIN

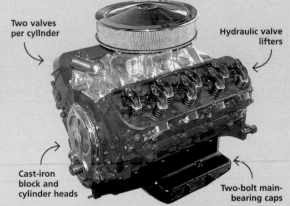

Body-on-frame construction

Power front disc brakes

Live rear axle

Big-block V8

Strong frame

For the 1965 model year, Chevrolet introduced a new perimeter chassis frame for the Impala, plus revised the suspension with a wider front and rear track which made the car more stable during high-speed cornering. The frame had to be strong so that the pillarless two-door coupe bodies of the SS versions could be fitted without flexing. The faster SS versions had superior rear axle location with four, rather than three, links.

THE POWER PACK

The fat rat

In 1966, Chevrolet launched its 427, an enlarged version of the 396-cubic inch V8 which was more common to find in a Corvette than a full-size car. The following year, it was available in full-size cars. The standard 427 engine returned for 1968 with a power output of 385 bhp and a four-barrel carburetor in full-size cars (GM outlawed multi-carb setups in 1967 on all models but the Corvette). The engine continued until 1969, by which time it thumped out 390 bhp.

Two valves per cylinder

Hydraulic valve lifters

Cast-iron block and cylinder heads

Two-bolt main-bearing caps

Milestone SS

1967 was a milestone for the SS Impala. The Impala was reskinned with larger, swoopier sheet metal. It was also the first and last year that the SS 427 was a model in its own right. Today, these cars make an interesting alternative to Chevelles and Camaros.

The 1967 Impala SS with fastback styling and the 427 is the one to go for.

Chevy IMPALA SS 427

'For the man who'd buy a sports car if it had this much room' was how Chevrolet marketed the Impala SS 427. It was a fine machine, with a huge torquey V8, seating for five and a well-engineered suspension.

Four transmissions

The big V8s could be matched to a variety of transmissions: a three- or four-speed heavy-duty manual; Powerglide; or strong TurboHydramatic 400 three-speed automatic.

V8 engine

The fastest of all the Impalas, the SS 427 is powered by the same short-stroke cast-iron 427-cubic inch engine found in the Corvette. Despite its size, it is happy to rev and produces its maximum power at 5,200 rpm with maximum torque coming in at 3,400 rpm. In its highest state of tune, Chevrolet claimed 385 bhp for the Impala engine.

Front disc brakes

Front disc brakes are a necessity for the faster SS models with their high performance and weight. For the SS, Chevrolet made front discs an option, which came with different wheels for $121.15.

Heavy-duty suspension

The best-handling SS Impalas use the optional heavy-duty F41 suspension with its stiffer springs and shocks. At just $31.60, it was a very small price to pay for the extra handling security.

Fastback style

The fastback style was very fashionable in the 1960s and helped give a sporty look to very large cars. The size of cars like the Impala and the Ford Galaxie meant they could have a long sloping rear roof line and still have room for rear passengers.

Front parking lights

The ends of the front fenders contain what look like turn signals. In fact, they are just parking lights, with the turn signals located in the lower grill assembly.

Pillarless construction

Chevrolet gave the Impala its sleek look by the use of two styling features. As well as the long, sloping rear fastback, the car has pillarless construction. This accentuates the side window glass area and makes it appear bigger than it really is.

Specifications
1968 Chevrolet Impala SS 427

ENGINE
Type: V8
Construction: Cast-iron block and heads
Valve gear: Two valves per cylinder operated by a single camshaft with pushrods and rockers
Bore and stroke: 4.25 in. x 3.76 in.
Displacement: 427 c.i.
Compression ratio: 10.3:1
Induction system: Single four-barrel carburetor
Maximum power: 305 bhp at 5,200 rpm
Maximum torque: 460 lb-ft at 3,400 rpm
Top speed: 125 mph
0-60 mph: 8.4 sec.

TRANSMISSION
M21 four-speed manual

BODY/CHASSIS
Box-section perimeter chassis with two-door fastback hardtop body

SPECIAL FEATURES

In 1968, the 427-cubic-inch V8 was offered in 390- or 425-bhp form.

For 1968, all cars sold in the U.S. had to have side marker lights. In addition to the lights the SS also had proper engine identification.

RUNNING GEAR
Steering: Recirculating ball
Front suspension: Double wishbones with coil springs, telescopic shock absorbers and anti-roll bar
Rear suspension: Live axle with four links, Panhard rod, coil springs and telescopic shock absorbers
Brakes: Discs, 11-in. dia. (front), drums, 11-in. dia. (rear)
Wheels: Steel discs, 6 x 15 in.
Tires: 8.25 x 15 in.

DIMENSIONS
Length: 213.2 in.   **Width:** 79.9 in.
Height: 55.4 in.   **Wheelbase:** 119.0 in.
Track: 62.5 in. (front), 62.4 in. (rear)
Weight: 3,835 lbs.

Chevrolet **CAMARO Z28**

General Motors' answer to the Ford Mustang needed plenty of power to compete with the original pony car. The Z28 performance option on the Chevrolet Camaro was the answer. It dramatically improved handling and power.

" ...factory built race car."

"Designed to compete in Trans Am racing, the high-revving Z28 is a factory built race car. Underrated at 290 bhp, the over-square 302 V8 engine is peaky and nothing much happens until the engine revs past 4,000 rpm. Suddenly the tachometer needle is pointing to 7,000 rpm and the car really comes to life. It's upper end power like this where the Z28 gives you easy 120 mph performance. Complementing the overabundance of high end power, the Z28 is garnished with a four-speed transmission, seven-inch rims and competition suspension."

The interior of this race-modified Z28 uses bucket seat, roll cage and a fire extinguisher.

Milestones

1966 First Camaro appears based on the Chevy II frame. The standard powertrain is only a 230-cubic inch six cylinder.

Only 602 Camaro Z28s were built in its first year, 1967.

1967 Regular production option Z28 is introduced with a 302-cubic inch engine, just inside the 305-cubic inch limit set for Trans Am racing. Z28s finish third and fourth at the Sebring 12 Hours, winning the Trans Am category.

1968 Z28 dominates Trans Am, easily winning the championship with the Roger Penske-prepared cars. Driver Mark Donohue wins 10 out of the 13 rounds.

The Camaro's styling was radically altered for 1970.

1969 Crossram induction is made available, but is put in only 205 cars.

1970 Model restyled to be longer and heavier with egg-crate type grill, but the Z28 option lives on and is still found on today's hottest Camaros.

UNDER THE SKIN

Multi-leaf rear springs

Close-ratio Muncie transmission

Seven-inch wheels

Quick-ratio steering

Short-stroke V8

Tightened up

Detail changes transformed the basic and simple Camaro. The steering ratio was improved to give 'quicker' steering. It also had harder brake linings, stiffer rear multi-leaf springs, and revalved shock absorbers were fitted all around. There was a host of other options to add to the Z28 package, such as even quicker steering and a Muncie M-22 close-ratio four speed transmission.

THE POWER PACK

Hybrid V8

For the Z28, GM used the 327 cast iron block to give a four-inch bore and added a forged crankshaft (similar to the 283) with a three-inch stroke to make a rev-happy, over-square 302-cubic inch V8. It operated a high (11.0:1) compression ratio, had 'Camelback' cylinder heads fitted with large 2.02-inch intake and 1.60-inch exhaust valves and had very radical valve timing. The engine is designed to give loads of top end performance with its maximum power not coming in until 6,000 rpm.

Holley carburetor

2.02/1.60 valves

Shorter-stroke crankshaft

11.0:1 compression ratio

Longer, sleeker

The distinctive egg-crate grill is a definitive feature on the second-generation Camaro and was included on the Z28. It may not be the original, the rarest, or the most collectable Camaro variant, but it has a more obvious, overtly-sporting image. This shape remained in production, largely unchanged, until 1974.

The 1970 Camaros are more streamlined than first generation cars.

Chevrolet CAMARO Z28

To compete in the prestigious Trans Am championship, the rules required that Chevrolet had to build 1,000 suitable cars ready for sale to the public to homologate the car for racing. The result was the Z28, a racing car for the road.

Performance V8

Chevrolet originally rated the Z28's short-stroke V8 at 290 bhp. Some critics thought its potential was being deliberately underrated, and it could really produce something nearer to 350 bhp at well over 6,000 rpm.

Coupe-only body style

You could not order the Z28 package with the convertible body because Chevrolet only needed to homologate the coupe for Trans Am racing.

Vented disc brakes

Z28s are heavy cars, so with the performance available they have to have vented front disc brakes. Even with the harder pads though, the Z28's braking isn't its strongest feature.

Close-ratio transmission

Standard Z28 transmission was an automatic but for $184 a Muncie four-speed manual was available that could also be ordered with close-ratio gears.

Harder brake linings

Although the Z28 carries rear drum brakes, just like stock Camaros, the linings are a harder compound to improve performance under sustained high-speed braking.

Rear spoiler

The rear spoiler is as much about adding just a touch of style to the rear of the Camaro as managing the airflow over the car to improve rear downforce.

Wide tires
The Z28 used Goodyear WideTread tires on relatively wide (for the time) seven-inch rims.

Stiffer rear springs
The one major suspension change was the switch to multi-leaf instead of the stock single leaf rear springs which were 25 percent stiffer than standard. Despite this change, the front spring rates did not need to be altered at all.

Specifications
1968 Chevrolet Camaro Z28

ENGINE
Type: V8
Construction: Cast-iron block and heads
Valve gear: Two valves per cylinder operated by single block-mounted camshaft via pushrods and hydraulic lifters
Bore and stroke: 4.0 in. x 3.0 in.
Displacement: 302 c.i.
Compression ratio: 11.0:1
Induction system: Single four-barrel 800-cfm Holley carburetor
Maximum power: 290 bhp at 5,800 rpm
Maximum torque: 290 lb-ft at 4,200 rpm
Top speed: 123 mph
0-60 mph: 6.5 sec

TRANSMISSION
Three-speed automatic or four-speed manual

BODY/CHASSIS
Unitary steel construction with two-door coupe body

SPECIAL FEATURES

The 302-cubic inch engine was new for the Z28. It combined 327 block with a 283 crank to achieve a capacity of less than 305 cubic inches for SCCA racing.

This car has been fitted with a roll cage to comply with SCCA racing regulations.

RUNNING GEAR
Steering: Recirculating ball
Front suspension: Double wishbones with coil springs, telescopic shocks and anti-roll bar
Rear suspension: Live axle with multi-leaf semi-elliptic springs and telescopic shocks
Brakes: Front vented discs, 11 in. dia., and rear drums, 9 in. dia.
Wheels: Steel disc, 7 in. x 15 in.
Tires:: Goodyear WideTread E70-15

DIMENSIONS
Length: 184.7 in.   **Width:** 72.5 in.
Height: 51.4 in.   **Wheelbase:** 108 in.
Track: 59.6 in. (front), 59.5 in. (rear)
Weight: 3525 lbs.

Chrysler 300 G

As a major player of Chrysler's infamous 'letter' dynasty, the 1961 300 G was one of the finest performance/luxury packages on the road during its day, something that endears it to car enthusiasts all over the world.

"...Subtly deceptive."

"With swivelling front bucket seats, access to the cabin is almost effortless. From behind the wheel it becomes all too obvious why few cars can match the 300 G's charisma. Start the engine and just listen to the subtly deceptive sound of the cross-ram 413 V8. The unique pushbutton-operated TorqueFlite transmission is perfectly mated to the engine's torque curve. Despite its size, the 300 feels quite nimble through corners, helped by a finely tuned suspension."

A well-appointed interior and wide bucket seats make the G inviting.

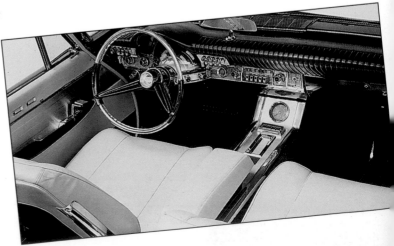

Milestones

1959 Replacing the costly
392-cubic inch Hemi in this year's 300 E is a more conventional 413-cubic inch wedge head. Packing 375 bhp, it is one of the fastest U.S.-built cars on the road.

The first incarnation of the 'letter' cars was the 1955 C300.

1960 Unitary construction
and substantially revised styling appear on the heavily revised 300F. It comes with a French-built Pont-a-Mousson four-speed or TorqueFlite automatic. A 400-bhp, 413 V8 is a performance enthusiast's dream option.

In 1957, Chrysler introduced its 300 convertible.

1961 Canted headlights
and mild styling revisions are seen on the 300 G. Taller wheels and tires fill its wheelwells. The four-speed option is dropped, but prices are unchanged from 1960.

1962 The 300 sheds its fins
on the new H model.

UNDER THE SKIN

Unitary construction

Dana rear axle with 3.23:1 gears

Torsion-bar front suspension

413 max-wedge V8

Trademark traits
For 1960, all Chryslers adopted a unitary body/chassis foundation, and this was carried over for the 1961 model year. The 300 G also has another Chrysler characteristic—a torsion-bar front suspension supplemented by a leaf-sprung live rear axle. The 300 G features stiffer spring rates and has a tough Dana rear end with 3.23:1 gears. Four-wheel drum brakes are standard.

THE POWER PACK

Cross-ram credence
All 300 Gs were powered by the incredible 413-cubic inch max-wedge V8. An outgrowth of the 383 unit that arrived for 1959, the 413 was procured as a less expensive and more practical alternative to the original, first-generation Hemi. This heavy engine offers an incredible 495-lb-ft of torque at a low rpm, making the 300 G very quick from 0-60 mph. Atop the malicious max wedge is a highly unusual, though very effective, cross-ram intake manifold with a Carter four-barrel carb on each side of its seemingly endless ports. The long runners force the air/fuel mixture at a high velocity into the heads and combustion chambers, further maximizing its power.

Hard or soft
Without question one of the most powerful and polished cars of its time, the 300 G is highly regarded today. Two body-styles were offered, and although the hardtop was more popular when new, it is the convertible that captures hearts today.

Extremely stylish though sadly elusive, only 337 drop-top 300 Gs were built.

Chrysler 300 G

Unleashing an overabundance of output from its dual-quad, cross-ram, max-wedge engine, the Chrysler 300 G became a legend on the street. However, its first-class styling and massive size kept its brutality well concealed.

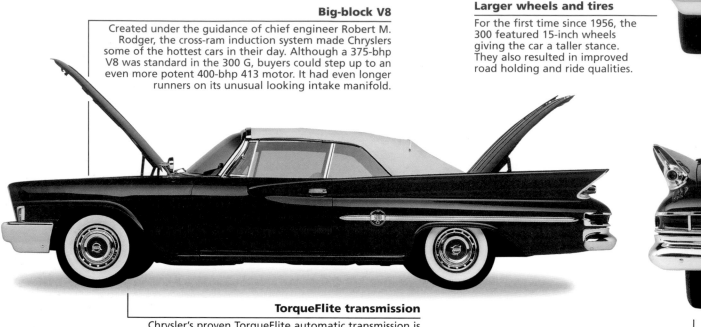

Big-block V8

Created under the guidance of chief engineer Robert M. Rodger, the cross-ram induction system made Chryslers some of the hottest cars in their day. Although a 375-bhp V8 was standard in the 300 G, buyers could step up to an even more potent 400-bhp 413 motor. It had even longer runners on its unusual looking intake manifold.

Larger wheels and tires

For the first time since 1956, the 300 featured 15-inch wheels giving the car a taller stance. They also resulted in improved road holding and ride qualities.

TorqueFlite transmission

Chrysler's proven TorqueFlite automatic transmission is operated by pushbutton controls mounted on the dashboard. A three-speed manual was listed on the options list, but few 300 Gs were ordered with it.

Generous list

As befitting its flagship status, the 300 G came loaded with equipment, including power steering, brakes and windows, a safety cushion dashboard, waterproof ignition, tachometer and front and rear center armrests.

Crisp styling

The 300 G was the last of the 'letter' cars to really bear the hallmarks of what is perhaps Virgil Exner's finest work. Canted fins were dramatic and futuristic but times were changing, and for the 1962 300 H they were discarded completely, marking the end of the tail-fin era.

Specifications
1961 Chrysler 300 G

ENGINE
Type: V8

Construction: Cast-iron block and heads

Valve gear: Two valves per cylinder operated by pushrods and rockers

Bore and stroke: 4.18 in. x 3.75 in.

Displacement: 413 c.i.

Compression ratio: 10.0:1

Induction system: Twin Carter four-barrel carburetors, cross-ram intake manifold

Maximum power: 375 bhp at 5,000 rpm

Maximum torque: 495 lb-ft at 2,800 rpm

Top speed: 130 mph

0-60 mph: 8.4 sec.

TRANSMISSION
TorqueFlite 727 three-speed automatic

BODY/CHASSIS
Steel unitary chassis with two-door convertible body

SPECIAL FEATURES

The 300 G's swivelling seats were a popular feature on lavish Chryslers.

The year 1961 was significant because it was the final appearance of large, pointed fins on 300s.

RUNNING GEAR
Steering: Recirculating ball

Front suspension: Unequal-length A-arms with longitudinal torsion bars and telescopic shock absorbers

Rear suspension: Live axle with semi-elliptic leaf springs and telescopic shock absorbers

Brakes: Drums (front and rear)

Wheels: Steel disc, 15-in. dia.

Tires: Blue Streak, 8.00 x 15

DIMENSIONS
Length: 219.8 in   **Width:** 79.4 in.

Height: 55.6 in.   **Wheelbase:** 126.0 in.

Track: 61.2 in. (front and rear)

Weight: 4,315 lbs.

Stiffer suspension
The 300 G has a stiffer suspension than other Chryslers, making this 4,315-lb. cruiser one of the most nimble big cars of its time.

Popular options
Besides the extensive standard equipment that garnished the 300, popular options included air conditioning, electric mirrors and a Music Master radio.

 **FRANCE** 1955-1975

Citroën **DS**

When Citroën launched the DS at the Paris Motor Show, the motoring world was astonished. The styling was space-age and the car bristled with technical innovations, such as hydraulically-operated self-levelling suspension, brakes, and steering.

"...magic carpet ride."

"Everything about the DS is geared toward comfort. The ride is superbly smooth and the car floats along the highways but becomes a bit of a handful on twisty byways because of excessive body roll. The brake pedal looks more like half a tennis ball than a pedal and is extremely sensitive: Until you're used to it, smooth progress is difficult to maintain. The 2.3-liter engine is the least high-tech bit of the car and dates back to before World War II."

The DS is dramatically styled inside and out. The shifter selects gears semi-automatically and also operates the starter motor.

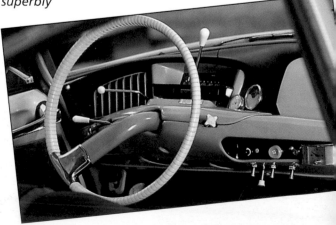

Milestones

1955 Citroën reveals its new sedan at the Paris Motor Show—a show-stopper, bristling with innovation.

1957 Cheaper and less sophisticated ID version is introduced, and a station wagon follows the next year.

1965 Engine enlarged to 2.2 liters for the DS21, and dynamic headlight control arrives.

Traction Avant lent its overhead-valve, four-cylinder engine to DS.

1969 Electronic fuel injection lifts DS21 power. Production reaches one million.

1971 Borg Warner automatic and 5-speed manual transmission are finally introduced.

1972 DS23 appears with a 2.3-liter engine.

Three bodystyles are shown: convertible, wagon and sedan.

1975 DS is discontinued.

UNDER THE SKIN

Bolt-on rear fenders

Roof-level rear lights

Transmission mounted in-line ahead of engine

Self-levelling suspension

Inboard front brakes

Long-stroke four

No jack required

All the body panels, including the plastic roof, are bolted to the steel monocoque. The hydro-pneumatic self-levelling suspension uses hydraulic fluid and gas for springing, and will keep the car level regardless of how it is loaded. The car needs no jack: if there's a puncture, simply raise the suspension, prop up the appropriate corner of the car, lower the suspension, and the wheel lifts off the ground.

THE POWER PACK

Convention reigns

First used in the Traction Avant of 1934, the engine of the DS is a conventional cast-iron, four-cylinder, overhead-valve unit. In its initial 1,911-cc form, it produced 63 bhp, and both capacity and power were gradually increased until it reached 141 bhp in its final 2.3-liter fuel-injected guise. This level of power is sufficient to propel the large DS to about 115 mph. Two flat-six engines were designed for the original DS, one air-cooled and one water-cooled, but neither made it to production due to high cost.

One dual-choke carburetor

Overhead valves with pushrods

Aluminum-alloy head

Cast-iron block

Décapotable

The Décapotable (convertible DS) was built by French Coachbuilder Chapron. He converted the bodies to two-door form, strengthened the chassis and added a folding fabric roof. It is the most valuable DS variant, with good examples worth about four times that of the sedan.

The Décapotable DS looks more elegant with the roof down.

Citroën DS ■■

When it was introduced in 1955, the revolutionary DS set new standards for family sedans. Though not much to look at, the DS was innovative and very much ahead of its time.

Fiberglass roof

Although the rest of the panels were steel, the bolt-on roof panel was manufactured from fiberglass. Early ID models had unpainted and untrimmed roofs that allowed light to filter into the cabin.

Swivelling headlights

When the headlights were faired in and the system changed to a four-light design, the inner pair turned with the front wheels to illuminate the driver's way through corners.

Pushrod engine

Citroën wanted to have an engine as advanced as the car itself but DS development cost such a fortune it couldn't afford the water- and air-cooled sixes that had been developed for the car. Instead, Citroën installed a modified Light 15 engine.

Hydropneumatic gearchange

The high-pressure hydraulic system was originally intended to power the brakes, the clutch, the steering and even the shifter, but eventually a manual gearshift was used.

Hydropneumatic suspension

The DS's greatest innovation was the hydropneumatic suspension, which relied on a pressurized hydraulic system run by an engine-driven pump. It also operated the power-assisted steering, the brakes and semi-automatic gearshift.

Self jacking

The high-pressure hydraulics gave the DS the ability to rise up on its suspension to allow the driver or mechanic to look underneath. It was also useful for crossing bumpy terrain.

Removable rear panels

The rear fenders of the DS could be detached in a matter of seconds to allow access to the rear wheel or to change a flat tire.

Specifications
1971 Citroën DS21

ENGINE
Type: In-line four cylinder
Construction: Cast-iron block and alloy head
Valve gear: Two valves per cylinder operated by single block-mounted cam, via pushrods and rockers
Bore and stroke: 3.54 in. x 3.36 in.
Displacement: 2,175 cc
Compression ratio: 8.75:1
Induction system: Electronic fuel injection
Maximum power: 108 bhp at 5,500 rpm
Maximum torque: 123 lb-ft at 3,500 rpm
Top speed: 95 mph
0-60 mph: 18.4 sec.

TRANSMISSION
Five-speed manual

BODY/CHASSIS
Steel monocoque with four-door, four-seat sedan body

SPECIAL FEATURES

Roof-guttering leads the eye into an unusually located trumpet-shaped rear indicator.

Rear fenders can be removed by simply unfastening one bolt. The fender must be removed to change the wheel.

RUNNING GEAR
Steering: Rack-and-pinion
Front suspension: Upper and lower control arms, hydropneumatic combined spring/shock units and anti-roll bar
Rear suspension: Trailing arms and combined hydropneumatic spring/shock units
Brakes: Discs front, drums rear
Wheels: Steel disc
Tires: 185-400 Michelin XAS

DIMENSIONS
Length: 189 in.   **Width:** 70.5 in.
Wheelbase: 123 in.   **Height:** 63 in.
Track: 57 in. (front), 51.3 in. (rear)
Weight: 2,919 lbs.

Inboard front discs
Citroën took advantage of the empty space under the hood next to the transmission by moving the front discs inboard to save on unsprung weight.

Dodge CHARGER

Based on the intermediate Coronet, the Charger created a sensation when it arrived for 1966. The dramatic fastback shape also lends it to custom modifications, as demonstrated by this example.

"...modernized muscle car."

"This modified Charger is a uniquely modernized classic muscle car. The interior still looks cool, even today, and with a small-block, 360-cubic inch V8, performance is better than average. 0-60 mph takes just eight seconds and, thanks to its relatively tall gearing, this Charger can cruise happily at 100 mph. With a lowered suspension and modern tires, it holds the road too, and front disc brakes mean it stops far better than with the original drums."

A Le Carrera steering wheel and Auto Meter gauges give it a roadracing flair.

Milestones

1966 The Charger is launched

as a stylish two-door fastback based on the intermediate Coronet 117-inch wheelbase chassis. Flashy touches include a hidden headlight grill and a four-bucket-seat interior. Engines range from a 318-cubic inch unit to the monster 425-bhp, 426 Hemi.

A second-generation Charger arrived for 1968. This is the limited-production 1969 500.

1967 After selling

37,344 units in its debut year, the Charger returns with few changes. A new performance-oriented R/T package arrives with a standard 440-cubic inch V8 and heavy-duty suspension. Sales drop to 15,788 in its sophomore year.

A Ram pickup donated its 360 V8 for this particular Charger.

1968 An all-new, Coke-bottle

styled, second-generation Charger arrives.

UNDER THE SKIN

Making it handle

Derived from the intermediate Coronet, the new-for-1966 Charger shares its unitary construction, torsion-bar front suspension and leaf-sprung live rear axle. The torsion bars have been cranked lower to drop the front, and lowering springs have been fitted at the back—resulting in a 1.5-inch lower ride height. Front disc brakes and stainless-steel brake lines replace the stock items.

Unitary construction

Front disc brakes

Lowered suspension

Small-block V8

THE POWER PACK

Mid-1970s muscle

Back in 1966, this Charger had a 318-cubic inch V8 nestling between the fenders. Now long gone, the original V8 has been replaced with something a little more potent: a 1978 360-cubic inch engine taken from a Dodge Ram pickup. This 360, which is an excellent high-performance V8 in its own right, has been further improved with the aid of Sealed Power pistons, a high-lift Mopar Performance camshaft, Edelbrock performer intake manifold and four-barrel carburetor. Retaining the stock manifolds, the V8 delivers 365 bhp at 4,700 rpm and 400 lb-ft of torque, making an excellent, head-turning driver.

Base model

Most common of the first-generation Chargers are the 1966 models. The big-block cars are the most sought after, but regular examples are cheaper to buy and are more readily available. They easily accept more power and can be modified to handle well, too.

Eclipsed in popularity by later Chargers, the early cars are still a good buy.

Dodge CHARGER

First generation Chargers almost beg for custom treatment, and even with subtle modifications they are guaranteed head-turners on the street. This one has won numerous awards at shows and cruises.

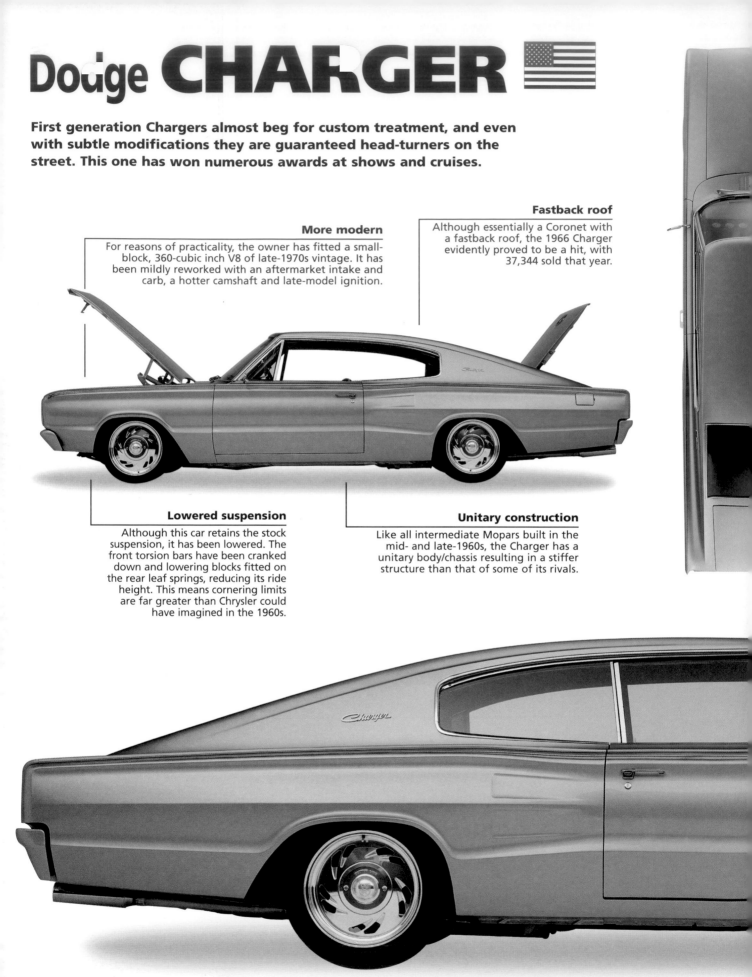

More modern

For reasons of practicality, the owner has fitted a small-block, 360-cubic inch V8 of late-1970s vintage. It has been mildly reworked with an aftermarket intake and carb, a hotter camshaft and late-model ignition.

Fastback roof

Although essentially a Coronet with a fastback roof, the 1966 Charger evidently proved to be a hit, with 37,344 sold that year.

Lowered suspension

Although this car retains the stock suspension, it has been lowered. The front torsion bars have been cranked down and lowering blocks fitted on the rear leaf springs, reducing its ride height. This means cornering limits are far greater than Chrysler could have imagined in the 1960s.

Unitary construction

Like all intermediate Mopars built in the mid- and late-1960s, the Charger has a unitary body/chassis resulting in a stiffer structure than that of some of its rivals.

Updated interior

Besides late-model seats, the transmission shift indicator on the console has been modified to read Skully (the car's name), instead of the normal P-R-N-D-2-1 pattern,

Low-profile tires

Besides the lowered suspension, modern BF Goodrich radial tires improve handling even further. Those at the rear are slightly larger than those at the front (255/45x17 versus 215/45x17), which gives excellent traction during standing-start acceleration.

Specifications
1966 Dodge Charger

ENGINE
Type: V8
Construction: Cast-iron block and heads
Valve gear: Two valves per cylinder operated by a single camshaft with pushrods and rocker arms
Bore and stroke: 4.00 in. x 3.58 in.
Displacement: 360 c.i.
Compression ratio: 9.1:1
Induction system: Edelbrock Performer four-barrel downdraft carburetor
Maximum power: 365 bhp at 4,700 rpm
Maximum torque: 400 lb-ft at 2,800 rpm
Top speed: 135 mph
0-60 mph: 8.0 sec

TRANSMISSION
TorqueFlite three-speed automatic

BODY/CHASSIS
Unitary steel chassis with two-door fastback body

SPECIAL FEATURES
Given the nickname 'Skully,' this car has subtle custom body graphics.

Full-length dual exhaust pipes help the 360 V8 produce its 365 bhp.

RUNNING GEAR
Steering: Recirculating ball
Front suspension: Unequal-length A-arms with torsion bars, telescopic shock absorbers and anti-roll bar
Rear suspension: Live axle with semi-elliptic leaf springs and telescopic shock absorbers
Brakes: Discs (front), drums (rear)
Wheels: Centerline Scorpion, 7 x 17 in. (front), 8 x 17 in. (rear)
Tires: BF Goodrich Comp ZR, 215/45x17 (front), 255/45x17 (rear)

DIMENSIONS
Length: 204.2 in.   **Width:** 75.0 in.
Height: 55.2 in.   **Wheelbase:** 117.0 in.
Track: 59.5 in. (front), 58.5 in. (rear)
Weight: 3,900 lbs.

Ferrari 330 GT

If you wanted an exotic four-seater in the 1960s, the car to choose was the Ferrari 330 GT. A genuine four seater, its 4-liter V12 engine gave exceptional performance.

"...excellent ride."

"The 330 feels most at home on open roads, where the big V12 can be kept at high revs and the fine chassis can be exploited through the bends. First gear has an awkward dog-leg, but the rest of the gearshift has a wonderfully quick feel. The steering isn't particularly sharp, but the chassis is so beautifully balanced it is easy to adjust the line with the throttle. Springs and dampers are stiff enough to virtually eliminate bodyroll but still give an excellent ride."

The 330 has an abundance of Italian chic, although the style is firmly 1960s.

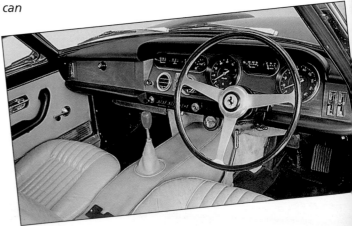

Milestones

1963 Ferrari unveils the 330 GT as a successor to its first production four-seater, the 250 GTE. Initial cars are known as Americas and feature twin headlights. It was also fitted with Ferrari's new Tipo 209 4-liter V12.

The 250 GTE was the first purpose-built Ferrari 2+2.

1965 A restyled front end sees single headlights replace the original double arrangement and the America name is dropped. The revised car also has a five-speed transmission in place of the previous four-speed transmission with overdrive. Alloy wheels are made standard as wire becomes optional.

The 365 GT 2+2, nicknamed Queen Mary, replaced the 330 GT.

1967 The 365 GT 2+2 is launched as a replacement for the 330 GT. It is larger and heavier than its predecessor.

UNDER THE SKIN

Disc brakes front and rear

Leaf-sprung rear suspension

Independent front suspension

V12 engine

Classic layout

As usual for Ferrari, there was a tubular-steel chassis frame under the Pininfarina-styled body, which was also built at the Pininfarina plant. The chassis frame carries independent front suspension that consists of wishbones, coil springs, anti-roll bar and telescopic shocks. At the rear there is a live axle with semi-elliptic leaf springs and radius arms. Earlier cars have a four-speed manual transmission with overdrive; later cars have a five-speed.

THE POWER PACK

All-alloy V12

For the 330 GT, Ferrari fitted one of the Gioacchino Colombo-designed, 60-degree V12s. The engine is all alloy with shrunk-in dry cylinder liners for the alloy pistons to run in and there are just two valves per cylinder in the alloy heads. They are angled in crossflow hemispherical combustion chambers even though there is only one overhead chain-driven camshaft per cylinder bank, so it has to work the valves by rockers. Fuel is fed in with three downdraft twin-choke Weber carburetors and there are twin distributors, each serving six cylinders.

America

The redesigned 330 GT is regarded as being one of Pininfarina's less successful creations. The twin headlights of the America give a more harmonious style that is augmented by the wire wheels. 330 GTs are too common for real classic status.

330s are affordable by Ferrari standards.

Ferrari 330 GT ▌▌

With real 150-mph performance, room for four passengers and one of the sweetest engines on the market, the Ferrari 330 GT was the epitome of luxurious freeway mile-eaters.

V12 engine

In many ways the all-alloy 4-liter V12 was a straightforward design with just a single cam per cylinder bank, two valves per cylinder and surprisingly low 8.8:1 compression ratio.

Four-seat interior

One of the major attractions of the 330 GT was its ability to seat four adults in comfort, making it ideal for long-distance touring. In Ferrari circles, this makes it less desirable.

Worm-and-roller steering

When the 330 GT was made Ferrari had yet to concede that rack-and-pinion steering was the best system for a high-performance car and kept the existing worm-and-roller arrangement, with 3.5 turns lock to lock.

Overdrive transmission

The first batch of Ferrari 330 GT Americas came with a manual four-speed transmission with overdrive on top gear only. This long final gearing was ideally suited to the V12's characteristics, helping it along to 150 mph plus. From 1965 onward a new five-speed transmission was fitted.

Disc brakes

Like Jaguar, Ferrari eventually conceded that disc brakes were really the only way to stop high-performance cars effectively, so large discs were fitted on the 330 GT.

Specifications
1967 Ferrari 330 GT

ENGINE
Type: V12
Construction: Alloy block and heads with cast-iron dry liners
Valve gear: Two valves per cylinder operated by single overhead cam per bank of cylinders with rockers
Bore and stroke: 3.03 in. x 2.80 in.
Displacement: 3,967 cc
Compression ratio: 8.8:1
Induction system: Three Weber 40 DFI twin-choke carburetors
Maximum power: 300 bhp at 6,600 rpm
Maximum torque: 415 lb-ft at 5,000 rpm
Top speed: 152 mph
0-60 mph: 6.3 sec

TRANSMISSION
Four-speed manual with overdrive

BODY/CHASSIS
Separate tubular-steel chassis with steel two-door coupe body

SPECIAL FEATURES

Side vents on the front fenders exhaust hot air from the crowded engine bay.

Early 330 GT Americas have the elegant twin-headlamps design.

RUNNING GEAR
Steering: Worm-and-roller
Front suspension: Double wishbones with coil springs, telescopic shock absorbers and anti-roll bar
Rear suspension: Live axle with semi-elliptic leaf springs, torque arms and shock absorbers
Brakes: Discs all around, 12.4-in. dia. front, 11.74-in. dia. rear
Wheels: Wire center lock, 7 in. x 14 in.
Tires: 205 HR14

DIMENSIONS
Length: 189.0 in.   **Width:** 69.0 in.
Height: 52.0 in.   **Wheelbase:** 104.2 in.
Track: 55.0 in. front, 54.7 in. rear
Weight: 3,180 lbs.

Leaf-sprung rear suspension

When the 330 GTC two-seat version was introduced, it featured double wishbone rear suspension, complete with coil springs. However, the GT relied on conventional semi-elliptic leaf springs.

Ferrari 500 SUPERFAST

The 500 Superfast was unashamedly aimed at wealthy enthusiasts. The elegantly styled Ferrari was large enough to seat four, but had just two seats and a race-bred 400-bhp, 4.9-liter V12 engine, which made it the fastest car on the road in the mid 1960s.

"...incredible speeds."

"The name sums up this car. It needs to be taken out on open roads with long, fast, sweeping bends. There, the Superfast is in its element, and is able to fully exploit its superb stability at incredible speeds. There's no tendency for the car to lean or wallow despite its size. It's a consummate tourer in which you can switch in and out of overdrive rather than change gears, but floor the throttle and the Superfast requires all of your attention as you hurtle toward the horizon."

The 500 has a classic Ferrari dashboard with large dials and subtle use of wood.

Milestones

1956 The Superfast

name appears for the first time on a spectacular car based on the 410 at the Paris Show. Four years later another Superfast gives rise to the low-volume Aerodinamica.

Forerunner to the 500, the 410 Superamerica also uses a V12.

1964 Ferrari and Pininfarina

use lessons learned on the Aerodinamica to produce a low-production exotic—the Superfast. Just 25 are built between 1964 and 1965.

The super-rare, super-expensive 365 California took over where the 500 Superfast left off.

1965 Minor changes

distinguish the cars built from November onward. The style of the side vents is changed and the overdrive arrangement is replaced by a five-speed transmission. Only 12 of this type of Superfast are made.

1966 The last 500

Superfasts are built.

UNDER THE SKIN

Double-wishbone coil-spring front suspension

Semi-elliptic rear leaf springs

Disc brakes front and rear

Racing-bred V12

THE POWER PACK

Tubular chassis

Ferrari broke no new ground with the Superfast's chassis. Two large oval-section steel longitudinal tubes that sweep up at the rear to clear the axle give the chassis its strength. A double row of small outer tubes fortifies the sill area. Vertical tubes form a strong cowl section and other smaller tubes form a base for the roof. Suspension is by double wishbones and coils at the front and a live axle with semi-elliptic leaf springs at the rear.

Racing heritage

Aurelio Lampredi's short-stroke, 60-degree, 4.9-liter V12 that powered the victorious 1954 Le Mans car had fixed cylinder heads to avoid any gasket problems. The Superfast's V12 shares a similar Silumin alloy block with cast-iron wet liners but conventional detachable cylinder heads. These hold two angled valves per cylinder, operated by a single chain-driven camshaft with rockers to give an efficient crossflow cylinder-head design. Fuel is fed in through six Weber carburetors. This engine design made it one of the most powerful production engines in the world at the time, producing a massive 400 bhp at 6,500 rpm.

Final dream

Any Superfast is a collector's dream, but the best ones are the last 12 made, because they have the five-speed trans-mission rather than the four-speed manual. The side-vent treatment is also more elegant than the earlier design.

Later, five-speed Superfasts are the ultimate collector's dream.

Ferrari 500 SUPERFAST

Pininfarina's design for the Superfast is nothing short of a masterpiece with its perfectly proportioned flowing lines and long graceful tail. Yet at the same time it is muscular enough to radiate sheer power.

Overdrive

The first 25 Superfasts used a four-speed manual transmission with overdrive to make even 150 mph seem relaxed. The overdrive operates on top gear and gives over 25 mph per 1,000 rpm.

V12 engine

Although a single camshaft gives an ideal combustion-chamber shape, it does not allow for a centrally mounted spark plug, so the plugs are side-mounted.

Wishbone front suspension

A double-wishbone front suspension was standard Ferrari equipment by this time. Transverse leaf springs were abandoned in 1956. The 410 Superamerica was the first Ferrari to use conventional coil springs, telescopic shocks and an anti-roll bar.

Four-wheel discs

The 170-mph Superfast requires large brakes. Therefore it is fitted with 12.4-inch diameter discs at the front and 11.7-inch discs at the rear. Twin-vacuum servo assistance insures that enough pressure can be applied.

Separate chassis

Ferrari used a separate chassis frame on all its cars, but for short production run models like the Superfast, it would certainly have made no sense to tool up to make either a stamped floorpan or monocoque body/chassis.

Side vents

The huge V12 engine needs good ventilation to keep under-hood temperatures down. Consequently, the Superfast has a large radiator grill and two large side vents to expel hot air.

Specifications
1965 Ferrari 500 Superfast

ENGINE
Type: V12

Construction: Alloy block with pressed-in cast-iron wet liners and alloy heads

Valve gear: Two valves per cylinder operated by a single overhead camshaft per bank of cylinders

Bore and stroke: 3.46 in. x 2.68 in.

Displacement: 4,962 cc

Compression ratio: 8.8:1

Induction system: Six Weber 40 DC2/6 carburetors

Maximum power: 400 bhp at 6,500 rpm

Maximum torque: 351 lb-ft at 4,750 rpm

Top speed: 174 mph

0-60 mph: 7.6 sec.

TRANSMISSION
Four-speed manual with overdrive

BODY/CHASSIS
Separate tubular-steel body with steel two-door coupe body

SPECIAL FEATURES

Aside from the 365 California, the 500 Super-fast was the last Ferrari to have wire wheels.

The tail of the 500 is understated but perfectly proportioned.

RUNNING GEAR
Steering: Worm-and-roller

Front suspension: Double wishbones with coil springs, telescopic shock absorbers and anti-roll bar

Rear suspension: Live rear axle with semi-elliptic leaf springs, radius arms and telescopic shock absorbers

Brakes: Dunlop discs, 12.4-in. dia. (front), 11.7-in. dia. (rear)

Wheels: Borrani wire spoke, 15-in. dia.

Tires: 205-15

DIMENSIONS
Length: 189.8 in.   **Width:** 70.1 in.

Height: 50.4 in.   **Wheelbase:** 104.3 in.

Track: 55.0 in. (front), 54.7 in. (rear)

Weight: 3,087 lbs.

Ford GALAXIE

Ford Galaxie Starliners are powerful even in stock form. This particular model has been fitted with a variety of vintage Ford high performance running gear such as the infamous, ultra-rare, marginally street legal 427 SOHC.

"...prowess of performance."

"No matter what car you put the outlawed-by-NASCAR 427 SOHC engine in, it is guaranteed to give it an extraordinary prowess of performance. The only factor that keeps this Starliner from dropping its 0-60 mph elapsed time is the tires. Complimenting the hand-built 625-bhp engine is perhaps Ford's finest driveline. It includes a Top-Loader' 4-speed and a 9-inch rear that houses 4.30:1 gears. Though it's far from original, this street machine was sure done right."

Drop the pedal and hang on! Soon everything outside the windshield becomes a blur.

Milestones

1960 Ford introduces
a new full-size hardtop line, and a new Starliner fastback hardtop joins the Galaxie series. It is conceived to reduce aerodynamic drag on NASCAR tracks and helps Ford to win the championship this year.

For 1960 the full-size Fords were completely revised.

1961 The Starliner
returns, although full-size Fords are reduced by four inches in length and two in width. The FE series 352-cubic inch engine is stroked to 390 and the most powerful version produces 375 bhp at 6,000 rpm. Only 29,669 Starliners are built this year and poor sales ensure that it does not return for 1962.

Like their GM rivals, Ford 'biggies' had shorter and narrower bodies in 1961.

1965 A restyled
full-size Ford, with all-coil suspension, goes on sale. A single overhead-cam version of the 427 is made available to racers.

UNDER THE SKIN

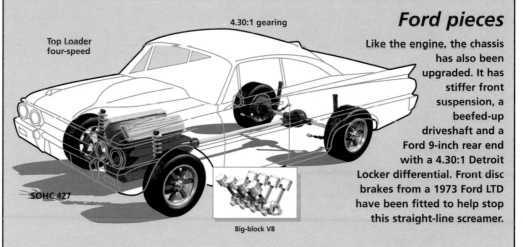

Top Loader four-speed

4.30:1 gearing

SOHC 427

Big-block V8

Ford pieces

Like the engine, the chassis has also been upgraded. It has stiffer front suspension, a beefed-up driveshaft and a Ford 9-inch rear end with a 4.30:1 Detroit Locker differential. Front disc brakes from a 1973 Ford LTD have been fitted to help stop this straight-line screamer.

THE POWER PACK

SOHC it to ya!

In 1965, Ford built the 427 SOHC in retaliation to Chrysler's 427 Hemi engines that were tearing up the NASCAR and NHRA circuits. The engine had single overhead cams and hemispherical combustion chambers. On Ford's dynamometer it made 675 bhp. The monster 427 mill proved to be so wicked that NASCAR disapproved the use of the engine. Seven factory sponsored A/FX cars that ran in NHRA in 1965 used the mighty engine and won the championship that year. The rest were never available in production models, but detuned versions could be bought over the counter form Ford. Though rare, some were used in street machines like this 1961 Starliner.

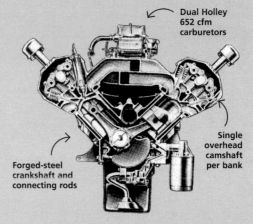

Dual Holley 652 cfm carburetors

Single overhead camshaft per bank

Forged-steel crankshaft and connecting rods

Fastback style

The Galaxie Starliner arrived in 1960—its main purpose was to keep Ford competitive in NASCAR. In its day the Starliner was one of the best looking Fords. Today its fastback design and low stance makes it a natural to be transformed into a street machine.

The Starliner debuted in 1960 but only lasted until the following year.

Ford GALAXIE

The 427 SOHC engines were never installed in any production cars. Although the handful that were offered were scoffed up by racers and hot rodders alike nearly as soon as they were available in 1965, their status is still legendary today.

Ultra-rare engine
Originally fitted with a 390, the owner of this car has installed a 427-cubic inch single overhead cam engine. This very rare power unit was developed by Ford to compete with the hemi Chryslers in NASCAR and NHRA sanctioned racing.

Manual transmission
Most Starliners are equipped with C6 automatics, but this one has a Borg-Warner T-10. To cope with the torque of the big V8, it has a heavy-duty clutch linkage.

Fastback styling
The fastback roof not only looks good, but it had a purpose. In 1961 Ford designed this car to be as aerodynamic as possible for specially prepared cars that raced in NASCAR. This was done to help reduce high speed aerodynamic drag.

Custom exhaust headers
For less restricted exhaust flow, the stock manifolds have been replaced by custom-fabricated tubular units. Doug Thorley was one of the largest suppliers of headers to drag racers in the 1960s.

Teardrop hood

Because the engine's induction system used a high rise intake manifold and dual carburetors, extra clearance was necessary. This stylish 'teardrop' shaped scoop was molded to a fiberglass hood to give the engine the space it required. Another added benefit was the two openings at the cowl that allowed hot air from the engine to escape. This hood style was immortalized in the 1964 lightweight Galaxie and Thunderbolt factory race cars. It quickly became a popular add-on for many other Ford models.

Full interior

As it is a street machine rather than a factory drag racer, this Galaxie still has a full stock interior and two-tone upholstery.

Specifications
1961 Ford
Galaxie Starliner

ENGINE
Type: V8

Construction: Cast-iron block and heads

Valve gear: Two valves per cylinder operated by a single overhead camshaft per bank via rockers

Bore and stroke: 4.23 in. x 3.78 in.

Displacement: 427 c.i.

Compression ratio: 12.5:1

Induction system: Twin Holley four-barrel carburetors

Maximum power: 625 bhp at 7,000 rpm

Maximum torque: 515 lb-ft at 3,800 rpm

Top speed: 130 mph

0-60 mph: 5.4 sec.

TRANSMISSION
Borg-Warner 'Top-Loader' T-10 four-speed

BODY/CHASSIS
Perimeter steel chassis with two-door steel hardtop body

SPECIAL FEATURES

Starliner emblems garnish the rear quarter panels.

Round tail lights and a simulated grill treatment on the rear valance are hallmarks of early 1960s Fords.

RUNNING GEAR
Steering: Recirculating ball

Front suspension: Unequal length wishbones with coil springs and telescopic shock absorbers

Rear suspension: Live rear axle with semi-elliptic leaf springs and telescopic shock absorbers

Brakes: Drums (front and rear)

Wheels: Torque Thrust magnesium, 15-in. dia.

Tires: BFG radials

DIMENSIONS
Length: 463.0 in. **Width:** 190.0 in.

Height: 124.0 in. **Wheelbase:** 119.0 in.

Track: 145.0 in. (front), 136.0 in. (rear)

Weight: 3,660 lbs.

Ford **FALCON**

Super Gas is one of the toughest categories in NHRA drag racing, and most competitors run Chevy-powered vehicles. It is not so with this Falcon, which screams down the ¼-mile with Ford's finest under the hood.

"...breathtaking experience."

"Power and speed are everything at this level of NHRA racing, and one drive in this Falcon will show you that this little car delivers a lot of both. Strap yourself securely into the lightweight bucket seat, switch on the fuel pump and flip the starter switch. With around 700 bhp, the driving experience is breathtaking. Once you hit the gas, all you can do is just sit there and hold on as the car starts up and then rockets down the strip covering the ¼-mile in less than 10 seconds."

A custom-built interior houses a pair of lightweight buckets and a B&M shifter.

Milestones

1960 Ford launches its compact
Falcon, an utterly conventional car offered in two- and four-door sedan forms or as a station wagon. A 144-c.i. inline six is the only engine available. In its debut year an incredible 435,676 are built.

Sprints finally got a V8 in 1963, in keeping with their sporty nature.

1961 A bigger, 170-c.i. six
becomes available and a Futura coupe (with bucket seats) is added to the range, in an attempt to add sportiness. Falcon output this year numbers 474,191 units.

1965 was the last year for sprints and convertibles.

1963 The Futura becomes
a separate series and a convertible is added to the range. A 260-c.i. V8 is also made available in the Futura this year. A redesigned Falcon arrives for the 1964 model year.

UNDER THE SKIN

Narrowed live axle on upper and lower links

Four-wheel disc brakes

Tubular steel chassis

Monster big-block V8

Little stock

It may look like a 1963 Falcon from the outside, but underneath it bears little resemblance. The chassis is a custom-built tubular-steel affair, with a four-link rear suspension and a narrowed 9-inch axle on Koni coil-over shocks. At the front, the radical Falcon employs Morrison struts and a power rack-and-pinion steering rack. A Panhard rod helps control sideways movement at the rear and disc brakes help the car stop.

THE POWER PACK

Simply overkill

With 164 bhp from its 260 V8, the 1963 Falcon Futura Sprint was quite a peppy little mover in its day, but this one gets its motivation from something bigger. Sitting in the custom-built chassis is a huge 460 V8 (Ford's largest production passenger car engine). It has been bored and stroked and has steel Manley Chevy rods pinned to Probe 13.5:1-compression pistons. It has a solid-lifter Crane camshaft that opens and closes the valves in a pair of ported and polished J. Bittle heads. Up top there's a Ford Performance aluminum intake manifold and a monster 1050-cfm Holley Dominator carburetor.

Sprinter

If you ask any Falcon aficionado which would be the best pick, a 289-powered Sprint convertible from 1964-1965 would be it. The earlier cars are great machines; simple, plentiful and relatively easy to build into a killer street or strip warrior.

Falcons are quite rare in Southern California Super Gas events.

Ford **FALCON**

It may resemble a 1963 Falcon, but this car is almost totally custom fabricated. Perhaps the most interesting thing about it is that the shell is actually from a convertible, with a hardtop from another Falcon grafted on.

Killer V8

With a genuine 500 cubic inches and a huge 1050-cfm carburetor, this engine makes a tremendous amount of horsepower, more than 700, in fact. This enables the bantam weight Falcon to scream down the quarter-mile in just 9.2 seconds.

Lightweight bumpers

Shaving as many pounds as possible was of primary concern when building this car. That approach extends to the bumpers, which are fiberglass items and have been sectioned to make them fit as close to the body as possible.

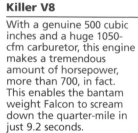

Strut front suspension

Stock Falcons came with a short-long-arm front suspension and coil-over shocks, but both the stock chassis and IFS have been replaced by a pair of Morrison struts. In the interest of weight transfer, the anti-roll bar has been omitted and lightweight wheels, with skinnies, have been fitted.

Custom interior

A whole new interior has been fabricated from aluminum sheeting, including the dash and the transmission tunnel (on which sits a B&M shifter for the Powerglide transmission). Safety is courtesy of a roll cage and Simpson twin harnesses.

Free-flowing exhaust

To expel the spent gases as quickly as possible, the big motor has a pair of Hooker 2½-inch diameter headers bolted to it. Besides getting rid of the spent gases, they help the engine make a truly thunderous trip down the strip.

Specifications
1963 Ford Falcon Sprint

ENGINE
Type: V8
Construction: Cast-iron block with alloy heads
Valve gear: Two valves per cylinder operated by a single V-mounted camshaft with pushrods and rockers
Bore and stroke: 4.39 in. x 4.125 in.
Displacement: 500 c.i.
Compression ratio: 13.5:1
Induction system: Holley Dominator 1050 cfm four barrel carburetor
Maximum power: 710 bhp at 7,000 rpm
Maximum torque: 685 lb-ft at 5,200 rpm
Top speed: 230 mph
0-60 mph: 2.8 sec

TRANSMISSION
Powerglide two-speed automatic

BODY/CHASSIS
Tubular-steel chassis with two-door hardtop body

SPECIAL FEATURES

Lexan glass is used for all windows to save as much weight as possible.

Wheelie bars help keep the car straight off the tree.

RUNNING GEAR
Steering: Rack-and-pinion
Front suspension: Morrison struts, lower control arms and telescopic shock absorbers
Rear suspension: Live axle, four-bar links, coil springs, telescopic shock absorbers and Panhard rod
Brakes: Discs (front and rear)
Wheels: Centerline lightweight
Tires: BFGoodrich radial T/A (front), Goodyear Drag Slicks (rear)

DIMENSIONS
Length: 183.7 in. **Width:** 70.8 in.
Height: 51.5 in. **Wheelbase:** 109.5 in.
Track: 56.9 in. (front), 48.5 in. (rear)
Weight: 2,015 lbs.

Ford MUSTANG 1966

Following its 1964 launch, the Mustang was a massive hit. Creating a place in the pony car market, its sales continued to increase. A modification of a 1966 car was the next step for this almost perfect package.

"...no ordinary Mustang."

"Do not be fooled by its looks; this is no ordinary Mustang. Underneath there have been a multitude of changes. The supercharged engine delivers considerable power, and the modified chassis gives more stability and poise than the original. Great attention has been paid to the interior, which blends well with the orange exterior. You would be hard-pressed to find a better example of a 1966 Mustang."

The carpet of this car is taken from Mercedes and it certainly looks elegant.

Milestones

1961 Inspirational Ford
President Lee Iacocca decides that the company should produce a sporty-looking car. Prototypes are built using a German four-cylinder engine.

1966 Mustangs came as convertibles as well as hardtops.

1964 Six months ahead
of the 1965 calendar year, Ford releases the Mustang. It is an instant hit, sparking a host of imitators from other manufacturers as the pony car war heats up.

The Mustang's first major design changes were introduced on the 1967 model, a bigger car.

1974 After a series of styling
changes, the original Mustang is replaced by the Mustang II. Initially a strong seller, it falls victim to the impending oil crisis and becomes a bloated, underpowered version of its previous self. Sales suffer as a result.

UNDER THE SKIN

Omni steering rack

Four wheel disc brakes

DOHC 4.6L modular engine shock absorbers

All-alloy V8

Uprated chassis

The original 1966 Mustang has a simple chassis layout that was adequate for the times, but feels its age now. Many changes have been made in the suspension. Up front, Mustang II parts have been incorporated and a chrome Ford 9-inch axle is in the rear. Disc brakes have been installed all around. Transmission is a Ford AOD-E automatic with a Lokar shifter. The rack-and-pinion steering is taken from a Dodge Omni.

THE POWER PACK

4.6 Liter "modular" V8

In 1966, the Mustang was available with a 200-c.i. inline six or a 289-c.i V8, in either 200 bhp or 225/271 bhp state of tune. The venerable cast-iron motor was considered too heavy for this Mustang and has been replaced by a 32-valve, 4.6 liter modular Ford V8 unit with all-alloy construction. From its relatively small displacement, 281 c.i., it produces 392 bhp with the aid of a Kenne Bell twin-screw whipplecharger running at 6 pounds of boost. This is in combination with a multipoint electronic fuel-injection system and a modern engine layout of four valves per cylinder operated by four chain-driven overhead camshafts.

Dynamite

For some people, the pre-1967 Mustangs are the best of the breed. The lines are uncluttered and classic. When mated with a stiff chassis and powerful engine, excellence is created—exactly what this 1966 example is.

Tasteful modifications have not betrayed the Mustang's good looks.

Ford MUSTANG 1966

If you like the looks but not the performance, what can you do?
Build your ideal car, of course. With nearly 400 bhp and a chassis
that can handle the power, this Mustang would be your dream car.

Supercharged engine

To get phenomenal performance from the
Mustang, a 32-valve, all-alloy 4.6 liter "modular"
Ford V8 engine, from a late-model Mustang
Cobra, has been fitted. The power has been
upped to 392 bhp by the addition of a Kenne
Bell supercharger running at 6 pounds of boost.

Tangerine dream

Completing the modified look is the
tangerine pearl custom paint scheme.
The side scallops are finished in a blend
of gold pearl and candy root beer.

Billet grill

A lot of attention
has been paid to
the look of this car.
This is illustrated by
the six-bar chrome
front grill and the
five-bar rear fascia,
which incorporates
900 LEDs.

Four-wheel disc brakes

To balance the enhanced
performance, disc brakes have
been installed. At the front these
are 11 inches in diameter with
9-inch ones at the rear.

Custom interior

As much work has gone into customizing the interior as modifying the mechanicals of this car. There are two shades of leather upholstery, cream and biscuit. There is also a wool carpet from a Mercedes, as well as modified 1965 T-Bird front seats.

Upgraded suspension

As with many modified first-generation Mustangs, this car uses the coil-sprung front suspension from the Mustang II. A chrome 9-inch rear axle combines with a Global West stage III suspension system out back.

Specifications

1966 Ford Mustang

ENGINE
Type: V8

Construction: Alloy block and heads

Valve gear: Four valves per cylinder operated by four chain-driven overhead cams.

Bore and stroke: 3.61 in. x 3.60 in.

Displacement: 281 c.i.

Compression ratio: 9.8:1

Induction system: Multipoint fuel injection with Kenne Bell twin-screw whipple supercharger

Maximum power: 392 bhp at 5,800 rpm

Maximum torque: 405 lb-ft at 4,500 rpm

Top speed: 141 mph

0-60 mph: 4.3 sec.

TRANSMISSION
Three-speed automatic

BODY/CHASSIS
Steel chassis with steel body

SPECIAL FEATURES

Even the trunk has been upholstered in matching fabrics.

Budnick alloy wheels are a fine addition to the car.

RUNNING GEAR
Steering: Rack-and-pinion

Front suspension: A-arms with coil springs and telescopic shock absorbers

Rear suspension: Live rear axle with leaf springs and telescopic shock absorbers

Brakes: Discs, 11-in. dia. (front), 9-in. dia. (rear)

Wheels: Alloy, 17 x 7 in. (front); 17 x 8 in. (rear)

Tires: Toyo 215/45ZR17 (front), 245/45ZR17 (rear)

DIMENSIONS
Length: 176.0 in.   **Width:** 71.0 in.

Height: 50.3 in.   **Wheelbase:** 108.0 in.

Track: 58.6 in. (front and rear)

Weight: 2,358 lbs.

Ford **GT40**

The GT40 showed that when a company the size of Ford decides to go into racing, their vast resources will ensure success. After some initial teething trouble, the mighty V8 Ford humiliated the Ferraris with a sweep at Le Mans in 1966.

"...V8 thumps you in the back."

"Even in the road car, with its milder engine and rubber-bushed suspension it's easy to get a realistic impression of what it was like to drive the GT40s through the June heat at Le Mans. The open road and wide, sweeping corners soon beckon; somewhere you can floor the throttle and feel the gutsy V8 thump you in the back as it tears to 100 mph in just 12 seconds. If it's this good on the road, it must have been fantastic on the Mulsanne Straight."

The cabin is small and claustrophobic. Tall drivers cannot even fit in and miss out on one of the greatest driving experiences available.

Milestones

1963 After failing to buy Ferrari, Ford joins forces with Lola to turn the Lola GT into the prototype Ford GT.

1964 Now known as the GT40, the Ford makes its racing debut at the Nurburgring 1000 km. It is forced to retire, as it does in every race this year.

GT40 was so named because its overall height was 40 inches.

1965 Production starts for homologation and a GT40 wins its first race: the 2000-km Daytona Continental.

1966 The big-block cars finish 1-2-3 at Le Mans and win the International Sports Car Championship for GTs.

GT40 won Le Mans in 1968 and '69 after Ford had withdrawn from sports car racing in '67.

1967 Once again the car wins both the International Sports Car Championship and the 24 Hours of Le Mans. Although Ford withdraws from racing at the end of '67, the GT40 races on in the hands of the Gulf team, winning Le Mans again in '68 and '69.

UNDER THE SKIN

Sheet steel semi-monocoque structure

Fuel tanks in deep sills

Suspension mounted in subframes

Sedan-derived V8

Mid-mounted engine

Stiff and strong

As a race car, the GT40 needed to be light as well as stiff and strong. To achieve this, it uses a sheet steel semi-monocoque structure with very deep sills (which hold the fuel cells). At either end of the center monocoque are subframes to hold the engine, transmission and suspension. The later MkIV racers use a more advanced alloy honeycomb construction.

THE POWER PACK

Tuning potential

Most GT40s used the 289-cubic inch V8 also found in the Sunbeam Tiger, Ford Mustang and early AC Cobra. With a cast-iron block and cylinder heads, a single camshaft operating two valves per cylinder via pushrods and rockers, it is not a sophisticated engine. Its design dates back to the 1950s, but it has huge tuning potential. In full racing tune, it can produce around 400 bhp which was more than enough to blow past the more sophisticated, but often less reliable, Ferraris.

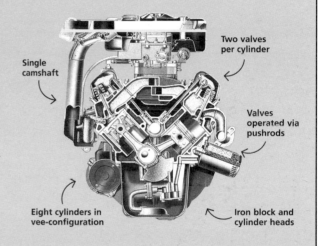

Single camshaft

Two valves per cylinder

Valves operated via pushrods

Eight cylinders in vee-configuration

Iron block and cylinder heads

Big blocks

Ford's first Le Mans-winning GT40 used the big-block 427-cubic inch engine; a unit that proved in the tough world of NASCAR racing it had the strength required for 24-hour racing. Only a few big-block cars were built.

Big-block cars had extra power and strength to compete in endurance racing.

Ford GT40 🇺🇸

Fast and immensely strong, the GT40 showed what a production car company could do when it wanted to go racing, particularly with Carroll Shelby, father of the AC Cobra, running the racing program.

Final specification

Although this car first raced in 1965, it was later brought up to the final racing specs, those of the Le Mans-winning cars of 1968 and '69.

Mid-engined design

By the 1960s, it was obvious that a successful racing car had to be mid-engined and Ford followed suit. The engine is behind the driver, mounted lengthwise, and by 1968, the displacement of the small-block engine had risen to 302 cubic inches. With Gurney-Weslake-developed cylinder heads, as on this car, power output was up to 435 bhp.

Front-mounted radiator

Ford decided to keep the radiator in its conventional position rather than mounting it alongside or behind the engine as on some modern mid-engined designs.

Four-speed transmission

The first racers are equipped with a four-speed Colotti transmission with right-hand change. Road cars have a ZF five-speed box with conventional central shifter.

Opening side windows

GT40s get incredibly hot inside and although the main side windows do not open, there are small hinged windows to allow air to pass through the cockpit.

Fiberglass body

The GT40's body played no structural role, so it was made from fiberglass and consisted basically of two large hinged sections, which gave the best access during pit stops.

Radiator outlet

By 1968, the air passing through the radiator was exhausted through this one large vent. It has a small upturned lip on the leading edge to accelerate air flow through the radiator.

Competition record

This car was one of the first driven at Le Mans, in 1965 by Bob Bondurant, but it failed to finish after cylinder head gasket failure. Three years later, it came fourth in the 1000 km at Spa Francorchamps.

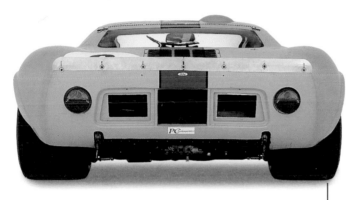

Magnesium suspension components

The GT40 is a heavyweight racing car, but some effort was still made to save weight—the magnesium suspension uprights, for example.

Halibrand wheels

The wide Halibrand wheels are made from magnesium, so they are very light. The design also provides good cooling for the disc brakes. They are a knock-off design for quick changes at pit stops.

Specifications
1967 Ford GT40 MkIII (road spec)

ENGINE
Type: V8
Construction: Cast-iron block and heads
Valve gear: Two valves per cylinder operated by single camshaft via pushrods and rockers
Bore and stroke: 4 in. x 2.87 in.
Displacement: 289 c.i.
Compression ratio: 10.5:1
Induction system: Single four-barrel Holley carburetor
Maximum power: 306 bhp at 6,000 rpm
Maximum torque: 328 lb-ft at 4,200 rpm
Top speed: 165 mph
0-60 mph: 5.5 sec.

TRANSMISSION
Five-speed ZF manual transaxle

BODY/CHASSIS
Sheet steel central semi-monocoque with front and rear subframes and fiberglass two-door, two-seat GT body

SPECIAL FEATURES

The GT40 was made as low as possible to help its aerodynamics. On this car, to help fit a driver with helmet into the cockpit, this bump was added onto the roof.

To help achieve a low overall height, the exhaust pipes run over the top of the transmission.

RUNNING GEAR
Steering: Rack-and-pinion
Front suspension: Double wishbones with coil springs, telescopic shocks and anti-roll bar
Rear suspension: Trailing arms and wishbones with coil springs, telescopic shocks and anti-roll bar
Brakes: Discs, 11.5 in. dia. (front), 11.2 in. dia. (rear)
Wheels: Halibrand magnesium 6.5 in. x 15 in. (front), 8.5 in. x 15 in. (rear)
Tires: 5.5 in. x 15 in. (front), 7 in. x 15 in. (rear)

DIMENSIONS
Length: 169 in.   **Width:** 70 in.
Height: 40 in.   **Wheelbase:** 95.3 in.
Track: 55 in. (front), 53.5 in. (rear)
Weight: 2,200 lbs.

Ford FAIRLANE 427

To fight its opposition on the street Ford built the Fairlane 427, which had widened shock towers and larger front coil springs to fit a detuned 427 V8. Unfortunately, the Fairlane 427 was costly to build so only 70 units were made in 1966 and 200 in 1967. Most went to pro racers for NHRA Super Stock competition.

"...uses a detuned race engine."

"Only a Borg-Warner 'Top-Loader' four-speed transmission was able to handle the 480 lb-ft of torque that the massive engine was capable of making. Though it uses a detuned version of its race engine, the brutal 427, if equipped with dual four-barrel carbs, it 'only' makes 425 bhp. On the street, the Fairlane 427 was very competitive. Only a handful were made and at $5,100 were very pricey, thus giving a slight edge to the competition.

The only indication of power from the vinyl-clad interior was a 9,000 rpm tachometer.

Milestones

1964 After minimal success on the drag strips with the larger Galaxies, Ford creates the Thunderbolt—a specially prepared 427-powered lightweight Fairlane sedan. These factory-built race cars helped Ford secure the NHRA manufacturers' championship.

The first Fairlanes to be equipped with the 427 were the competition-only Thunderbolts.

1966 A new, bigger Fairlane is released, which has plenty of room for 427 FE V8 engines. Only 70 white hardtops and coupes are built to qualify for Super Stock drag racing.

The 1966 Fairlane has similar styling to the 1966-67 Galaxie.

1967 The 427 returns as a regular production option for its second and final season. Only 200 Fairlanes are equipped with the side-oiler 427 and are available in a variety of colors and optional trim packages.

UNDER THE SKIN

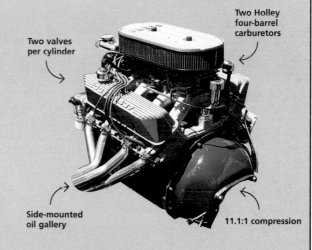

Larger rear leaf springs

Front-disc brakes

Special handling package

427 FE V8

Muscle bound

The 1966 Fairlane is larger and wider than its predecessor. It has a unitary body chassis, with a leaf-sprung live axle at the rear and coil-sprung wishbones at the front. A special handling package, front disc brakes, longer leaf springs and 15-inch wheels and tires were included. Only a 'Top Loader' transmission was available with the 427.

THE POWER PACK

The side-oiler

Oiling was always a problem on the 406 and 427 FE engines, and so in 1965 Ford introduced a new block design known as the 'side-oiler'. It is this version of the 427-cubic inch engine that powers the Fairlane. Instead of routing the main oil gallery down the center of the block, like other FE engines, the side-oiler has the main oil gallery positioned low on the left side near the pump outlet. It is rated at 410 bhp with a single four-barrel carburetor and 425 bhp with a dual carburetor set up.

Two valves per cylinder

Two Holley four-barrel carburetors

Side-mounted oil gallery

11.1:1 compression

Rare beast

Although the 1966 models are very rare, this no frills homologation special isn't very refined. For 1967, Ford offered the Fairlane 427 in a variety of colors and exterior trim. The cars still had the potent 427 V8 and also carried the equally potent price tag.

The 1967 Fairlane 427s were a serious threat on the streets and at the track.

Ford FAIRLANE 427

Although it was one of the quickest muscle cars around in 1966, the rarity of the Fairlane 427 prevented it from having the same impact among street racers as a Chevelle SS396 or a tri-power GTO.

Heavy-duty suspension

To cope with the weight and power of the 427 engine, the standard Fairlane suspension was reworked with stiffer spring rates and larger front coil springs. This unit also took up considerable space, which necessitated relocating the front shock towers.

Race-derived engine

The 427-cubic inch engine was only available with the base model trim and was never used in the plusher GT/GTA model. After all, it was a thinly-disguised race car and potential purchasers were carefully screened by dealers.

Four-speed transmission

Unlike the Fairlane GT/GTA, the 427 was only available with one transmission: a Borg-Warner 'Top Loader' T-10 four-speed.

Handling package

A special handling package, consisting of manual front disc brakes, longer rear leaf springs and larger blackwall tires, was available. This particular car is one of the very few to be fitted with these items.

Smooth styling

For 1966, the Fairlane hardtop received similar styling to the Pontiac GTO, with stacked headlights and smooth-flowing contours.

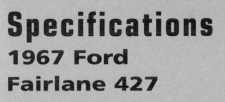

ENGINE
Type: V8
Construction: Cast-iron block and heads
Valve gear: Two valves per cylinder actuated by a single camshaft via pushrods, rockers and solid lifters
Bore and stroke: 4.23 in. x 3.78 in.
Displacement: 427 c.i.
Compression ratio: 11.1:1
Induction system: Two Holley four-barrel downdraft carburetors with aluminum intake manifold
Maximum power: 425 bhp at 6,000 rpm
Maximum torque: 480 lb-ft at 3,700 rpm
Top speed: 121 mph
0-60 mph: 6.0 sec

TRANSMISSION
Borg-Warner 'Top Loader' T-10 four-speed

BODY/CHASSIS
Steel unitary chassis with two-door body

SPECIAL FEATURES

Stacked headlights are a feature of 1966-1967 Fairlanes. The lower units are the high beams.

Dual 652 cfm Holley four barrel carburetors are housed beneath an open element aircleaner

RUNNING GEAR
Steering: Recirculating ball
Front suspension: Double wishbones with heavy duty coil springs, telescopic shock absorbers, anti-sway bar
Rear suspension: Live axle with long semi-elliptic leaf springs and telescopic shock absorbers
Brakes: Discs front, drums rear
Wheels: 14 x 5.5-in.
Tires: 7.75 x 14

DIMENSIONS
Length: 197.0 in.   **Width:** 74.7 in.
Height: 54.3 in.   **Wheelbase:** 116.0 in.
Track: 58.0 in.   **Weight:** 4,100 lbs.

Fiberglass hood

In 1966 all 427 Fairlanes were built with a fiberglass lift-off hood with four tie-down pins. For 1967 a steel hood was available alongside the fiberglass unit.

Ford GALAXIE 500

Although it became progressively more formal during the 1960s, the Galaxie still remained a hot seller. However, few people then would have considered it to be a great basis for a street rod.

"...eye-popping paint."

"You may not remember much about driving a stock a 1968 Galaxie, but you won't forget this one. The custom interior is a world away from Ford's, with special seats, steering wheel and high-quality trim. A very low stance really helps this huge car corner, and stiff springs reduce body lean under high g loads. Handling, however, is incidental—this car's primary role is to turn heads, which it does with flames from the tailpipes and its eye-popping paint."

The billet aluminum wheel and painted metal dash are far removed from the stock interior.

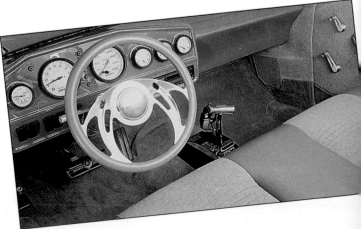

Milestones

1965 With the intermediate

Fairlane assuming the performance mantle, the new, redesigned big Fords adopt more formal lines and have stacked quad headlights. Engines range from a humble straight six to the big 427 V8. The top-of-the-line Galaxie range includes a new luxury model, the LTD.

The 1966 7-Litre marked a more formal role for the Galaxie.

1966 The Thunderbird's

345-bhp, 428-cubic inch V8 becomes an option and is standard on the new 7-Litre models. Styling is only slightly changed from 1965.

In 1968, the Mustang could also be ordered with a 390-cubic inch V8 engine.

1967 More fluid styling

marks the big Fords this year.

1968 A new grill with

hidden headlights is the major change.

UNDER THE SKIN

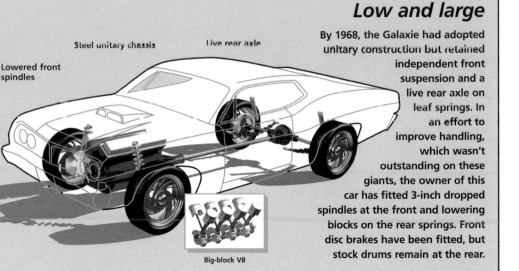

Low and large

By 1968, the Galaxie had adopted unitary construction but retained independent front suspension and a live rear axle on leaf springs. In an effort to improve handling, which wasn't outstanding on these giants, the owner of this car has fitted 3-inch dropped spindles at the front and lowering blocks on the rear springs. Front disc brakes have been fitted, but stock drums remain at the rear.

Steel unitary chassis

Live rear axle

Lowered front spindles

Big-block V8

THE POWER PACK

Fiery FE

The 345-bhp 428 engine could have been ordered in a Galaxie, but the buyer of this car chose the smaller 390-cubic inch V8. Like the 428, it is a member of the FE family of Ford big-blocks. Its basic construction consists of a cast-iron block, a crankshaft running on five main bearings, and a single central camshaft working the overhead valves with pushrods and hydraulic lifters. This motor has been fitted with a set of Hooker Super Comp exhaust headers, and an Edelbrock intake manifold and carburetors. Power is boosted from 315 bhp to an estimated 365 bhp.

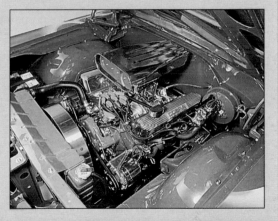

Bargain buy

When it comes to street machines, most hot rodders choose intermediate-size cars, although really big cars, like the Galaxie, should not be forgotten. A 1968 hardtop or convertible is the best bodystyle. There are plenty around and they're very affordable.

1968 Galaxies in good condition can be bought for less than $2,000.

Ford GALAXIE 500

The stock 1968 Galaxie was a clean and rather understated design. That look has been totally transformed on this car by a combination of paint, perfect detailing, massive alloy wheels and flames—both painted and real.

Custom interior
Totally unique to this car are the combination of tweed and vinyl covering on the custom-made seats and the painted dashboard with Auto Meter phantom gauges. Not only has the steering wheel been changed to a Billet Specialities design, but it is now on a GM rather than Ford tilt steering column.

Modified V8
The 1968 Galaxie could be fitted with the 390-cubic inch V8 in various states of tune, from 265 bhp up to 315 bhp. This car has the base 390, but with a more efficient Edelbrock intake and four-barrel carburetor, plus a set of Hooker Super Comp headers.

Independent suspension
Throughout the 1960s, Ford altered its A-arm and coil-spring front suspension design, trying to achieve the right degree of wheel control as well as the greatest comfort by minimizing the road shocks fed through the system. This was partly achieved by working on the bushings in the lower A-arm to give compliance in one direction only. In this case spring and shock rates have been increased to cope with the reduced suspension travel of a lowered car.

Live rear axle
Live axles were still the industry standard in 1968. This one is a simple arrangement with angled telescopic shocks and long semi-elliptic leaf springs doing the dual task of suspending and locating the axle.

Low ride height

Wide and flat, the original 1968 Galaxie was fairly low, but this one has been fitted with 3-inch drop spindles to lower the whole car, front and rear, to under 49 inches—about the height of a Porsche 928.

Seam-welded body

This Galaxie's body is much stiffer and stronger than any that left the production line in 1968. Instead of rows of individual spot-welds joining the body panels, there's a continuous run of weld along each seam.

Specifications
1968 Ford Galaxie 500

ENGINE
Type: V8
Construction: Cast-iron block and heads
Valve gear: Two valves per cylinder operated by a single V-mounted camshaft with pushrods, rockers and hydraulic valve lifters
Bore and stroke: 4.05 in. x 3.78 in.
Displacement: 390 c.i.
Compression ratio: 9.5:1
Induction system: Single Edelbrock four-barrel carburetor
Maximum power: 365 bhp at 5,800 rpm
Maximum torque: 370 lb-ft at 3,400 rpm
Top speed: 110 mph
0-60 mph: 7.9 sec

TRANSMISSION
Three-speed automatic

BODY/CHASSIS
Unitary steel construction

SPECIAL FEATURES

A set of spark plugs in the tailpipe enables this Galaxie to spit flames from its exhaust.

The hood has a central cut-out to clear the custom 'bug catcher'-style scoop.

RUNNING GEAR
Steering: Recirculating-ball
Front suspension: Independent A-arms with coil springs, telescopic shock absorbers and anti-roll bar
Rear suspension: Live axle with semi-elliptic leaf springs and telescopic shock absorbers
Brakes: Drums, 11.0 x 3 in. (front), 11.0 x 2.5 in. (rear)
Wheels: Billet Specialities alloy, 8 x 17 in. (front), 9.5 x 17 in. (rear)
Tires: Toyo Proxes

DIMENSIONS
Length: 213.3 in.   **Width:** 78.0 in.
Height: 48.9 in.   **Wheelbase:** 119.0 in.
Track: 63.0 in. (front), 64.0 in. (rear)
Weight: 3,554 lbs.

Ford LOTUS CORTINA

It took the manufacturing power of Ford and the engineering skills of Lotus to produce one of the most effective competition sedans of the 1960s—the Lotus Cortina.

"...an absolute delight."

"There is only one way to drive the Lotus Cortina— very quickly. Taking fast corners is an absolute delight, as the Cortina sticks to the road like glue. The Lotus-enhanced twin-cam engine makes a delightful sound and the gears are slick and the clutch light. It is a car in which you can drive for miles without getting tired. But best of all, because it is based on a family sedan, it has four seats and a sizeable trunk that makes it practical, too."

The inside of the Lotus Cortina is very user friendly and tastefully restrained.

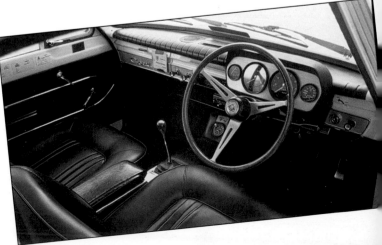

Milestones

1963 Ford's Walter Hayes persuades Lotus' Colin Chapman to produce a limited run of Cortinas with Lotus engines.

Most Mk 1 Lotus Cortinas retain their original white paint.

1964 Jim Clark wins the British Saloon Car Championship in a Lotus Cortina, which has had many of the light aluminum components replaced by steel ones.

1965 Sir John Whitmore triumphs in the European Championship driving a red and gold car. It uses the standard Cortina GT leaf-spring suspension.

The Mk 2 Lotus Cortina of 1967 has much boxier styling.

1966 After winning the RAC Rally, the production of Lotus Cortinas ends. Nearly three times the planned 1,000 production run have been made. A more ordinary Mk 2 replaces it and lasts until 1970.

UNDER THE SKIN

Lowered suspension all around

Aluminum hood and trunk

Unitary construction

Tweaked in-line four

Hot family sedan

While it may look like a regular Ford Cortina sedan, underneath Colin Chapman made a number of changes to justify the 'Lotus' name. The front suspension has new springs and revalved shocks which reduces the ride height. The rear end is located by a completely different arrangement of an A-frame and twin radius arms with coil spring/shock units. To save weight, the clutch housing is made from aluminum.

THE POWER PACK

Lotus twin-cam

The whole point of the Lotus Cortina was to fit a Lotus engine under the hood. The right powerplant had already been devised in the form of Harry Mundy's twin-cam head combined with the unbreakable Ford 1500 Kent bottom end. Mike Costin and Keith Duckworth were asked to develop the engine for racing and production, and increased the capacity to 1,558 cc. Twin Weber 40DCOE carburetors help to push power up to 105 bhp, and the torque figure is extremely impressive at 108 lb-ft.

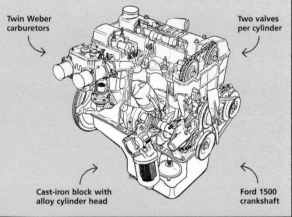

Twin Weber carburetors

Two valves per cylinder

Cast-iron block with alloy cylinder head

Ford 1500 crankshaft

Mk 1 favorite

Although it was also produced in Mk 2 form, the original Lotus Cortina is much more desirable and expensive. It has style, pace, and grace. Historic racers really value the Lotus Cortina and good surviving examples can bring a high price.

Lotus Cortinas often compete in historic sedan car racing.

Ford **LOTUS CORTINA**

In the 1960s both Lotus and Ford were making huge waves in racing, and the Lotus Cortina was a fine advertisement for the road/race crossover aspirations of Ford. Today, it is rated as a true classic.

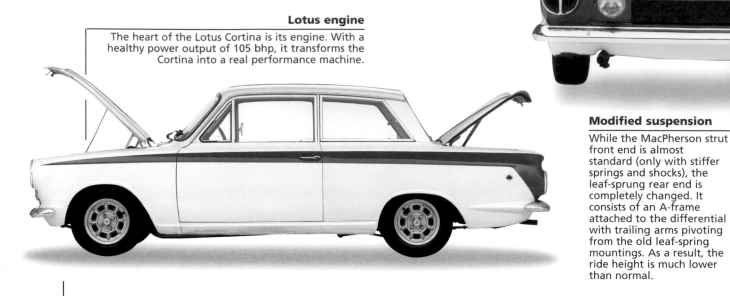

Lotus engine

The heart of the Lotus Cortina is its engine. With a healthy power output of 105 bhp, it transforms the Cortina into a real performance machine.

Modified suspension

While the MacPherson strut front end is almost standard (only with stiffer springs and shocks), the leaf-sprung rear end is completely changed. It consists of an A-frame attached to the differential with trailing arms pivoting from the old leaf-spring mountings. As a result, the ride height is much lower than normal.

Lightweight drivetrain

Colin Chapman was called in to re-engineer the transmission to match the new engine. The close-ratio four-speed manual unit from the Elan is used, but the clutch housing, differential casing and remote gearshift extension are made from light alloy.

Sensible styling

Ford of England often played it safe regarding styling. The Cortina may not be much to look at, but this was exactly what the public wanted.

Aluminum body parts

When launched, the Lotus Cortina boasted lightweight aluminum panels. These included the skins on the doors, hood and trunk lid. However, in July 1964 these reverted to ordinary steel, and you had to pay extra if you wanted light alloy panels.

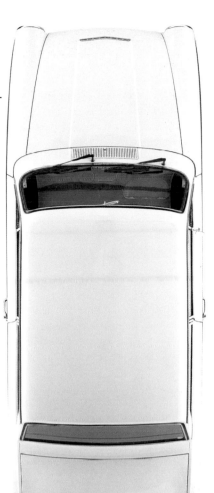

Unique paint scheme

The distinctive paintwork of the Lotus Cortina became its trademark. Virtually all cars were delivered from Lotus' Cheshunt factory in England painted in Ermine White with a Sherwood Green flash applied by Lotus.

Specifications
1964 Ford Lotus Cortina

ENGINE
Type: In-line four-cylinder
Construction: Cast-iron block and aluminum head
Valve gear: Two valves per cylinder operated by dual overhead camshafts
Bore and stroke: 3.25 in. x 2.87 in.
Displacement: 1,558 cc
Compression ratio: 9.5:1
Induction system: Twin Weber downdraft carburetors
Maximum power: 105 bhp at 5,500 rpm
Maximum torque: 108 lb-ft at 4,000 rpm
Top speed: 106 mph
0-60 mph: 9.9 sec

TRANSMISSION
Four-speed manual

BODY/CHASSIS
Integral chassis with two-door steel sedan body

SPECIAL FEATURES

Auxiliary driving lights are fitted to many Lotus Cortinas and together with the stripes add a dash of sportiness.

Minilite wheels were a popular aftermarket addition to British sports cars in the 1960s, and the Lotus Cortina was no exception.

RUNNING GEAR
Steering: Recirculating ball
Front suspension: MacPherson struts with coil springs, shock absorbers, track control arms and anti-roll bar
Rear suspension: Live axle with A-frame, coil springs, trailing arms and shock absorbers
Brakes: Discs (front), drums (rear)
Wheels: Steel, 13-in. dia.
Tires: 6.00 x 13

DIMENSIONS
Length: 168.3 in.   **Width:** 62.5 in.
Height: 53.7 in.   **Wheelbase:** 98.4 in.
Track: 51.5 in. (front), 50.5 in. (rear)
Weight: 2,038 lbs.

Jaguar **MK 2**

Jaguar invented the compact luxury car with the Mk 2. It was fast in 3.8-liter guise, comfortable, spacious and had a hand-built, quality feel to it. Today, the Mk 2 is an undisputed classic.

"...inspiring to drive."

"It's a wonderful feeling to step inside a Jaguar Mk 2 for the first time. The car oozes high class—a feeling of robust quality and good taste. The superb six-cylinder engine both purrs and growls. At low revs the Mk 2 sounds quiet and behaves in a docile manner, but put your foot to the floor and it sounds great. The body has a tendency to roll through corners, but the Mk 2 is inspiring to drive and caresses its occupants."

In typical Jaguar fashion the interior is leather-trimmed with lots of wood.

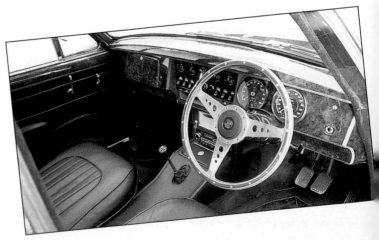

Milestones

1955 Jaguar shows

its '2.4-Liter' (now known as the Mk 1); a 3.4-Liter model joins it soon after.

1959 The prettier,

more luxurious Mk 2 is introduced at the London Motor Show. It is available with a 3.8-liter engine.

Mk 2s also did well in the British Saloon Car Championship.

1965 The manual transmission model

receives the XK-E's synchromesh four-speed.

1966 Specification is

downgraded with no foglights, lower grade carpet and Ambla upholstery instead of leather.

The basic engineering of the Mk 2 dates back to the Mk 1 of 1955.

1967 The Mk 2 is finally retired and replaced

by the slim-bumper Jaguar 240 and 340 models.

1969 All Mk 2-style

models are discontinued.

UNDER THE SKIN

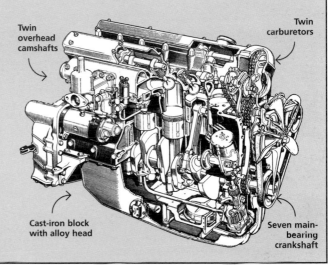

Four-wheel disc brakes

Unitary construction

All-independent suspension

Gutsy in-line six

High-tech

The Mk 2 was a clear development of the Mk 1, which, in its day, was very advanced and the first Jaguar with unitized monocoque construction. The body is immensely rigid due to its beefy box-section structure. Front suspension is independent with coil springs, while at the rear there is a leaf-sprung axle.

THE POWER PACK

An XK jewel

Mk 2s could be ordered with a magnificent 3.8-liter powerplant, which was taken directly from the Mk IX sedan that was first seen in October 1958. This engine, born in 1948, was bored to 3,781 cc and had a new lined block for the Mk 2, although the 'B'-type cylinder head was retained. With its twin SU carbs, the engine produces a very strong 220 bhp and about 11 percent more torque than the smaller 3.4-liter unit.

Twin overhead camshafts

Twin carburetors

Cast-iron block with alloy head

Seven main-bearing crankshaft

Speedy sedan

There is really only one choice as far as the Mk 2 is concerned: the 3.8-liter model. Both the British police and criminals used them in the 1960s because they were the fastest European sedans produced at the time. Today, collectors cherish 3.8-liter models.

The 3.8-liter engine endows the Mk 2 with tremendous performance.

Jaguar MK 2

There is something about the shape of a Mk 2 that excites Jaguar enthusiasts. In addition, it is rewarding to drive and comfortable to be in, and has charm and grace aplenty.

XK power

Jaguar's acclaimed straight-six XK engine powers the Mk 2. Available in 2.4-, 3.4- and 3.8-liter sizes, the biggest one made the Mk 2 the quickest Bitish four-door sedan on the market in its day.

Stylish wheels

Although the Mk 2 was available with steel wheels with traditional Jaguar hub caps and a body-colored finish, the more stylish option was a set of chromed wires. These suit the Mk 2's sporty temperament.

Choice of transmission

A four-speed manual transmission with overdrive is standard for the Mk 2, although many customers chose a three-speed automatic. Unlike the smaller-engined versions, the 3.8-liter Mk 2 has a standard limited-slip differential.

Luxury interior

Inside, the Mk 2 reached new levels of luxury. The upholstery is almost entirely leather and the floors have rich pile carpeting. Standard equipment includes a sports car-like instrument display, center console and foldaway tables for rear passengers.

Classic styling

Many people regard the Mk 2 as Jaguar's most elegant sedan. It has slimmer pillars, a much larger glass area, separate chromed window frames and more chrome than the earlier Mk 1.

Unibody construction

Unlike separate-chassis Jaguars of the 1950s, the Mk 2 uses monocoque construction. It is extremely rigid with two long box-sections welded to a ribbed steel floorpan, linked by transverse crossmembers and bulkheads.

Specifications

1960 Jaguar Mk 2 3.8

ENGINE

Type: In-line six-cylinder

Construction: Cast-iron cylinder block and alloy head

Valve gear: Two valves per cylinder operated by two overhead camshafts

Bore and stroke: 3.42 in. x 4.17 in.

Displacement: 3,781 cc

Compression ratio: 8.0:1

Induction system: Two SU sidedraft carburetors

Maximum power: 220 bhp at 5,500 rpm

Maximum torque: 240 lb-ft at 3,000 rpm

Top speed: 125 mph

0-60 mph: 9.2 sec.

TRANSMISSION

Four-speed manual with overdrive or three-speed automatic

BODY/CHASSIS

Unitized chassis with steel four-door sedan body

SPECIAL FEATURES

Wide wire wheels were a popular option on the Mk 2.

A classic Jaguar grill features vertical chrome bars. On early Mk 2s it is flanked by twin driving lights.

RUNNING GEAR

Steering: Recirculating ball

Front suspension: Wishbones with coil springs, shock absorbers and anti-roll bar

Rear suspension: Live axle with radius arms, leaf springs, Panhard rod and shock absorbers

Brakes: Discs (front and rear)

Wheels: Steel or wires, 15-in. dia.

Tires: 6.40 x 15 in.

DIMENSIONS

Length: 180.8 in.   **Width:** 66.75 in.

Height: 57.5 in.   **Wheelbase:** 107.4 in.

Track: 55.0 in. (front), 53.4 in. (rear)

Weight: 3,400 lbs.

UK 1961-1975

Jaguar E-TYPE

The E-type appeared like something from outer space in 1961. Nothing else at the price could compete with its combination of great beauty and amazing performance. It remains one of the all-time great sports cars.

"...the thrill of a lifetime."

"A combination of narrow bias-ply tires, 265 bhp and a 150 mph top speed sounds like a real challenge, but the E-type is a joy to drive. The view down the never-ending hood promises the thrill of a lifetime and that's just what the E-type delivers. Power flows smoothly from the superb straight-six engine and flooring the throttle, even at 100 mph, makes the nose rise as the car surges forward toward the 150 mph mark."

Simple but stylish—the E-type's dashboard is stocked with all the necessary gauges for a sports car.

Milestones

1961 Orders flood in

for the new Jaguar E-type, following its launch at the Geneva Motor Show.

1964 An enlarged,

4.2-liter engine is installed, giving more torque, but similar performance. An improved transmission is introduced.

The series was extended with addition of 2+2 with occasional rear seats.

1966 The larger 2+2

coupe, with small rear seats and a raised roofline is launched.

1968 Series II models have

larger hood opening, more prominent front and rear lights and unfaired headlights.

Series III cars have V12 engine and a more prominent grill.

1971 A new 272 bhp,

5.3-liter alloy V12 is installed to form the Series III Roadster and Coupe 2+2 (the two-seater coupe is dropped). These have flared wheel arches and bolder radiator grills. It has a top speed of more than 145 mph.

1975 Production ends

after 72,507 have been built.

UNDER THE SKIN

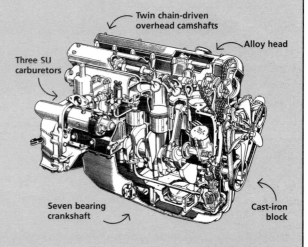

Independent rear suspension

Strong steel monocoque

Twin-cam, straight-six engine

Torsion bar front suspension

XK engine lasted more than four decades

D-type inspired

The E-type's construction was advanced, with a central monocoque inspired by the racing D-type Jaguars. A square-section tube frame carries the engine and front suspension and is bolted to the bulkhead. The rear suspension, mounted on a separate subframe, is also advanced with wishbones and double shock units while the driveshafts also act as suspension arms.

THE POWER PACK

Long-lived XK

One of the most famous and strong engines of all time powered the E-type. The XK straight-six twin-cam was developed during and after the war and first appeared in the successful XK120 sports car in 1948. As well as being installed on most of Jaguar's postwar cars, it also powered the all-conquering C- and D-types to victory at Le Mans. In fact, Jaguar continued to use the XK engine until 1992, when production of the 24-year-old Daimler DS420 limousine finally ended.

Twin chain-driven overhead camshafts

Alloy head

Three SU carburetors

Seven bearing crankshaft

Cast-iron block

Aluminum E-type

In 1963, Jaguar built a small series of Lightweight E-types. They had aluminum monocoque and body panels rather than steel and also alloy block engines to save weight. Despite producing between 320 and 344 bhp from their highly developed fuel-injected engines, they were outclassed on the track by Ferrari's 250 GTO.

Only 12 of the aluminum-bodied Lightweights were built.

Jaguar E-TYPE

It is no surprise the Jaguar E-type is sleek—it is the work of aerodynamicist Malcolm Sayer, with the usual input from Jaguar boss, William Lyons, himself one of the greatest English car stylists.

Short wheelbase

Although the E-type appears to be long and sleek, its wheelbase is actually shorter than those of the Jaguar XK120, 140 and 150 sports cars that came before it.

Front-hinged hood

To allow easy access to the E-type's long, straight-six engine for maintenance and repairs, the whole hood hinges forward.

Torsion bar front suspension

A classic double-wishbone setup is used for the front suspension, sprung by torsion bars running lengthwise rather than the more usual coil springs, which would take up more underhood space.

Knock-off wheels

Wire spoke wheels with knock-off hubs are standard equipment on the early E-type. When the Series II was launched, chrome steel disc wheels became available.

Semi-monocoque construction

The E-type was built around a very strong and rigid central monocoque of sheet steel rather than on a separate chassis like some of its rivals.

Independent rear suspension

Jaguar's first car to have independent suspension was the E-type. The complete assembly is encapsulated in a separate subframe, which is attached to the monocoque via bonded rubber mountings to reduce noise transference.

Faired-in headlights

To make the E-type even more aerodynamic, the headlights on the early cars have perspex covers, later removed due to changing Federal regulations in the U.S.

Inboard rear brakes

Not only does the E-type boast disc brakes all around, but they are mounted inboard at the rear, reducing unsprung weight and giving the suspension less work.

Louvered hood

E-types generate a lot of heat under the low hood, which escapes through 14 rows of louvers on the hood.

Specifications

1961 Jaguar E-Type Roadster

ENGINE
Type: Straight-six twin-cam
Construction: Cast-iron block and alloy cylinder head
Valve gear: Two valves per cylinder operated by twin chain-driven overhead camshafts
Bore and stroke: 3.43 in. x 4.17 in.
Displacement: 3,781 cc
Compression ratio: 9.0:1
Induction system: Three SU carburetors
Maximum power: 265 bhp at 5,500 rpm
Maximum torque: 260 lb-ft at 4,000 rpm
Top speed: 150 mph
0-60 mph: 7.3 sec

TRANSMISSION
Four-speed manual

BODY/CHASSIS
Steel two-seat convertible with center steel monocoque chassis and front and rear subframes

SPECIAL FEATURES

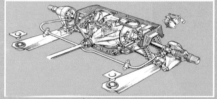

The advanced independent rear suspension can be removed complete from the car in its own separate subframe.

Shallow and wide windshield needs three short wipers to keep it clear.

RUNNING GEAR
Steering: Rack-and-pinion
Front suspension: Double wishbones with longitudinal torsion bars, shocks and anti-roll bar
Rear suspension: Lower wishbones with driveshafts as upper links and twin coil spring/shock units per side
Brakes: Discs all around, inboard at rear
Wheels: Wire spoked 5 in. x 15 in.
Tires: Dunlop 6.40 x 15 RS5 bias-plies

DIMENSIONS
Length: 175.5 in.   **Width:** 165.3 in.
Height: 48 in.   **Wheelbase:** 96 in.
Track: 50 in. (front and rear)
Weight: 2,463 lbs.

Jensen INTERCEPTOR

Unveiled in 1966, the Interceptor had everything: Italian styling, American V8 power and well-balanced handling. The original Interceptor remained in production, virtually unaltered, for 10 years and gained a cult following which lives on today.

"...a sense of refinement."

"More of a grand tourer than a sports car, the Interceptor has deep, comfortable seats. The powerful American V8 and automatic transmission are perfectly suited to a laid-back approach to driving and give the car a sense of refinement. Despite its mannerisms, the car is still quick and can reach 60 mph in just over six seconds. Despite its weight, the Jensen has predictable handling, but the brakes are hard pressed to stop the it from speeds above 124 mph."

Full instrumentation is standard and the interior trim is of the highest quality.

Milestones

1966 Jensen presents
two vehicles styled by Vingale at the London Motor Show. One is fitted with a specially-developed four-wheel drive system.

Jensen's 1954 541 had triple carburetors and four-wheel disc brakes

1969 An improved
Mk II Interceptor is launched. It has a bigger fuel tank, radial tires, and restyled bumpers.

1971 The Mk III and
an SP model with three two-barrel carburetors and 330 bhp are introduced. The FF is dropped this year.

1976 Jensen goes
out of business and the last original Interceptor is built.

The forerunner of the Interceptor was the bizarre-looking CV8.

1983 A new Mk IV
Interceptor enters production, built by Jensen Parts and Service.

UNDER THE SKIN

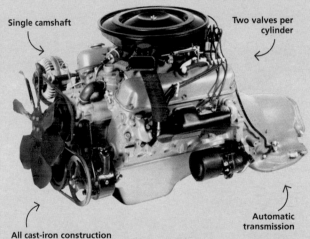

Box-section chassis

Live rear axle

Independent front suspension

Four-wheel disc brakes

Cast-iron V8

Built to last

Carried over from the CV8, the chassis is a steel box-section frame. Double-skinned bulkheads and welded steel panels add to the body's stiffness. Suspension is typical for the era with wishbones and coil springs up front and leaf springs at the rear supporting a solid axle. A Panhard rod helps rear axle location and disc brakes are fitted all around.

THE POWER PACK

Chrysler V8 power

Original Interceptors are powered by Chrysler 383-cubic inch (6.3-liter) and 440-cubic inch (7.2-liter) V8s. Both engines are made of cast-iron with chain-driven camshafts, a five main-bearing crankshaft and two valves per cylinder. With the larger unit acceleration is phenomenal, although handling naturally suffers. Mark IV cars use a small-block 5.9 liter V8, based on the early 340-cubic inch unit. This produced improved fuel economy and slightly better handling.

Single camshaft

Two valves per cylinder

All cast-iron construction

Automatic transmission

Hi-tech FF

Standing for Ferguson Formula, the Jensen FF has four-wheel drive, rack-and-pinion steering, and anti-lock brakes. Slightly longer than the standard Interceptor, it is a complex machine and only 320 were built. Only a small number still remain today.

The Jensen FF was in production from 1966 to 1971.

Jensen INTERCEPTOR

The Jensen Interceptor, launched in 1966 at the London Motor Show, is by far the company's best-remembered product and its biggest seller. The car was so good that it was reborn in the early 1980s.

Chrysler V8 engine

All interceptors are powered by Chrysler V8 engines. Mks I-III used either the 6.3- or 7.2-liter units. These are strong, reliable engines, but have high fuel consumption.

Steel bodywork

Unlike previous Jensen models like the CV8, which had fiberglass bodyshells, the Interceptor uses steel body panels which are better suited to high-volume production.

Limited-slip differential

To aid traction, which is rather poor, a limited-slip differential is installed to the rear axle.

Glass hatchback

The bulbous back window is not only attractive, but also functional. The whole unit lifts up to provide space for luggage.

Specifications

1968 Jensen Interceptor

ENGINE
Type: V8

Construction: Cast-iron block and heads

Valve gear: Two valves per cylinder operated by hydraulic tappets, pushrods and rockers

Bore and stroke: 4.25 in. x 3.38 in.

Displacement: 6,276 cc

Compression ratio: 10.0:1

Induction system: Single Carter AFB four-barrel carburetor

Maximum power: 330 bhp at 4,600 rpm

Maximum torque: 450 lb-ft at 2,800 rpm

Top speed: 137 mph

0-60 mph: 6.4 sec.

TRANSMISSION
Chrysler TorqueFlite 727 automatic

BODY/CHASSIS
Tubular and welded sheet steel monocoque with two-door body

SPECIAL FEATURES

The Mk II Interceptor has a different front bumper with the parking lights positioned beneath it.

Fender extractor vents aid engine cooling and help to distinguish the Interceptor from the four-wheel drive FF, which has two vents per side.

RUNNING GEAR
Steering: Recirculating ball

Front suspension: Independent wishbones with coil springs and telescopic shocks

Rear suspension: Live rear axle with semi-elliptical leaf springs, telescopic shocks and a Panhard rod

Brakes: Girling discs, 11.4-in. dia. (front), 10.7-in. dia. (rear)

Wheels: Rostyle pressed steel, 15-in. dia.

Tires: Dunlop 185 x 15

DIMENSIONS
Length: 188 in.	**Width:** 70 in.
Height: 53 in.	**Wheelbase:** 105 in.

Track: 56 in. (front and rear)

Weight: 3,696 lbs.

Adjustable shocks

Despite its archaic rear leaf springs, the Interceptor has adjustable telescopic shocks to help smooth out the ride.

Italian styling

The shape was originally penned by Touring of Milan and adapted by Vignale to produce the Interceptor.

Lagonda RAPIDE

The Lagonda name has a rich heritage that Aston Martin's David Brown tapped into with a 1961 revival of the marque. At launch, the Rapide was probably the world's most prestigious performance sedan.

"...thoroughbred quality."

"Classic, handbuilt charm does not come any more attractive than in the cabin of a Lagonda Rapide. Surprisingly, the six-cylinder engine has thoroughbred quality written all over it, sounds fabulous and provides gutsy straight line performance. The handling exploits a perfect 50/50 weight distribution and the car has a low center of gravity. Although this is a very bulky 4-door, it really feels like a grander version of an Aston Martin, even if the steering is a touch heavy."

Leather and wood styling grandly garnish the cabin, giving a decidedly sporty feel.

Milestones

1961 After a gap of
three years, Aston Martin revives the Lagonda name with the luxury high-performance Rapide sedan. Nevertheless, buyers are hesitant about the idiosyncratic front end styling and relatively compact cabin.

Aston's DB5 shares components with the Lagonda Rapide.

1964 After a disappointingly sparse
production run, the Rapide is dropped and the Lagonda marque is quietly forgotten.

Latest Aston Martin Lagondas are these Virage-based designs.

1974 The Lagonda name
is revived once again, after an absence of 10 years— the new car is called simply the Aston Martin Lagonda. It is followed two years later by the famous, wedge-shaped model.

UNDER THE SKIN

Twin fuel tanks

Steel-platform chassis

Four-wheel disc brakes

Alloy six

Like a longer DB4

Under its light-alloy bodywork, the Rapide is an engagingly engineered car, owing much to the Aston Martin DB4. It uses a very strong steel platform chassis with substantial box section stiffening and an independent front suspension. At the rear, a de Dion beam axle is used. It is sprung by torsion bars and has double-acting shock absorbers.

THE POWER PACK

Advanced straight six

Aston Martin Lagonda's highly talented engineer Tadek Marek used the same basic layout for the Rapide's engine as used in earlier Lagondas: twin overhead cam, six cylinders. The all-alloy, lightweight straight six is best known as the powerplant of the Aston Martin DB5 and DB6, but this 4.0-liter engine was first used in the Rapide three years before the Astons. The engine—advanced for its time—features double overhead camshafts, seven main bearings, twin Solex carburetors and a mechanical camshaft with solid lifters. More crucially, it pumps out a very healthy 236 bhp.

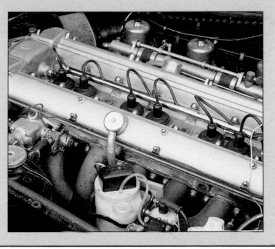

Quirky choice

If you were in the market for a high performance, handbuilt car with four doors in 1961, you had very few choices. Today, the Rapide remains a quirky and individual choice among classic car enthusiasts and also represents excellent value.

As a hand-built, David Brown creation, the Rapide is good value today.

Lagonda RAPIDE

The Rapide name recalled the glorious LG45 and V12 Lagondas of the 1930s, though in most respects the new Lagonda was a modern, cutting-edge car. Its construction followed Touring's 'superleggera' principles.

Italian styling

The Milanese styling house Touring had done an excellent job of designing the Aston Martin DB4 and so it was called in to design the Rapide. Its efforts here were more controversial, especially at the front end.

Traditional grill

The outline of the main air intake grill reflects the traditional Lagonda design. However, its overall effect is rather convoluted, thanks to an odd center bar in the main grill and ungainly side grills.

'Superleggera' construction

Touring of Milan pioneered the 'superleggera' method of construction, which was used for the Rapide. Basically, the aluminum body panels are unstressed and mounted on a solid frame constructed with channels and round tubes welded to the main chassis frame. This increases stiffness and keeps the car's overall weight down.

Auto or manual transmission

As standard, the Rapide came with a Borg-Warner torque converter and three-speed automatic transmission. To satisfy more sporty drivers, an all-synchromesh, four-speed, manual transmission was optional.

de Dion rear axle

To save space, the well located live rear axle of the DB4 was abandoned in favor of a de Dion layout. For the same reason, transverse torsion bars were used in place of coil springs. A Watt linkage provides lateral location and trailing arms locate the de Dion longitudinally.

Luxury interior

All five passengers enjoy true luxury travel. The seats are deeply upholstered in leather, and the front pair is fully adjustable. There is thick floor carpeting, twin heaters for front and rear and power windows all around.

Quad headlights

One of the controversial aspects of the styling was the headlight treatment. Lucas 'mixed' lights were fitted in oval shrouds, the outer pair measuring seven inches across, the inner pair five inches. The effect is dramatic but rather fussy for some enthusiast's tastes.

Specifications

1962 Lagonda Rapide

ENGINE

Type: In-line six-cylinder

Construction: Aluminum block and cylinder head

Valve gear: Two valves per cylinder operated by double overhead camshafts

Bore and stroke: 3.78 in. x 3.62 in.

Displacement: 3,995 cc

Compression ratio: 8.25:1

Induction system: Two Solex carburetors

Maximum power: 236 bhp at 5,000 rpm

Maximum torque: 265 lb-ft at 4,000 rpm

Top speed: 130 mph

0-60 mph: 8.9 sec.

TRANSMISSION

Four-speed manual or three-speed automatic

BODY/CHASSIS

Platform steel chassis with aluminum four-door sedan body

SPECIAL FEATURES

What was considered odd styling in 1961 now has idiosyncratic appeal.

Aston Martin's hallmark fender vents appear on a Lagonda for the first time.

RUNNING GEAR

Steering: Rack-and-pinion

Front suspension: Upper and lower wishbones with coil springs, telescopic shock absorbers and anti-roll bar

Rear suspension: De Dion axle with Watt linkage, trailing arms, torsion bars and telescopic shock absorbers

Brakes: Discs (front and rear)

Wheels: Steel, 15-in. dia.

Tires: 7.10 x 15

DIMENSIONS

Length: 195.5 in.   **Width:** 69.5 in.

Height: 56.0 in.   **Wheelbase:** 114.0 in.

Track: 54.0 in. (front), 55.5 in. (rear)

Weight: 3,780 lbs.

Lamborghini MIURA

With one stroke, Ferruccio Lamborghini made Enzo Ferrari look foolish and his cars appear obsolete. Lamborghini beat Ferrari to the punch, building the world's first mid-engined supercar and the first with a quad-cam V12 engine.

"...sensation of the decade."

"The sensation of the 1966 Geneva Motor Show was also the sensation of the decade. Now this superb Bertone design is before you, and as you slide low into this gorgeous automobile, you realize why this is still one of the most desired cars ever built. Everything about this car is over-the-top: the colors, the sci-fi body design, the power and even the zero body roll that tempts you to push it until it suddenly breaks away."

There can be few more inviting cockpits than the Lamborghini Miura's. It's a car that truly begs to be driven hard.

Milestones

1966 Lamborghini stuns the Geneva Motor Show by unveiling the 400 GT's replacement. The Miura is styled for Bertone by a rising star in the design world, Marcello Gandini.

The beautiful Touring-bodied 400 GT was Lamborghini's second model.

1967 Miura P400 production gets under way and 475 are built before the car is updated.

1969 The Miura S is introduced with the engine tuned to produce 370 bhp and torque increases to 286 lb-ft.

1971 The S turns into the SV with even more power, 385 bhp and an improved transmission, which makes the power easier to use.

1973 The world oil crisis helps bring about the end of Miura production.

Rear slats helped the style, but did little for rear visibility.

UNDER THE SKIN

Modern monocoque

While other Italian supercar builders were still using old-fashioned spaceframes, the Miura has a modern steel monocoque structure with the strength coming from massive sills and a large center tunnel, all three joined by large bulkheads. The engine is held in a folded steel frame behind the center bulkhead.

Front-mounted radiator

Mid-mounted engine

Double-wishbone rear suspension

Transverse V12

THE POWER PACK

Four Weber carburetors

Twin distributors

Transmission behind engine

Differential behind transmission

Racing V12

The Miura's V12 was designed by the man who led development on the legendary Ferrari 250 GTO. For the very first Lamborghini (the 350 GT), Giotto Bizzarrini designed a quad-cam V12, with alloy block and heads, twin distributors and classical hemispherical combustion chambers. Even though there are only two valves per cylinder, it was originally more like a race than a road engine. It was slightly altered and refined before being installed in the Miura with an integral transmission.

The Miura SV

Last and best of the Miura line is the SV, introduced in 1971. It has more power (385 bhp), enough to take the top speed to over 174 mph and drops the 0-60 mph time to 6.8 seconds. A wider track under larger wheel arches improves the Miura's handling.

The SV was the last and best of the Miuras.

Lamborghini MIURA ▮▮

Only three years after Lamborghini started making cars, the company produced the most exotic supercar the world had ever seen. It was as advanced as it was stunning, with its 4-liter V12 engine mounted behind the driver.

Alloy and steel bodywork
The main body section of the Miura is fabricated from steel for strength. Some panels, such as the engine cover and front section of the bodywork, are alloy to save weight.

Transverse V12
To make the Miura as compact as possible the engine is mounted transversely, making it the first transverse V12 supercar.

Transmission behind engine
With a transverse engine, there is no space for the transmission to be mounted in the usual place. The Miura's transmission is behind the engine, with the transmission and engine sharing the same oil.

Slatted engine cover
The great heat generated by a large V12 running fast in a small engine bay was vented through the open slatted engine cover, which did little to improve the view through the rear-view mirror.

Door frame air vents
One of the main styling features is the air vents—for the engine compartment—which are actually built into the door frame.

Tip forward lights

When not in use, the headlights fold back to follow the line of the bodywork, a styling feature used years later by Porsche on the 928.

Top-mounted anti-roll bar

The Miura follows racing car practice in many ways. For example, its rear anti-roll bar runs from the bottom wishbones up over the chassis.

Front-mounted radiator

Although the engine is mid-mounted, the radiator stays in the conventional place at the front where it is easier to cool with the help of two electric fans. It is angled to fit under the Miura's low sloping nose.

Specifications
1969 Lamborghini P400S

ENGINE
Type: V12
Construction: Light alloy block and heads
Valve gear: Two valves per cylinder operated by four chain-driven overhead camshafts
Bore and stroke: 3.23 in. x 2.44 in.
Displacement: 3,929 cc
Compression ratio: 10.7:1
Induction system: Four Weber downdraft carburetors
Maximum power: 370 bhp at 7,700 rpm
Maximum torque: 286 lb-ft at 5,500 rpm
Top speed: 172 mph
0-60 mph: 6.9 sec.

TRANSMISSION
Five-speed manual

BODY/CHASSIS
Steel monocoque platform with steel and alloy two-door, two-seat coupe body

SPECIAL FEATURES

Stylized vents behind the doors provide air to the mid-mounted engine. Door handle is cleverly shaped to blend in with the styling.

The sloping headlights have distinctive 'eyebrows'; purely a styling feature.

RUNNING GEAR
Steering: Rack-and-pinion
Front suspension: Double wishbones with coil springs, telescopic shocks and anti-roll bar
Rear suspension: Double wishbones, with coil springs, telescopic shocks and anti-roll bar
Brakes: Solid discs, 11.8 in. dia. (front),12.1 in. dia. (rear)
Wheels: Magnesium 7 in. x 15 in.
Tires: Pirelli Cinturato GT70 VR15

DIMENSIONS
Length: 171.6 in.   **Width:** 71 in.
Height: 42 in.   **Wheelbase:** 98.4 in.
Track: 55.6 in. (front and rear)
Weight: 2,850 lbs.

Lotus ELAN

The lithe and agile Lotus Elan is still regarded by many as one of the best-handling cars ever made—a masterpiece and tribute to Colin Chapman's innovative and intuitive engineering skill.

"...fantastic driver's car."

"The Lotus Elan is a lightweight compared to most other small sports cars. It remains a fantastic driver's car. First of all it is fast: 126 bhp in a car that weighs just over 1,500 lbs. means aggressive power in the lower gears all the way past 100 mph. But it is the handling that makes the Elan so memorable. It doesn't understeer or oversteer, but simply tracks faithfully around any curve generating high levels of lateral acceleration even on skinny tires."

Despite its light weight, the Elan still has a high-quality wooden dashboard.

Milestones

1962 The Elan 1500 is announced at the London Motor Show. All 1500s are recalled and fitted with 1,558-cc engines.

The Elan +2 four seater was launched in 1967.

1964 The Elan S2 is introduced with restyled taillights, larger front brake calipers and a new veneer fascia with a lockable glovebox.

1965 A fixed-head coupe version joins the convertible model.

The Elan replaced the fiberglass monocoque Elite.

1968 The new S4 convertible is announced.

1971 The Sprint is launched with a new 126-bhp version of the twin-cam engine.

1973 Production of the Elan is discontinued.

UNDER THE SKIN

Fiberglass bodyshell

Backbone chassis

Four-wheel disc brakes

Twin-cam four

Chapman's ace

The Elan uses a backbone chassis that was very simple to build. It is shaped like a tuning fork with the final drive and strut suspension mounted in high-angled outriggers. The rest of the rear suspension comprises tubular lower wishbones with driveshafts fitted with inner and outer rubber universal joints. The rack-and-pinion steering is from the Triumph Herald and there are four-wheel disc brakes.

THE POWER PACK

Lotus power

For the first time for Lotus, the engine was not entirely sourced from another manufacturer. The twin-cam cylinder head was fitted to the Ford cast-iron 1,499-cc block which was later increased to 1,558 cc. The Sprint, introduced in 1971, has larger intake valves, a new camshaft, reworked ports and combustion chambers and a higher 10.3:1 compression ratio. The drive-train is strengthened to take the extra power. Carburetor choices were twin Webers, Strombergs or Dellortos.

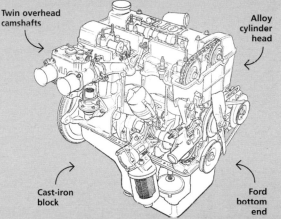

Twin overhead camshafts

Alloy cylinder head

Cast-iron block

Ford bottom end

More seats

To cater to Elan owners with young families, Lotus announced the +2 model in 1967. It has all the engineering features of the small Elan but is clothed in a larger body that offers 2+2 seating. It has all the performance of its smaller brother.

The Elan +2 four-seater is often overlooked by collectors.

Lotus ELAN

The Lotus Elan Sprint was one of the fastest sports cars built. Its speed, agility and compact dimensions mean it is now one of the most sought after of all classic Lotus models.

Twin-cam engine
Based on the Ford Cortina, the Elan's engine was originally supposed to have a smaller 1,340-cc capacity. It was designed by Harry Mundy, the technical editor of *Autocar* magazine.

Four- and five-speed transmissions
Most Elans came with the Ford four-speed, but in search of better high-speed cruising, a few later Sprints used the Lotus five-speed transmission (commonly found in the +2S 130), which used Austin internals.

Backbone chassis
Chapman's original intention was to make the Elan a fiberglass monocoque like the Elite. In fact, Elan prototypes used a separate chassis so that they could be built quickly for testing. They worked so well, however, that the production cars were built with separate chassis.

Fiberglass body

Lotus was a pioneer of fiberglass bodyshells. Fiberglass is ideal for low-volume production and has the advantages of strength, light weight and rust resistance.

Pop-up headlights

The Elan's pop-up headlights were a first on a production car and were a device intended to meet California headlight height regulations. They are vacuum-operated.

Advanced suspension

Chapman mixed and matched many parts to produce probably the best-handling and best-riding sports car of its generation. The front suspension parts are shared with the Triumph Herald, with coil springs and patented 'Chapman struts' at the rear.

Specifications

Lotus Elan Sprint

ENGINE

Type: In-line four

Construction: Cast-iron block and alloy cylinder head

Valve gear: Two valves per cylinder operated by twin overhead camshafts

Bore and stroke: 3.25 in. x 2.86 in.

Displacement: 1,558 cc

Compression ratio: 10.3:1

Induction system: Two Weber carburetors

Maximum power: 126 bhp at 6,500 rpm

Maximum torque: 113 lb-ft at 5,500 rpm

Top speed: 118 mph

0-60 mph: 7.0 sec.

TRANSMISSION

Four-speed manual

BODY/CHASSIS

Fiberglass body with steel backbone chassis

SPECIAL FEATURES

The hood bulge was incorporated to accommodate larger carburetors.

Pop-up headlights were a rarely seen feature in the 1960s.

RUNNING GEAR

Steering: Rack-and-pinion

Front suspension: Double wishbones with coil springs, telescopic shock absorbers and anti-roll bar

Rear suspension: Independent by Chapman struts, lower wishbones, coil springs and telescopic shock absorbers

Brakes: Discs (front and rear)

Wheels: Steel, 4.5 x 13.0 in.

Tires: Radials, 165 x 13

DIMENSIONS

Length: 145.0 in.   **Width:** 56.0 in.

Height: 45.2 in.   **Wheelbase:** 84.0 in.

Track: 45.0 in. (front), 48.4 in. (rear)

Weight: 1,515 lbs.

Maserati MISTRAL

In the early 1960s, although overshadowed by Ferrari and lacking the charisma of the Maranello marques' V12 engines, Maserati still produced real thoroughbreds like the stylish Mistral.

"...ample character."

"On the road, the Mistral owes few apologies to Ferrari or anyone else. It is a practical car, with lazy performance, a fine chassis and ample character. The injection has a 'choke' for starting, which needs care, but once warmed up the six is untemperamental and flexible. The ZF transmission has a delightfully short throw and the steering is pleasantly light, though a little low geared. In reality, the Mistral is more like a grand tourer than a sports car."

The cockpit is light, spacious and luxurious, with leather upholstery and wool carpets.

Milestones

1963 Maserati previews the Mistral at the Turin Motor Show—only 15 years after the first 'production' Maserati was introduced at the same venue.

The later Bora adopted a mid-mounted V8 engine.

1964 The Mistral reaches the showroom floor In coupe and convertible forms. In the first year of production, Maserati sells 99 coupes and 17 convertible Spyders, which were launched at the Geneva Motor Show.

AC's 428 grand tourer was also styled by Frua.

1966 The engine's capacity is enlarged from 3.7 to 4.0 liters. It produces 255 bhp and has even more impressive flexibility.

1970 The last three Mistrals are sold. The model is replaced by the V8-engined Mexico and Ghibli family.

UNDER THE SKIN

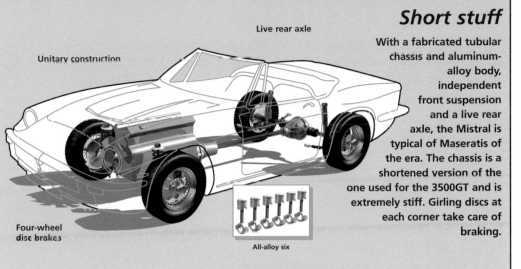

Unitary construction

Live rear axle

Four-wheel disc brakes

All-alloy six

Short stuff

With a fabricated tubular chassis and aluminum-alloy body, independent front suspension and a live rear axle, the Mistral is typical of Maseratis of the era. The chassis is a shortened version of the one used for the 3500GT and is extremely stiff. Girling discs at each corner take care of braking.

THE POWER PACK

Ultimate engine

The ultimate development of Maserati's long-stroke twin-cam straight-six, designed by Giulio Alfieri, is used in the Mistral. It is an all-alloy unlt with cast-iron cylinder liners and a fully-machined crankshaft running in seven main bearings. The twin-overhead camshafts are chain-driven and operate two large valves in each hemispherical combustion chamber. There are two spark plugs per cylinder, which fire simultaneously to maximize combustion.

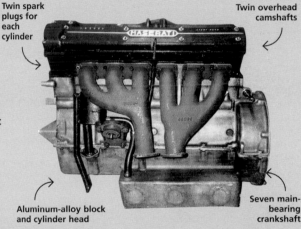

Twin spark plugs for each cylinder

Twin overhead camshafts

Aluminum-alloy block and cylinder head

Seven main-bearing crankshaft

Undervalued

Although it was in production for seven years, only 1,068 Mistrals left the factory. It is a stylish, fast, forgiving and practical car, but the Mistral is underrated. The most desirable model is the Spyder, of which only 120 were built.

Stylish and fast, the Mistral is relatively cheap to buy.

Maserati MINSTRAL

The Mistral marked the end of an era for Maserati—it was the company's last straight-six sports car. Despite having only six cylinders, the Mistral had excellent performance, particularly in its final 4.0-liter form.

Tubular-steel chassis

At the time the Mistral was introduced, all Maseratis were built with a separate tubular-steel chassis. In the Mistral's case this features an array of relatively small-diameter tubes in place of fewer, but larger, main chassis members.

Wishbone front suspension

The front suspension is compact with concentric coil spring/shock absorber units mounted between the unequal-length wishbones.

Frua styling

Pietro Frua styled the Mistral and it proved to be the best of all his designs. He virtually recreated it for a different manufacturer in the form of the AC 428.

Aluminum-alloy bodywork

Contrary to some accounts which describe the Mistral as having mainly steel bodywork with alloy doors, hood and trunk lid, all the body panels are made of aluminum.

Disc brakes

By the mid-1960s virtually all European high-performance cars used disc brakes. The Mistral is no exception, with Girling discs front and rear.

Live rear axle

The most traditional part of the specification is the rear suspension, which employs a live axle located by semi-elliptic leaf springs and assisted by a single torque reaction arm.

Specifications
1967 Maserati Mistral

ENGINE
Type: In-line six

Construction: Aluminum-alloy block and head

Valve gear: Two valves per cylinder operated by two chain-driven overhead camshafts via bucket tappets and shims

Bore and stroke: 3.46 in. x 4.33 in.

Displacement: 4,014 cc

Compression ratio: 8.8:1

Induction system: Lucas mechanical fuel injection

Maximum power: 255 bhp at 5,200 rpm

Maximum torque: 267 lb-ft at 3,500 rpm

Top speed: 147 mph

0-60 mph: 6.5 sec.

TRANSMISSION
ZF five-speed manual

BODY/CHASSIS
Tubular-steel chassis with coupe or convertible aluminum-alloy body

SPECIAL FEATURES

Tear-drop marker lights supplement the main units under the bumper.

The scoop in the fender is mechanically-operated, allowing cool air into the car.

RUNNING GEAR
Steering: Recirculating ball

Front suspension: Double wishbones with coil springs, telescopic shock absorbers and anti-roll bar

Rear suspension: Live axle with semi-elliptic leaf springs, telescopic shock absorbers, single torque reaction arm and anti-roll bar

Brakes: Discs, 12.05-in. dia. (front), 11.5-in. dia (rear)

Wheels: Borrani wire, 7 x 15 in.

Tires: 225/70 VR15

DIMENSIONS
Length: 177.2 in.   **Width:** 64.9 in.

Height: 49.2 in.   **Wheelbase:** 94.5 in.

Track: 54.7 in. (front), 53.3 in. (rear)

Weight: 2,866 lbs.

Mercedes-Benz 600

With the 600 'Grosser' of 1963, Mercedes-Benz took luxury driving to a new level of sophistication, combining sports car performance with every kind of labor-saving device in a massive and beautifully built sedan.

"...surprisingly nimble."

"For such a heavyweight, the 600 is surprisingly nimble. Although the four-speed automatic transmission generally starts off in second, the V8 engine produces enough torque to make the bottom gear redundant, unless you're into racing. It kicks in only if you slam your foot hard to the floor from a standstill. The air suspension keeps cornering composed and the ride is steady and supple. The whole car feels impeccably built and totally solid."

Immaculate build quality is a Mercedes' hallmark and is exemplified by this cabin.

Milestones

1961 Mercedes announces
Its first air suspended model, the 300SE/SEL, based on the 'fintail' body.

1963 The 600 is launched
with a 'normal' wheelbase and 5-seater body, and a long-wheelbase limousine with an 8-seater capability. Some limousines have six doors.

European dignitaries usually used the six-door limo.

1968 A 6.3 V8 unit is used
in the 300SEL S-class body to become the 300SEL 6.3.

The current S-class, although more modestly proportioned, is a direct descendant of the 600.

1975 The 450SEL 6.9 is announced
with a 6,834-cc version of the 6.3-liter engine in the new-shape S-class body. It runs until 1980.

1981 600 production ends.
A modest but nevertheless significant total of 2,190 sedans and 487 limousines have been produced.

UNDER THE SKIN

Air suspension

Anti-dive geometry

All-new V8

Disc brakes

New hydraulics

A hydraulic circuit operating at 300 psi controls the windows, trunk lid, the closing of the doors (so they never need to be slammed), the sunroof and the glass partition on the long-wheelbase version. Mercedes-Benz pursued its commitment to air suspension with the 600. A self-leveling system pressurizes at 260 psi, and can raise the sedan by 2 inches. The front suspension features anti-dive geometry for the wishbones and the brake discs have twin calipers.

THE POWER PACK

A roadgoing first

The 600 uses an all-new overhead camshaft V8, the first in a roadgoing Mercedes. It is fuel injected and has an iron block and alloy heads with the camshafts driven by chains. Belts driven off the front of the engine drive all the hydraulic and compressed air functions. The 6.3 V8 is relatively low revving and produces its peak power—300 bhp SAE—at 4,100 rpm. It was only available with Mercedes-Benz's four-speed automatic transmission with a fluid coupling rather than a torque converter.

Fuel injection

Chain-driven camshafts

Belt-driven hydraulic functions

Iron block and alloy heads

Short stuff

Although the long-wheelbase limousines are more imposing, the short-wheelbase sedan is probably the better drive. Both versions have a lot more class and will turn more heads than any stretched Lincoln or Cadillac, old or new.

The shorter sedans are less expensive and have better driving characteristics.

Mercedes-Benz 600

With the 600, Mercedes aimed to beat Rolls-Royce at its own game with a car that set new standards in luxury travel for those who could afford it. At the time, the 600 was one of the most complex and expensive cars in the world.

V8 engine

This iron-block, overhead-camshaft engine was designed specifically to be used in the 600. It was intended to provide smooth, effortless operation combined with more performance than almost any other sedan in the world.

Four-speed automatic transmission

This is a strengthened version of the familiar four-speed Mercedes automatic transmission that was already becoming the favored option on most of the company's passenger cars.

Four-wheel disc brakes

Given its 130-mph capability, the heavy 600 sedan needed the best brakes money could buy. Mercedes realized this and fitted four-wheel discs that have separate hydraulic circuits front and rear. Each front disc has twin calipers.

Rear passenger luxury

As 600s were conceived for the most prestigious of customers, the rear section of the cabin is fitted with a host of convenience features. Radio controls are duplicated for rear-seat passengers, there are separate heating and ventilation systems, and there is an intercom for communication with the driver.

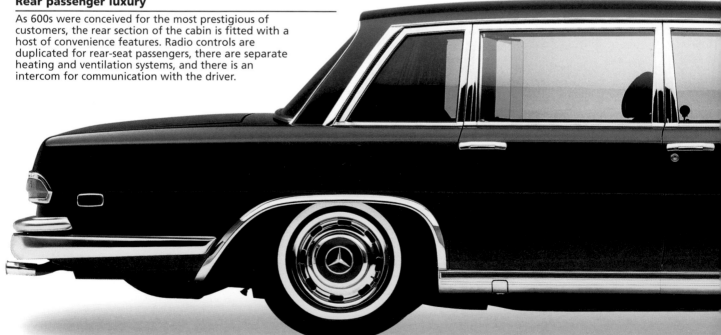

Air suspension

Rolling bag-type air suspension is a key feature of the 600. Pressurized at 260 psi, it is self-leveling by means of two sensing valves, front and rear. There are soft and hard settings, worked from a steering-column control. In addition, the suspension can be raised up to 2 inches for extra ground clearance.

Long and 'normal' wheelbase

The sedan version of the 600 has a 126-inch wheelbase and the limousine a 153.5-inch wheelbase. There are four- and six-door versions of the limo and a handful were built with State Landaulet bodywork.

Modern, brutal styling

The square, uncompromising styling of the 600 isn't liked by everybody, but its very simplicity means it has never really gone out of fashion; it looked as modern in 1981 as it did in 1963.

Specifications
1963 Mercedes-Benz 600

ENGINE
Type: V8

Construction: Cast-iron block and alloy heads

Valve gear: Two valves per cylinder operated by single overhead camshafts

Bore and stroke: 4.06 in. x 3.74 in.

Displacement: 6,332 cc

Compression ratio: 9.0:1

Induction system: Bosch electronic fuel injection

Maximum power: 300 bhp at 4,100 rpm

Maximum torque: 434 lb-ft at 3,000 rpm

Top speed: 130 mph

0-60 mph: 9.4 sec.

TRANSMISSION
Four-speed automatic

BODY/CHASSIS
Unitary monocoque construction with steel four-door sedan

SPECIAL FEATURES

This pressed-steel hubcap design is featured on most Mercedes-Benz models made in the 1960s.

Mercedes-Benz's prominent, upright headlight arrangement emphasizes the car's square-cut styling.

RUNNING GEAR
Steering: Recirculating ball

Front suspension: Double wishbones with air springs and anti-roll bar

Rear suspension: Low-pivot swing axle with trailing arms each side and air springs

Brakes: Dunlop/ATE discs, 11.3-in. dia. (front), 11.6-in. dia.(rear)

Wheels: Steel, 15-in. dia.

Tires: Fulda super sport, 9.00 x 15 in.

DIMENSIONS
Length: 218.0 in.   **Width:** 76.8 in.
Height: 59.5 in.   **Wheelbase:** 126.0 in.
Track: 62.5 in. (front), 62.0 in. (rear)
Weight: 5,380 lbs

MGB

One of the best-loved sports cars the world has ever known, the MGB also still retains its status as one of the longest-lived. In Roadster form it quickly became the archetypal British sports car of the post-war era.

"...pure enjoyment."

"In 1962 the MGB was a fine expression of the ideal sports car, and one of the most affordable on the market. The steering is communicative and the handling predictable—at least until you hit a bump, when it gets knocked out of shape all too easily. The B-series engine is tractable from low revs but does not have a high redline. For pure enjoyment the MGB was hard to beat and it is a fine value today."

The MGB has a classic and simple interior, although the steering wheel seems huge for a sports car by today's standards.

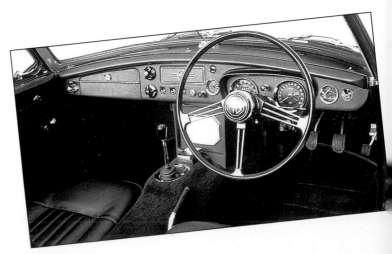

Milestones

1962 After a four-year development period, the MGB Roadster is first shown to the public at the Motor Show at Earl's Court in England.

1963 A fiberglass hardtop becomes a popular and inexpensive option.

The six-cylinder MGC can be recognized by the big hood bulge.

1964 The engine receives a five-bearing crankshaft and an oil cooler becomes standard.

1965 The Roadster is joined by a GT coupe model.

The MGB was available in GT and Roadster forms. These are post-1974 'rubber bumper' models.

1967 A new Mk II model receives an all-synchromesh transmission and the option of automatic transmission. The MGB remains in production until 1980.

UNDER THE SKIN

Classically British

The MGB was designed by the company's Chief Engineer, Sydney Enever, following the principles of and using many components from his previous MGA. It therefore has the proven coil spring and wishbone front suspension and a live rear axle with semi-elliptic leaf springs. The MGB departs from previous MG practice in its use of unitary (monocoque) construction.

Coil-sprung front suspension

Live rear axle

Monocoque construction

Trusty B-series

THE POWER PACK

Rugged engine

MG could have opted to fit the powerful 108-bhp, twin-cam engine which it had developed for the MGA in the MGB. However, the poor reliability record of this powerplant led to the choice of the well-proven overhead-valve B-series engine. For the MGB it is bored out to 1,796 cc, and power has increased from 86 bhp to 95 bhp. The bore castings are siamesed and the main bearings beefed up, but the head gear remains as before. One of its best characteristics is a flat torque curve.

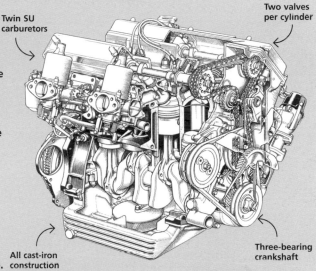

Twin SU carburetors

Two valves per cylinder

Three-bearing crankshaft

All cast-iron construction

Prized original

In MG circles, an early example of the original Roadster with the three-bearing engine is highly desirable. Built for only two years, it is rare to find in good condition and is keenly sought after. The earliest car represents the purest expression of the MGB form.

The early MGB is a prized collector's car.

MGB

There is no doubt that the MGB is what sports cars are supposed to be like. An open-topped, two-seater, front-engined, rear-wheel drive car is the way to travel.

Monocoque construction

Unlike all previous MG cars, the 'B' was designed around monocoque principles, using strong, double-skinned sills. This simplified the production process, reduced build costs and made the overall package more effective.

Leaf-sprung rear

Although MG experimented with an independently sprung rear end, the MGB has a live rear axle. It is suspended by semi-elliptic leaf springs and uses lever-arm shock absorbers.

Wind-up windows

Unlike all previous MG sports cars, which stuck with the old British custom of removable side windows or curtains, the MGB has glass windows that are opened and closed using a hand crank. Though this is a matter of course in U.S. built cars, it's considered a a luxury for MG owners.

Chrome bumpers

Early MGBs are colloquially known as 'chrome bumper' cars to distinguish them from the Federal-equipped 'rubber bumper' cars. Aesthetically, the original chrome finish is more pleasing and retains the familiar slatted grill of the older MGs.

Spacious cabin
By sports car standards, room inside the cockpit is very generous and the driver and passenger have no difficulty getting comfortable.

Specifications

1962 MGB Roadster

ENGINE
Type: In-line four-cylinder
Construction: Cast-iron block and head
Valve gear: Two valves per cylinder operated by a single camshaft via pushrods
Bore and stroke: 3.16 in. x 3.5 in.
Displacement: 1,796 cc
Compression ratio: 8.8:1
Induction system: Two SU carburetors
Maximum power: 95 bhp at 5,500 rpm
Maximum torque: 110 lb-ft at 3,500 rpm
Top speed: 105 mph
0-60 mph: 12.5 sec.

TRANSMISSION
Four-speed manual (overdrive optional)

BODY/CHASSIS
Monocoque chassis with two-door steel open body

SPECIAL FEATURES

The early three-bearing MGB is recognizable by its 'pull' door handles.

The MGB was designed with chrome bumpers, but post-1974 cars have rubber bumpers to meet the U.S. safety regulations.

RUNNING GEAR
Steering: Rack-and-pinion
Front suspension: Wishbones with coil springs and lever-arm shock absorbers
Rear suspension: Live axle with semi-elliptic springs and lever-arm shock absorbers
Brakes: Discs (front), drums (rear)
Wheels: Steel, 14-in. dia.
Tires: 165/70 14

DIMENSIONS
Length: 153.2 in.   **Width:** 59.9 in.
Height: 49.4 in.   **Wheelbase:** 91 in.
Track: 49.2 in. (front), 49.2 in. (rear)
Weight: 2,080 lbs.

Mini **COOPER**

When Formula 1 constructor John Cooper showed that the basic Mini could be transformed with a more powerful engine and disc brakes, the startling result instantly became one of the world's best rally cars.

"...amazing handling."

"Forget the upright driving position with its horrible seats and bus-like angle of the steering wheel. Dynamically everything else about the Cooper S is perfect. It has immediate response to the steering, amazing handling characteristics, grip that was unmatched, even on those tiny tires, and a feel that made you drive it absolutely flat out around every corner it went around. The transmission howls and it's undergeared, which makes it too noisy for highways but it's in its element on twisty country roads and rally circuits."

It may not be too comfortable at the wheel of a Mini Cooper, but it's certainly entertaining.

Milestones

1959 Mini introduced

in Austin and Morris forms.

Issigonis' Mini soon showed a capability to take more power.

1961 First Mini Cooper appears with a

bigger engine and disc brakes.

1963 Cooper given 998-cc engine. First Mini

Cooper S is launched, with 1,031-cc, 70-bhp engine. It is produced for just a year.

Mini Coopers had a huge impact on world rallying.

1964 Coopers given

998-cc engines and the new Hydrolastic suspension. The 970-cc Cooper S is built for homologation: only 963 are made. In March the 1,275-cc Cooper S appears with 76-bhp engine.

1970 MkII Cooper S

(essentially just a minor restyle launched in 1967) turns into the MkIII with better seats and wind-up windows.

UNDER THE SKIN

Square design maximizes room

Exposed seams on bodywork

Transverse mounted engine

Gearbox under engine

Four cylinders

Perfect package

The Mini was a brilliant piece of packaging. By placing the transmission below the engine, a space-efficient (if upright) design was created with more room inside for its external dimensions than any other car. The other really innovative part of the design is the use of small rubber cones in place of conventional coil springs. They, like the rear trailing-arm suspension design, are also very space efficient.

THE POWER PACK

Tunable four

The A-series engine was an old design even when the Mini was new. It is a simple all-iron, overhead-valve design with in-line valves, and the carburetor and exhaust ports are on the same side of the head. The first Minis were 848 cc with only 34 bhp but the first Coopers had 997-cc and then 998-cc versions with twin carburetors and 55 bhp. Biggest of the A-series variants used was the 1,275 cc, which, in the Cooper S, produced 76 bhp.

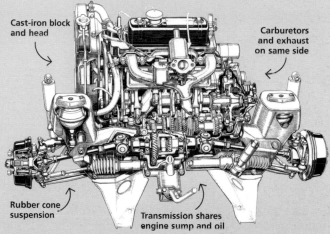

Cast-iron block and head

Carburetors and exhaust on same side

Rubber cone suspension

Transmission shares engine sump and oil

Superior S

The smaller-engined Coopers were fun, but the extra power and torque of the 1,275-cc engine in the Cooper S and its better brakes makes it more desirable. For those who don't mind bouncing around, the original rubber cone suspended car is the one to have.

Cooper S was a match for far larger race and rally cars.

Mini COOPER

The Mini Cooper's amazing road holding comes from its wheel at each corner design and its light weight. It quickly became the best small sporting sedan in the world, at home on the race track as well as rally stage.

Transmission in sump

Placing the transmission below the engine meant that it had to share the engine's oil instead of the special high-pressure oil normally used for transmissions, but this was never a problem.

Sliding windows

Because the Mini was so narrow, and designed to be cheap, the windows were the cheaper sliding type so that the doors could be single skin and fitted with storage-useful pockets.

Disc brakes

All Coopers and Cooper Ss are fitted with front Lockhead disc brakes, the Cooper Ss with larger, 7.48-inch diameter, discs than the 7-inch discs fitted to the lesser-powered cars.

Small wheels

No other cars had been built with such tiny 10-inch diameter wheels as the Mini. The tires had to be made specially by Dunlop. In later years, after the Cooper went out of production, the Mini was equipped with taller wheels.

Hydrolastic suspension

In 1964 the rubber cone 'dry' suspension was replaced by the Hydrolastic type in which a pressurized fluid-filled hydraulic unit supplies the springing for each wheel. Each front unit is interconnected to the corresponding rear unit so that no separate shocks are needed.

Side radiator

To keep the car as short as possible there was no room for the radiator ahead of the engine and it is mounted to one side at right angles to the air stream, but it still functions adequately.

Rubber suspension

Early Coopers use special rubber cones instead of coil springs; compressing them had just the same effect but they take up much less space.

Exposed side seams

The seams where the body panels join together were deliberately exposed on the outside and made into a styling feature.

Twin fuel tanks

The popular misconception is that all Cooper S models had twin fuel tanks but in fact the right-hand tank was an option.

A-series engine

BMC's A-series engine may have been all cast iron, with a single block-mounted camshaft and two overhead valves per cylinder but it was an excellent design with considerable tuning potential.

Specifications
1964 970-cc Mini Cooper S

ENGINE

Type: In-line four cylinder
Construction: Cast-iron block and head
Valve gear: Two in-line valves per cylinder operated by single block-mounted camshaft, pushrods and rockers
Bore and stroke: 2.78 in. x 2.44 in.
Displacement: 970 cc
Compression ratio: 9.75:1
Induction system: Two SU HS2 carburetors
Maximum power: 65 bhp at 6,500 rpm
Maximum torque: 76 lb-ft at 3,500 rpm
Top speed: 97 mph
0-60 mph: 10.9 sec.

TRANSMISSION

Four-speed manual

BODY/CHASSIS

Steel monocoque two-door, four-seat sedan

SPECIAL FEATURES

The deliberately exposed seams on the bodywork became a Mini hallmark. External door hinges identify an early Mini.

To increase the Mini's carrying capacity it could be driven with the trunk lid half open, in which case the license plate folded down so it could still be seen.

RUNNING GEAR

Steering: Rack-and-pinion
Front suspension: Double wishbones with rubber cone springs and Girling telescopic shocks
Rear suspension: Longitudinal trailing arms, rubber cone springs and Girling telescopic shocks
Brakes: Discs (front), 7.48 in., drums (rear)
Wheels: Steel, 4.5 in. x 10 in.
Tires: Dunlop C41 5.20 x 10 or Dunlop SP41 145/10

DIMENSIONS

Length: 120 in.   **Width:** 55.5 in.
Wheelbase: 80.1 in.   **Height:** 53 in.
Track: 47.5 in. (front), 46.3 in. (rear)
Weight: 1,275 lbs.

Monteverdi **375**

One of the rarest of all the American V8-engined European supercars, the Chrysler-powered and Swiss-built Monteverdi 375S had staggering performance and exotic Italian-styled looks.

"...hangs on through curves."

"As well as elegant looks, this car has solid muscle. The massive Chrysler V8 hurls the 375S forward with contemptuous ease, 100 mph coming up in less than 16 seconds. But it has far more than impressive straight-line performance. With its clever de Dion rear end, the Monteverdi hangs on tenaciously through curves, yet the ride is still very smooth, helped by the car's considerable weight. The brakes are outstanding, too."

A well-trimmed interior is dominated by an enormous center console.

Milestones

1967 The 375S appears, curiously, at the Frankfurt rather than the Geneva Motor Show. It goes on to be built in both coupe and convertible forms.

The Jensen Interceptor also used Chrysler V8 engines.

1972 The Standard two-door coupe gains a restyled nose and a new name— Berlinetta. The 2+2 and 375/4 retain their nomenclature.

Peter Monteverdi began selling Ferraris, but he quarreled with Enzo and set up his own business to build rival GT machines.

1975 The Berlinetta is supplemented by a convertible version, known as the Palm Beach. It is extremely rare.

1977 The last of the 375-based coupes and convertibles are built. Peter Monteverdi turns his attentions to hugely successful modified luxury four-wheel drive vehicles.

UNDER THE SKIN

Separate steel body and chassis

De Dion rear axle

Four-wheel disc brakes

Wishbone front suspension

Big displacement V8

Classic supercar

The Monteverdi uses a separate perimeter chassis composed of square-section steel tubing, onto which the steel body is welded. The 375S is of front-engine, rear-drive configuration, with double wishbone front suspension and a de Dion rear axle located by a Watt linkage and sprung by coils. For braking, the Monteverdi relies on four-wheel discs with dual piston calipers.

THE POWER PACK

Magnum force

Monteverdi used the Chrysler Magnum 440 for the 375S. First seen in 1966 in Chrysler's full-size cars, it was strengthened for 1967 for use in performance Dodges and Plymouths, with a higher lift cam and larger four-barrel Carter AFB carburetor, resulting in 375 bhp and 481 lb-ft of torque. It is a tremendously tractable engine, and simple construction—with a very strong crankshaft, connecting rods and hydraulic lifters—made it ideal for large, fast grand tourers.

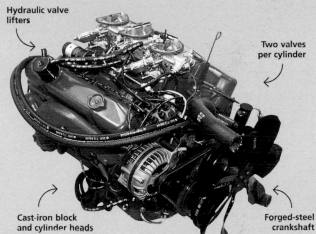

Hydraulic valve lifters

Two valves per cylinder

Cast-iron block and cylinder heads

Forged-steel crankshaft

Variety

All Monteverdis are rare and desirable. Besides the standard 375S coupe, there are also the two-seater 375C, the 375L 2+2 (shown) and the ultra-exclusive 375/4 luxury sedan. A few cars are powered by Hemi 426 engines and are worth tracking down.

All Monteverdi 375s wear Frua (later Fissore) steel bodies.

Monteverdi 375 ✚

Although very elegant, the Monteverdi's classic Italian styling by Frua was already beginning to look dated by the late 1960s as the supercar world turned to more dramatic-looking mid-engined exotics.

Steel body

Although the 375S body was made by Italian craftsmen—there was no tradition of car building in Switzerland—the bodies were made of steel rather than alloy as might have been expected. The chassis were trucked from Switzerland to Italy to have the bodies fitted, first at Frua's factory and then at the Fissore company.

Chrysler engine

The standard 440-cubic inch Chrysler Magnum V8 in the 375S gave it impressive performance, but for those who wanted more, there was also the 400SS. This uses a more powerful 406 bhp version with twin four-barrel Carter carburetors giving the car a claimed top speed of 168 mph.

Automatic transmission

Although a manual option was available, most of the 375s built had Chrysler's TorqueFlite 727 three-speed automatic unit fitted.

De Dion rear axle

The rear was a very well thought out and designed system using a de Dion axle to connect the two wheel hubs together. The axle itself is well located, with trailing arms for longitudinal location, and a Watt linkage to stop lateral movement.

Opening rear windows

Although the 375S has a luxury leather interior with air conditioning as standard, the design still incorporates rear quarter windows which can open outward to help air flow through the cabin.

Specifications

1969 Monteverdi 375S

ENGINE

Type: V8

Construction: Cast-iron block and heads

Valve gear: Two valves per cylinder operated by a single camshaft with pushrods and rockers

Bore and stroke: 4.32 in. x 3.75 in.

Displacement: 7,206 cc

Compression ratio: 10.1:1

Induction system: Single four-barrel Carter AFB carburetor

Maximum power: 375 bhp at 4,600 rpm

Maximum torque: 481 lb-ft at 3,200 rpm

Top speed: 152 mph

0-60 mph: 5.9 sec.

TRANSMISSION

TorqueFlite 727 three-speed automatic

BODY/CHASSIS

Separate chassis of square-section steel tubes with steel two-door coupe body

SPECIAL FEATURES

The driver's side windshield wiper has a built-in air deflector.

The headlights on pre-1972 375s bear a strong resemblance to those of the Maserati Mistral.

RUNNING GEAR

Steering: Worm-and-roller

Front suspension: Double wishbones with coil springs, telescopic shock absorbers and anti-roll bar

Rear suspension: De Dion axle with trailing arms, Watt linkage, coil springs, telescopic shock absorbers and anti-roll bar

Brakes: Girling discs, 12-in. dia. (front), 11.8-in. dia. (rear)

Wheels: Campagnolo knock-on alloy, 7 x 15 in.

Tires: Michelin radial, 205/70 R15

DIMENSIONS

Length: 181.1 in. **Width:** 70.7 in.

Height: 48.4 in. **Wheelbase:** 98.8 in.

Track: 59.5 in. (front), 57.9 in. (rear)

Weight: 3,528 lbs.

Separate chassis

The Monteverdi has a separate steel tubular chassis, onto which the body is welded. Extensive use of rubber bushings reduces vibrations and road shocks.

Frua styling

With no established Swiss stylists, Monteverdi selected the Italian company Frua to shape the look of the 375. The design bore a strong resemblance to other cars styled by the Italian firm, notably the Maserati Mistral and AC 428.

Morris **1100/1300**

Following Alec Issigonis' triumph with the Mini, the Morris 1100 was in many ways more advanced than its predecessor, boasting sealed cooling and disc brakes.

"...highly integrated package."

"For such a compact car, it is impressive how much room there is in the Morris. The driving position, overall feel, and even the sound of the engine are all very Mini-like. Thanks to front-wheel drive, handling is predictable and safe, with plenty of understeer. The ride quality on the Hydrolastic fluid suspension is wonderful, far superior to any rival of the time. The engine is willing, if not very exciting, and the overall impression is of a highly integrated package."

The roomy cabin, with the wooden door finish, has a very British feel to it.

Milestones

1962 BMC launches the Morris 1100 and MG 1100.

The rear seats of the estate fold flat to make a double bed.

1963 The Austin version is launched.

1965 Automatic transmission becomes an option, and Wolseley and Riley Kestrel-badged models arrive.

1967 The MKII is launched, with chopped tailfins and two engine sizes.

1968 As the Austin America, the 1300 is launched in the U.S.

The Austin version of the 1300 survived until 1974.

1971 The MKIII arrives, with wooden dash.

1973 The MG, Morris and Wolseley versions disappear.

1974 The last Austin and Vanden Plas cars are built.

UNDER THE SKIN

Shock absorber-less
Hydrolastic suspension

Rear torsion
bars

Front disc brakes

Mark of Issigonis

The fact that Alec Issigonis was heavily involved in project ADO16 shines through. The car shares its brilliant front-wheel-drive packaging with the immortal Mini. The centerpiece is its Hydro-lastic suspension—an all-fluid system that does away with conventional shock absorbers. The rack-and-pinion steering is based on a Jaguar design, and it has front disc brakes (unique in this class of car) and a choice of manual or automatic transmissions.

Inline four

THE POWER PACK

Ardent A-series

As the bigger brother of the Mini, the BMC 1100 received a larger version of the classic BMC A-series engine, first seen as early as 1951. Both the bore and stroke were larger than those of the tiny 848-cc Mini engine, to produce a 1,098-cc powerplant with a power output of 48 bhp. The engine was mounted transversely and drove the front wheels, just like the Mini. In 1967, the engine capacity was upped to 1,275 cc, sharing internal dimensions with, if not the power output of, the engine of the Mini Cooper. In standard guise it produced 58 bhp, but in the 1300 GT, power rose to 70 bhp.

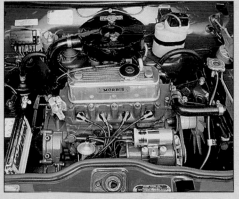

1300 GT

The most satisfying of the BMC midrange models is the twin-carb 1300 GT. Other sought after ADO16 models are the plush Vanden Plas Princess with its upper-crust grill, the MG and the Riley Kestrel, a hybrid of extra power and also a little snob appeal.

The two-tone MG variant has a sporty twin-carb engine.

Morris **1100/1300**

Under the codename ADO16, the British Motor Corporation built a huge badge-engineered range of models. The 1100/1300 range became Britain's best-selling car for many years.

Automatic transmission option
For 1965, a four-speed AP automatic transmission was available as an option. When launched in the U.S., BMC claimed it was the cheapest car with an automatic.

Front disc brakes
Almost unique in its class, the 1100/1300 boasted standard front disc brakes. A compact 8.4 inches across, they provide excellent stopping power and have a limiting valve that prevents wheel lockup.

Rubber-insulated subframes
As on the Mini, the main mechanical components are mounted on separate rubber-insulated subframes to keep vibration and noise to a minimum.

Pininfarina/Issigonis design
BMC had connections with the Italian Pininfarina design house and asked for its contribution to the new car. The new car's shape was widely admired and anticipated the 'two-box' design of a future generation of hatchbacks.

Masterful packaging

Thanks to Issigonis' input, the 1100/1300 shares the Mini's layout. The bored-out A-series engine is mounted transversely with the transmission in unit with the engine—a very compact arrangement. The lack of coil springs and shock absorbers also freed up more room inside, making it very spacious.

Sealed cooling

The water-cooling system is sealed for as little maintenance as possible, reflecting the setup of the sealed Hydrolastic suspension system.

Specifications

1966 Morris 1100/1300

ENGINE

Type: Inline four-cylinder

Construction: Cast-iron block and head

Valve gear: Two valves per cylinder operated by a single camshaft with pushrods and rockers

Bore and stroke: 2.82 in. x 3.25 in.

Displacement: 1,275 cc

Compression ratio: 8.8:1

Induction system: Single SU carburetor

Maximum power: 58 bhp at 5,250 rpm

Maximum torque: 67 lb-ft at 3,000 rpm

Top speed: 88 mph

0-60 mph: 17.3 sec.

TRANSMISSION

Four-speed manual

BODY/CHASSIS

Unitary monocoque construction with steel four-door sedan body

SPECIAL FEATURES

Mounting the gas tank under the rear seat helped maximize interior and trunk space. The gas cap is mounted on the left side.

Fins were toned down on most 1966 cars.

RUNNING GEAR

Steering: Rack-and-pinion

Front suspension: Wishbones with Hydrolastic shock absorbers and spring units

Rear suspension: Swinging trailing arms with Hydrolastic shock absorbers and spring units

Brakes: Discs (front), drums (rear)

Wheels: Steel, 12-in. dia.

Tires: 5.50 x 12

DIMENSIONS

Length: 146.7 in.   **Width:** 60.4 in.

Height: 52.7 in.   **Wheelbase:** 93.5 in.

Track: 51.5 in. (front), 50.9 in. (rear)

Weight: 1,860 lbs.

NSU **WANKEL SPIDER**

NSU was the first company in the world to sell a rotary-engine car, the Wankel Spider. The concept was cutting edge, even if the reality of high fuel consumption and poor reliability put customers off.

"...ingenious and unique."

"The whole Spider driving experience centers around the engine. Its turbine smoothness is ingenious and unique. Power delivery is progressive and the engine is so willing to rev that it will easily reach 8,000 rpm. Indeed you need to keep the revs up because low rpm torque is not the NSU's strongest feature. The handling is adequate for a rear-engined car with a low center of gravity. Braking, too, is also strong, thanks to front discs."

The most conventional feature of the NSU Spider is its interior.

Milestones

1957 The first running Wankel rotary
engine is produced.

The basis for the Spider's chassis comes from the NSU Prinz.

1963 A prototype of NSU's Wankel-engine
Spider is introduced.

1964 Production
of the NSU Spider begins.

1966 Karl-Heinz Panowitz takes the
German GT Rally Championship in a Spider.

The NSU Ro80 also uses the Wankel engine.

1967 NSU's rotary program switches to the
Ro80 sedan, and the little Spider is discontinued after 2,375 examples have been produced.

1967 NSU merges with Audi and the
Volkswagen group.

Prinz charming

In almost all respects, the Wankel Spider shares its underpinnings with the Sport Prinz coupe. This is a steel unibody car with a rear-mounted engine hanging behind the rear axle line. The motorcycle-style four-speed all-synchromesh transmission sits in front of the engine. All-independent suspension is employed, with wishbones and coils at the front end and semi-trailing arms at the rear.

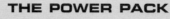

Front disc brakes

Coil-sprung front suspension

Rear-mounted rotary engine

Single-rotor engine

THE POWER PACK

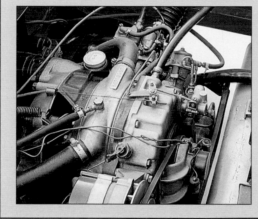

World's first rotary

NSU was brave enough to bite the bullet and build the first ever working rotary engine based on Felix Wankel's design in 1957. The idea grew out of experiments with rotary valves for torpedo engines. He realized that the four-stroke cycle of a regular engine could be achieved by using a single bore with an equilateral rotor as the piston. It would spin around on its combustion cycle rather than up and down. With a nominal capacity of 497 cc, the engine produces an impressive 64 bhp (SAE) at 5,000 rpm and 54 lb-ft of torque.

Wankel Spider

Every car museum ought to have an NSU Wankel Spider because of its historic place as the world's first rotary-engine car. The sad truth is that the Wankel engine has such a poor reputation (largely unjustified) that the little NSU never got the respect it deserves.

For such a tiny engine, the Spider has very lively performance.

NSU WANKEL SPIDER

The world was probably not ready for the Wankel engine when NSU launched its Spider in 1964, but there is no doubting the technical genius that lay behind it. The technology continues with Mazda to this day.

Convertible roof

Whereas the conventionally engined Sport Prinz was sold in coupe form, the Wankel Spider was made only as a roadster. The soft-top stowed in the rear deck. Alternatively, a detachable hardtop was available.

Rotary engine

The simplicity of Felix Wankel's idea for a rotary engine did not receive commercial success. With only one rotating piston and a capacity of 497 cc, it develops an impressive 64 bhp with turbine-like smoothness.

Front-mounted radiator

Unlike the Sport Prinz, which has a rear-mounted radiator, the cooling for the Wankel engine comes from a radiator installed in the nose. In turn, that meant that the spare wheel had to be repositioned in the tail.

Bertone styling

While the original NSU Prinz sedan was nothing much to look at, the Spider was a design jewel. Styled by Bertone's Franco Scaglione (better known for his Alfa Romeo designs), it looked right from every angle, which is the best judge of a car's overall design effectiveness.

Front disc brakes

Priced just under $3,000, the Spider was an expensive little car. The front disc brakes did little to justify the price.

Low center of gravity

Because the engine is so compact, the center of gravity over the rear is kept very low. This has beneficial effects on handling and stability. The transmission is mounted in line with the engine and transaxle.

Specifications

1967 NSU Wankel Spider

ENGINE

Type: Single-rotor Wankel
Construction: Cast-iron cylinder block
Valve gear: Circumferential porting
Bore and stroke: N/A
Displacement: 497 cc
Compression ratio: 8.6:1
Induction system: Single Solex sidedraft carburetor
Maximum power: 50 bhp at 5,000 rpm
Maximum torque: 54 lb ft at 3,000 rpm
Top speed: 98 mph
0-60 mph: 15.0 sec.

TRANSMISSION

Four-speed manual

BODY/CHASSIS

Unitary monocoque construction with steel two-door roadster body

SPECIAL FEATURES

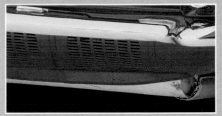

Vents are positioned under the rear fender to assist engine cooling.

The rear deck lifts backward for access to the engine.

RUNNING GEAR

Steering: Rack-and-pinion
Front suspension: Wishbones with anti-roll bar, coil springs and shocks
Rear suspension: Semi-trailing arms with coil springs and shocks
Brakes: Discs (front), drums (rear)
Wheels: Steel, 12-in. dia.
Tires: 5.00 x 12

DIMENSIONS

Length: 141.0 in. **Width:** 60.0 in.
Height: 49.5 in. **Wheelbase:** 79.5 in.
Track: 49.0 in. (front), 48.3 in. (rear)
Weight: 1,543 lbs.

Oldsmobile **TORONADO**

Ultraconservative Oldsmobile produced one of the most innovative cars of the 1960s with its Toronado coupe. The bold styling was just a teaser, for underneath lay Detroit's first front-wheel drive layouts. This endowed the Toronado with first-rate handling finesse.

"...fantastic front wheeler."

"The Toronado was one of the most well balanced drivers that came out of Detroit in the 1960s. The first thing you'll notice about this fantastic front wheeler is the lack of any transmission tunnel. Fire up the engine and the muted Rocket V8 revs happily and is an eager performer on the road. The real revelation comes when you turn your first corner—the car really handles. The payoff is a rather hard ride, but its light steering and easy cruising keep you smiling."

Needles and rocker switches fill the dash-board, but it's all clear and accessible.

Milestones

1966 General Motors turns history on its head with its most radical car of the decade, the front-drive Oldsmobile Toronado.

1967 Optional front disc brakes and radial tires improve the package.

The second generation 1971-1978 Toronado was bigger and heavier.

1968 A semi-notchback rear end is grafted on. Under the hood the engine displacement grows to 455 cubic inches, although standard power output falls by 10 bhp.

E-bodies, including the Toronado, were downsized in 1979.

1970 In its final year before being replaced by an all-new Toronado, fixed headlights replace the pop-up ones.

UNDER THE SKIN

Perimeter frame

All-around drum brakes

Front-wheel drive

Rocket V8

A front-drive first

America had not built a front-wheel-drive car since the Cord 812 of the 1930s, so the Toronado grabbed buyers' attention. The layout set the tone for GM cars for the next two decades. The torque converter sits directly behind the engine, with a remote three-speed Hydramatic transmission linked forward to the differential.

THE POWER PACK

Full-size V8

Originally, chief engineer John Beltz requested an all-alloy transverse V6 engine in the Toronado, but the GM chiefs knew that the market wanted a V8 in a flagship model. So Oldsmobile turned to the familiar full-size Rocket V8. Standard in Olds' big cars, the 425-cubic inch, cast-iron engine was rated at 385 bhp in the Toronado. Engineers mounted it in a rubber-insulated subframe, resulting in less cabin noise and vibration. From 1968, the engine size grew to 455 cubic inches and, though power dropped to 375 bhp, there was an optional W-34 package with twin exhausts and a special cam, capable of 400 bhp.

'66 Toronado

The original is the best when it comes to Toronados, and the first fastback body-style is preferred over the semi-notchback form adopted for 1968. And unless you find a modified 400-bhp version, the original 1966 Toronado has more power than later cars.

Today, the earlier models are the most sought after.

Oldsmobile TORONADO

Front-wheel drive was one thing, but an innovative engine/transmission layout freed up a lot of space inside and allowed engineers to deliver class-leading handling.

Concealed headlights

In all but 1970 models, the quad headlights are hidden away in pods. These swing up at the press of a button, increasing the sense of drama around the car.

Split transmission

For packaging reasons, the transmission is not an all-in-one unit. Instead, there is a torque converter mounted behind the engine with a two-inch Morse chain running to the Turbohydramatic three-speed.

Beam rear axle

In contrast with the innovative front end, the rear is conventional. The beam axle is suspended on rudimentary single-leaf, semi-elliptic springs. Two sets of shock absorbers are fitted, one pair mounted horizontally.

Bold styling

The Toronado combines European and American styling influences. Its designer, David North, created a clean and dramatic shape dominated by swoopy rear pillars, smooth flanks and heavy chrome bumpers.

Big cabin

Enormous doors open wide to provide access to a very spacious six-passenger interior. A long, 119-inch wheelbase coupled with the compact drivetrain gives ample room for passengers.

Front-wheel drive

In 1966, front-wheel drive cars were unique to the U.S market. The Toronado was easily the world's biggest example.

Specifications

1966 Oldsmobile Toronado

ENGINE

Type: V8

Construction: Cast-iron block and heads

Valve gear: Two valves per cylinder operated by a single camshaft with pushrods and rockers

Bore and stroke: 4.13 in. x 3.98 in.

Displacement: 425 c.i.

Compression ratio: 10.5:1

Induction system: Single four-barrel carburetor

Maximum power: 385 bhp at 4,800 rpm

Maximum torque: 475 lb-ft at 3,200 rpm

Top speed: 124 mph

0-60 mph: 9.9 sec.

TRANSMISSION

Turbohydramatic three-speed automatic

BODY/CHASSIS

Separate chassis with steel two-door coupe body

SPECIAL FEATURES

Cornering lights on the front fenders were an option on 1967 Toronados.

The heavily chromed rear bumper has cutouts for twin exhaust pipes.

RUNNING GEAR

Steering: Recirculating ball

Front suspension: Wishbones with longitudinal torsion bars, shock absorbers and anti-roll bar

Rear suspension: Beam axle with semi-elliptic springs and shock absorbers

Brakes: Drums, front and rear

Wheels: Steel 15-in. dia.

Tires: 8.85 x 15

DIMENSIONS

Length: 211.0 in.   **Width:** 78.5 in.

Height: 52.8 in.   **Wheelbase:** 119.0 in.

Track: 63.5 in. (front), 63.0 in. (rear)

Weight: 4,655 lbs.

Oldsmobile 4-4-2

While the 1968 4-4-2 had plenty of power with its 400-cubic inch V8 engine, this stock-looking Oldsmobile street machine has been modified with a massive 455 V8 that makes the kind of power found only in the limited edition Hurst-modified cars.

"...fast and fun street machine."

"The 1968 Oldsmobile 4-4-2 came with a W-30 360-bhp 400-cubic inch engine with the new, forced-air option. This custom example, however, has a full-size 455-cubic inch Rocket motor with added performance parts, similar to the Hurst/Olds introduced that same year. With a 410 bhp under the hood and a convertible top, this 4-4-2 is a fast and fun street machine. It accelerates like a rocket and handles better than most cars of its era."

The interior remains relatively stock, but the engine under the hood is a different story.

Milestones

1964 The 4-4-2
nameplate debuts as a package option on the mid-size F-85™.

1965 The standard
4-4-2 engine is a destroked and debored 425 V8 creating the new 400-cubic inch V8.

Early 4-4-2s have more square bodywork than the later cars.

1967 Tri-power
induction is offered for one year and the engine makes 360 bhp.

1968 A restyled body
gives the 4-4-2 a more elegant look. 3,000 modified versions known as the Hurst/Olds are offered with 455 engines.

The 1970 W-30 came with a big 455 V8 and fiberglass hood.

1970 A 455-cubic
inch engine becomes available with Oldsmobile's "select fit" parts. The W-30 455 makes 370 bhp, but its 14.3 quarter mile time suggests this car made more power. These cars had fiberglass hoods and plastic fender liners.

UNDER THE SKIN

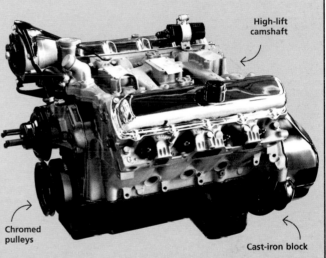

Steel body | Separate chassis

Coil springs

Large displacement engine

Toronado™ V8

One of the best muscle cars

The 1968 4-4-2 has something that many other auto manufacturers' hastily-conceived large-horsepower cars didn't have—a decent chassis. Although it still has a separate frame and steel body, like the Chevelle® and GTO®, the 4-4-2 offered better springs, and large anti-sway bars for an improved ride and handling.

THE POWER PACK

Full-size V8

After 1965 the first '4' in 4-4-2 stood for the size of the standard 400-cubic inch engine. Oldsmobile destroked and debored its full-size 425 V8 engine just for the 4-4-2. For 1966, Olds™ offered a tri-carburetors boosting power to 360 bhp (right). In 1970, its size was increased again to 455. It was the biggest and most powerful engine Olds ever offered. The owner of the model featured here has replaced the factory 400 V8 engine with a 455-cubic inch Rocket motor that makes 410 bhp thanks to special modifications.

High-lift camshaft

Chromed pulleys

Cast-iron block

Convertible

The new 1968 range of 4-4-2 models updated the earlier cars. At the top of the new range, above the hardtop coupe, was the convertible. It offered incredible value for this type of car, not to mention loads of fun with the top down in the summer.

The convertible top and stock wheels give this 4-4-2 a stealth-like look.

Oldsmobile 4-4-2

The 4-4-2 was one of the best muscle cars of the 1960s. It has incredible performance and, unlike many of its rivals, it also has the agility and braking to match the speed.

4-4-2 badging
By 1968 the 4-4-2 nameplate had become familiar and sought-after property. Badging in the grill announced that you were driving something special.

Custom paint
The bodywork has been sprayed with a base coat of Infinity White paint, followed by a clear coat to give a deep, high gloss finish.

Uprated wheels and tires
The 1968 4-4-2 had 14-inch diameter wheels, but the owner of this car has chosen to upgrade to 15-inch Super Stock II rims, shod with Goodyear Eagle ST tires.

Improved cabin
As well as 1970 Gold Madrid interior, this particular car features full GM and AutoGauge instruments and a 'Rallye' steering wheel.

Heavy-duty suspension
The rear end has been beefed up by replacing the stock coil springs with heavy-duty springs from a station wagon. Modern polyurethane bushings and $1\frac{7}{8}$-inch thick front and rear anti-roll bars have also been added to tighten the suspension further.

Specifications

Oldsmobile 4-4-2 Convertible

ENGINE

Type: V8

Construction: Cast-iron cylinder block and cylinder heads

Valve gear: Two valves per cylinder operated by a single camshaft

Bore and stroke: 4.12 in. x 4.25 in.

Displacement: 455 c.i.

Compression ratio: 10.5:1

Induction system: Four-barrel carburetor

Maximum power: 410 bhp at 5,500 rpm

Maximum torque: 517 lb-ft at 3,500 rpm

Top speed: 134 mph

0-60 mph: 6.2 sec.

TRANSMISSION

Turbo HydraMatic 350 three-speed automatic

BODY/CHASSIS

Separate chassis with two-door convertible steel body

SPECIAL FEATURES

The interior has been taken from a 1970 Oldsmobile and features Gold Madrid vinyl upholstery.

On this modified car, the exhaust tips exit behind the rear tires rather than out of the back as on the standard 4-4-2s.

RUNNING GEAR

Steering: Recirculating ball

Front suspension: Wishbones with coil springs, shocks, and anti-roll bar

Rear suspension: Rigid axle with coil springs, shocks, and anti-roll bar

Brakes: Discs front, drums rear

Wheels: Super Stock II, 15-in. dia.

Tires: Goodyear Eagle ST

DIMENSIONS

Length: 201.6 in.   **Width:** 76.2 in.

Height: 52.8 in.   **Wheelbase:** 112 in.

Track: 59.1 in. (front), 59.1 in. (rear)

Curb weight: 3,890 lbs.

Sharp steering

To improve handling, the owner installed a quick-ratio steering box. This means the wheel has to be turned less when cornering.

Big 455 V8

Although the 455 V8 engine was not offered in the 1968 4-4-2, it was available in a special edition called the Hurst/Olds. It became standard for all 4-4-2 models in 1970.

Opel **GT**

The shark-nose front and curvaceous sports coupe styling of Opel's GT led to its nickname, the 'mini Corvette.' It sold in the U.S. through select Buick dealers. Though it faced strong competition, the GT was extremely successful.

"...pleasing and precise."

"Sliding into the GT takes you back to the late 1960s, with deeply set gauges and vinyl upholstery everywhere. The 1.9-liter engine is not a bad unit but it betrays its sedan origins. Performance is fair but not outstanding; however, the manual shifter is pleasing and precise in action. Despite its simple underpinnings, the GT corners well, with only mild body roll and a trace of understeer. The brakes are adequate and the ride is excellent for a sports car."

Even inside, the GT mimics the contemporary Corvette's styling.

Milestones

1965 Opel displays a GT show car concept to widespread public acclaim at the Frankfurt Motor Show.

A second-generation Opel Kadett appeared for 1973.

1968 Looking remarkably similar to the original show car, the production GT is launched with 1.1- and 1.9-liter engines.

1970 The 1.1-liter engine is dropped.

The 90-bhp, 1.9-liter engine later found a home in the Manta SR.

1971 A new GT/J (Junior) base version is added to the range.

1973 The GT goes out of production with no direct successor.

UNDER THE SKIN

Front disc brakes

Unitary construction

Coil-sprung live rear axle

Sedan origins

To keep costs low, the GT is based on the conventional unitary chassis of the Kadett sedan. The front suspension uses a transverse leaf spring with wishbones, while the live rear axle is suspended by coils and radius arms. A four-speed manual transmission was standard, but there was an optional Opel three-speed automatic.

Sedan-derived four

THE POWER PACK

Playing it safe

Under the hood of the GT is a fairly conventional in-line four-cylinder engine, as used in several other Opel models. It has a cast-iron block and an aluminum cylinder head using a single overhead camshaft. There are four main bearings, a single Solex twin-barrel carburetor and a compression ratio of 9.0:1. The power output is not especially high at 102 bhp, but torque is a fairly healthy 121 lb-ft. A smaller 1,077-cc engine was offered until 1970.

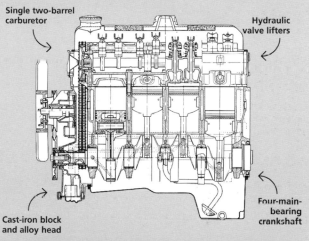

Single two-barrel carburetor

Hydraulic valve lifters

Four-main-bearing crankshaft

Cast-iron block and alloy head

Baby Vette

The definitive GT is, without question, the 1.9-liter model. It has decent styling, superb roadholding and lively performance. In their native Germany, these cars have become recognized as 'baby' Corvettes.

A choice of 1.1- and 1.9-liter engines was offered in the GT.

Opel GT

Opel had no real intention of making the GT when it first appeared at the 1965 Frankfurt Motor Show, but public reaction soon changed that thinking.

2+2 cabin

Although described as a four-seater, there is really only room for two passengers sitting on high-back bucket seats. In the rear, a simple platform can be used for passengers but is more useful for luggage.

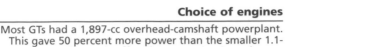

Choice of engines

Most GTs had a 1,897-cc overhead-camshaft powerplant. This gave 50 percent more power than the smaller 1.1-liter unit offered as an option in early cars.

Cut-off tail

Echoing the style of the Corvette, the GT's tail is sharply cut off, partly for aerodynamic reasons and partly for style. The kicked-up, built-in spoiler certainly helps airflow. Notice that there is no trunk lid.

Kadett platform

The GT is essentially a shortened Kadett sedan. This was done in the interest of economy, although the engine and cockpit were moved back by about a foot to improve weight distribution and handling.

American styling

General Motors stylist Clare MacKichan worked on the GT. It therefore comes as little surprise that the car bears many Corvette styling cues.

Concealed headlights

The Corvette-inspired shark nose was given an even more dramatic profile by concealing the headlights under vacuum-operated covers. They are activated by a lever on the transmission tunnel.

French-built bodywork

The steel bodies were built in France by Chausson (based near Paris) and then trimmed by Brissoneau & Lotz before being dispatched to the Opel factory in Bochum, Germany, to be mated with the engine and running gear.

Specifications

1969 Opel GT 1900

ENGINE

Type: In-line four-cylinder

Construction: Cast-iron block and aluminum head

Valve gear: Two valves per cylinder operated by a single overhead camshaft

Bore and stroke: 3.66 in. x 2.75 in.

Displacement: 1,897 cc

Compression ratio: 9.0:1

Induction system: Single Solex two-barrel carburetor

Maximum power: 102 bhp at 5,200 rpm

Maximum torque: 121 lb-ft at 3,600 rpm

Top speed: 110 mph

0-60 mph: 10.1 sec.

TRANSMISSION

Four-speed manual or three-speed automatic

BODY/CHASSIS

Integral chassis with steel two-door coupe body

SPECIAL FEATURES

The pop-up headlights rotate 180 degrees to lie flat when not in use.

Opel GTs have standard 13-inch steel wheels. This car has been fitted with modern radial tires.

RUNNING GEAR

Steering: Rack-and-pinion

Front suspension: Unequal length wishbones with leaf spring and shock absorbers

Rear suspension: Live axle with coil springs, radius arms, Panhard rod and shock absorbers

Brakes: Discs (front), drums (rear)

Wheels: Steel, 13-in. dia.

Tires: 165 HR13

DIMENSIONS

Length: 161.9 in.   **Width:** 62.2 in.

Height: 48.2 in.   **Wheelbase:** 95.7 in.

Track: 49.4 in. (front), 50.6 in. (rear)

Weight: 2,100 lbs.

Plymouth **BARRACUDA**

The Barracuda was the result of Chrysler's determination not to be left out of the 'pony car' market. Plymouth took an existing compact platform from the Valiant, added unique bodywork and options and there it was—Chrysler's very own version of the Mustang.

"...exhilarating experience."

"The 1967 Barracuda was part of the new wave of smaller, more powerful cars that swept across the U.S. during the mid-to-late 1960s. Chrysler followed the trend by providing an exhilarating driving experience, combining compact dimensions with awesome power. The Barracuda has decent handling characteristics. However, with legendary 383 V8 grunt it can be quite a handful when driven at the limit. Nonetheless, it's high on the fun factor."

The Barracuda's large steering wheel dominates the cabin and is typical of the era.

Milestones

1964 The Plymouth Barracuda
is launched on April 1st, two weeks before the Ford Mustang. Though it appears mid-1964, it is branded a 1965 model. It features folding rear seats that are quite novel for the time.

Modified Cudas became a common site on drag strips.

1967 The Barracuda undergoes
its first major restyle, which includes a 2-inch wheelbase extension. Convertible and hardtop coupe models are also introduced.

The Road Runner was Plymouth's full-size muscle car.

1970 Lower, wider and shorter,
the Barracuda begins the new decade with a total redesign. The legendary Hemi engine is now available.

1974 Production of the Barracuda
comes to an end—a victim of the fuel crisis and emissions controls.

UNDER THE SKIN

Drum brakes front and rear

Leaf-sprung rear suspension

Torsion-bar front suspension

Big-block V8

THE POWER PACK

A Valiant start

The Barracuda was originally based on the Chrysler Valiant platform to keep costs down. By 1967, it had evolved almost into its own separate line and the car developed away from its humble origins. In 1967, the Barracuda was lengthened almost 4 inches to 108 inches. Checking the front disc brakes and power-brake option boxes were recommended to ensure that it stopped as well as it accelerated.

Solid performance

The big-block, 383-cubic inch engine dates back to 1960, when the Golden Commando unit, complete with 'Ram Induction' was created for the Fury/Sport Suburban models. It is a simple design with a cast-iron block and cylinder heads. Hemi-engined Plymouths may have offered the ultimate in power output, but with Carter four-barrel carburetors, the 383-equipped Barracuda pumps out 280 bhp and an impressive 400 lb-ft of torque at 2,400 rpm. The 383 is a very flexible motor and can be easily tuned or modified with components from other Chrysler engines.

Formula S

Starting in 1968, Barracudas were available with a performance option package called 'Formula S.' These cars were available with a four-speed manual transmission, dual exhaust, anti-roll bars, wider tires and, of course, Formula S badging.

The stylish lines of the Barracuda are some of the finest seen on a Plymouth.

159

Plymouth BARRACUDA

The Barracuda, along with the Mustang, is in many ways the quintessential pony car. It offered the buyer a practical car that could be driven every day, yet had awesome performance potential—especially with the 383 engine.

Engine options

In 1967, buyers could choose either the base 145-bhp, 225-cubic inch slant-six engine or the 273- or 383-cubic inch V8. The following year, Plymouth offered another V8, the 340-cubic inch, to fill the gap between the earlier engines.

Transmission choices

Barracudas may have come as standard with a three-speed manual, but the options list also included a four-speed manual, as well as a TorqueFlite three-speed automatic transmission.

Restyled rear window

Although the first-generation Barracuda sported a distinctive wraparound rear window, the styling cue could not entirely disguise its Valiant origins. New bodystyles for 1967 included a convertible and a hardtop.

Stretched chassis

For 1967, the Barracuda's wheelbase was stretched by 2 inches and the car grew by about 4 inches overall. It still remained in proportion, however, and the motoring press universally applauded its modest, yet distinctive, good looks.

Sporty options

Buyers could specify a range of options to give the car a sporty feel, from cosmetic items—such as bucket seats, consoles and stripes—to real performance hardware—like a Sure-Grip differential or the 383 V8 engine.

Specifications

1967 Plymouth Barracuda

ENGINE

Type: V8

Construction: Cast-iron block and heads

Valve gear: Two valves per cylinder operated by a single camshaft

Bore and stroke: 4.25 in. x 3.38 in.

Displacement: 383 c.i.

Compression ratio: 10.0:1

Induction system: Carter four-barrel carburetor

Maximum power: 280 bhp at 4,200 rpm

Maximum torque: 400 lb-ft at 2,400 rpm

Top speed: 120 mph

0-60 mph: 7.0 sec.

TRANSMISSION

Three-speed manual/four-speed manual or three-speed auto

BODY/CHASSIS

Unitary construction with steel body panels

SPECIAL FEATURES

The rear seats fold down to create cavernous luggage space.

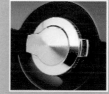

The race inspired style of the fuel-filler cap is unique to the Barracuda.

RUNNING GEAR

Steering: Worm-and-roller

Front suspension: A-arms with torsion bars and telescopic shock absorbers

Rear suspension: Live axle with semi-elliptic leaf springs and telescopic shock absorbers

Brakes: Drums (front and rear)

Wheels: Steel, 14-in. dia.

Tires: Firestone wide ovals, D70 x 14

DIMENSIONS

Length: 192.8 in.   **Width:** 69.6 in.

Height: 52.7 in.   **Wheelbase:** 108.0 in.

Track: 57.4 in. (front), 55.6 in. (rear)

Weight: 2,940 lbs.

Plymouth ROAD RUNNER

By the late 1960s, many muscle cars were beyond the financial reach of their would-be buyers. To corner this segment of the market, Plymouth offered the Road Runner. It was a no-frills coupe with a 383 V8 engine as standard power. The result proved to be an instant sales success and owners were well respected on the street.

"...back to the basics."

"Getting back to the basics is what the Road Runner is all about. It is all business, from the steel wheels to the rubber floormats. The 383 is a strong engine and thrives at low rpm. With the four-speed shifter in your right hand and your foot on the gas, its acceleration is unreal. Because it was a bare-bones muscle car its weight was kept as low as possible for an even better power-to-weight ratio. With 335 bhp, this was a car that really lived up to its name."

The 1968 model is the Road Runner in its purest form with a no-frills interior.

Milestones

1968 With a growing number of enthusiasts wanting a no-frills factory hot rod, Plymouth decides to take the plunge and offer the Road Runner—a two-door coupe with a standard 383-cubic inch V8. Chrysler pays Warner Bros. $50,000 to use the Road Runner name. Projected sales are 2,500, but in the end, 44,589 are sold.

The Super Bee was Dodge Division's equivalent to the Road Runner.

1969 The Road Runner goes upmarket. A convertible model is added to the range. Mid-year, a new 440-cubic inch Six-Barrel joins the 383 and 426 Hemi engine options.

The sporty Road Runner was extensively revamped for 1971.

1970 A new loop-type grill and revised taillights mark the 1970 edition. Fifteen inch Rallye wheels are now a popular option.

UNDER THE SKIN

Unitary body and chassis

Four-wheel drum brakes

Torsion-bar front suspension

Big-block V8

Belvedere based

Essentially a two-door Belvedere fitted with a huge engine, the Road Runner follows Chrysler engineering practice for the period, with a unitary body/chassis and a separate front subframe. Double A-arm suspension is carried up front, sprung by torsion bars, while the live axle at the rear rides on semi-elliptic leaf springs. Standard rear gearing is 3.23:1, although higher ratios were available.

THE POWER PACK

Big block brawler

While other muscle cars relied on increasingly complex engines for propulsion, Plymouth decided that simplicity was essential to the Road Runner. For maximum effect and in order to keep costs down, the division decided to install the 383-cubic inch big-block as the standard engine. This cast-iron V8 had been in production since the 1950s, but for the Road Runner it received some upgrades. The heads, exhaust manifolds, camshaft, heavy-duty valve springs, and crankshaft windage tray are all from the 440. With a four-barrel carburetor and a low-restriction air cleaner, it makes 335 bhp at 5,200 rpm.

Hemi first

The first-generation Road Runner is an undisputed muscle car classic, and the first-year (1968) model is its purest form. Collectors prefer the 426 Hemi-engined cars. They can easily run 13-second ¼-mile ETs, but only 1,019 were built.

Steel wheels were standard on 1968 Road Runners.

Plymouth ROAD RUNNER

The Road Runner was so successful that it inspired rival manufacturers to offer budget muscle cars of their own. Anyone who drove a Road Runner was soon mesmerized by its incredible performance.

Torsion-bar front suspension

A typical 1960s Chrysler feature is a torsion-bar front suspension. Twin longitudinal bars provide springing for the front wishbones and give a smoother ride than coil setups. Road Runners have bigger front bars in an attempt to improve handling.

Big-block V8

Inexpensive to build, yet with a few simple tweaks mightily effective, the 383 V8 was the ideal engine for Plymouth's budget muscle-car. Packing 335 bhp and a monster 425 lb-ft of torque, even in stock trim it was a street terror.

Drum brakes

Most muscle cars are about going fast in a straight line and little else. Stopping the Road Runner could be quite entertaining, with the standard four-wheel drums, so ordering front discs was a wise option.

Hardtop styling

When introduced, the Road Runner was only available in one body-style—a pillared coupe. A hardtop version appeared mid year and a convertible was introduced in 1969.

Four-speed transmission

An essential performance ingredient on any real street racer is a manual transmission, and the Road Runner has a standard four-on-the-floor. A TorqueFlite automatic was optional.

Steel wheels

In keeping with its frugal image, the Road Runner came with standard 14-inch steel wheels and center hub caps. However, 14-inch Magnum 500 rims were a popular upgrade.

Specifications

1968 Plymouth Road Runner

ENGINE

Type: V8

Construction: Cast-iron block and heads

Valve gear: Two valves per cylinder operated by a single camshaft

Bore and stroke: 4.25 in. x 3.38 in.

Displacement: 383 c.i.

Compression ratio: 10.0:1

Induction system: Carter AFB four-barrel downdraft carburetor

Maximum power: 335 bhp at 5,200 rpm

Maximum torque: 425 lb-ft at 3,400 rpm

Top speed: 130 mph

0-60 mph: 6.7 sec.

TRANSMISSION

Four-speed manual

BODY/CHASSIS

Unitary steel construction with stamped steel body panels

SPECIAL FEATURES

To extract the most power out of the engine, Road Runners were equipped with standard dual exhaust.

The flat black hood center gave this potent Plymouth a very aggressive look.

RUNNING GEAR

Steering: Recirculating-ball

Front suspension: Unequal-length A-arms with torsion bars, telescopic shock absorbers and anti-roll bar

Rear suspension: Live axle with semi-elliptic leaf springs and telescopic shock absorbers

Brakes: Drums (front and rear)

Wheels: Pressed steel, 14-in. dia.

Tires: F70-14

DIMENSIONS

Length: 202.7 in.   **Width:** 81.7 in.

Height: 56.3 in.   **Wheelbase:** 116.0 in.

Track: 59.5 in. (front and rear).

Weight: 3,400 lbs.

Pontiac VENTURA

Stylish, both then and now, the 1961 Ventura combines both luxury and performance. The owner of this car has chosen to upgrade its performance while retaining the Ventura's classic looks.

"...plenty of power to spare."

"With its big V8 and four-barrel carburetor, the 1961 Ventura has plenty of power to spare, taking less than seven seconds to reach 60 mph. In a straight line, the heavy Ventura can outrun plenty of modern sports cars. Around corners, though, the car shows its age. The steering is vague and there's a lot of body roll, and despite its modern tires, the back end easily breaks loose."

The dash is original, but the seats have been reupholstered for a custom look.

Milestones

1960 Pontiac
introduces the Ventura nameplate as a trim level on its Catalina™ line. Two body styles, a hardtop coupe and Vista sedan, are available.

Ed 'Fireball' Roberts was a highly successful stock-car racer in early 1960s full-size Pontiacs.

1961 Slightly
shorter and lighter, this year's full-size Pontiacs are established as performance cars. Pontiacs take the first three places in the NASCAR Daytona 500 Stock Car race.

Roberts won the Daytona 500 in 1962 in this Pontiac Catalina.

1962 The Ventura
is dropped, although a sporty new Grand Prix™ makes its debut. It features bucket seats and a full instrumentation pack. A 389-cubic inch V8 is the only engine available.

UNDER THE SKIN

X braced chassis

Coil springs

Four-wheel drum brakes

Big-block V8

Like an anvil
Following conventional Detroit practice, the Ventura has a separate X-braced frame. Suspension consists of unequal length wishbones up front and a live axle with coil springs at the rear. Drum brakes are fitted all around.

THE POWER PACK

Torque monster
The biggest engine available in the 1961 Ventura was a 389-cubic inch V8 with up to 348 bhp. This car has been fitted with a later Pontiac engine, a 400-cubic inch from a 1969 GTO®. The top engine was the Ram Air IV that gave 370 bhp, but the engine in this car is a tuned Ram Air III that gives more power than the radical Ram Air IV. With free-flow exhaust and ported cylinder heads, this engine makes 380 bhp. Torque has also been increased to 450 lb-ft.

Ported cylinder heads

Four-barrel carburetor

Cast-iron block and heads

Forged-steel crankshaft

Down-sized
The 1961 Pontiacs received shorter, narrower bodies and weighed slightly less. The Ventura was based on the Catalina platform and came in just two body styles. The hardtop coupe proved to be the least popular, though 13,297 were built.

Full size and full power; this Ventura is a stunning customized street machine.

Pontiac VENTURA

Full-size early-1960s Pontiacs have a special feel about them. This Ventura, with its Tri-Power induction and Torque Thrust wheels, is straight from the muscle-car era.

Custom paint

Many customizers adopt late-model paint finishes. This Ventura has been resprayed in 1993 Ford 'Coronado Red' paint.

Racing wheels

This Pontiac has been fitted with a set of American Racing Torque Thrust wheels, a popular aftermarket item in the 1960s.

Youthful appeal

The Pontiac was emerging as a more sporty, younger person's car in the early 1960s and the Ventura was available with bucket seats and a four-speed manual transmission. This example, however, retains the traditional front bench seat.

Bubble-top fastback

The 'bubble'-type rear window looks stylish and actually improved aerodynamics on the NASCAR Pontiacs.

Chrome accents

The huge chrome side spears running along the beltline are a trademark of General Motors cars from the period.

Wide-track ride

Since 1959, the large Pontiacs adopted a wider track, helping to make them some of the most stable full-size cars of the era.

Stainless-steel exhaust

To extract maximum power, an Edelbrock stainless-steel exhaust with 2½-inch diameter pipes has been fitted.

Ram Air III engine

This particular car has a Ram Air III 400-cubic inch engine from a 1969 Pontiac GTO. Mild tuning means it gives 380 bhp.

Specifications

1961 Pontiac Ventura

ENGINE

Type: V8

Construction: Cast-iron block and heads

Valve gear: Single camshaft operated by pushrods and rockers

Bore and stroke: 4.12 in. x 3.75 in.

Displacement: 400 c.i.

Compression ratio: 10.75:1

Induction system: Single four-barrel carburetor

Maximum power: 380 bhp at 5,500 rpm

Maximum torque: 450 lb-ft at 3,900 rpm

Top speed: 124 mph

0-60 mph: 6.5 sec.

TRANSMISSION

GM TurboHydramatic 400 three-speed automatic with a 2,000-rpm stall converter

BODY/CHASSIS

Steel X-braced frame with separate two-door coupe steel body

SPECIAL FEATURES

Torque Thrust wheels add a period touch to this Ventura.

Although toned down, there is still plenty of chrome.

RUNNING GEAR

Steering: Recirculating ball with power assistance

Front suspension: Unequal length upper and lower wishbones with coil springs and telescopic shocks

Rear suspension: Live rear axle with coil springs and telescopic shocks

Brakes: Drums (front and rear)

Wheels: Cast-magnesium, 15 in.

Tyres: BF Goodrich radial T/A 215/65-15 (front), 235/75-15 (rear)

DIMENSIONS

Length: 207.8 in.   **Width:** 118.9 in.

Height: 66.1 in.   **Wheelbase:** 119 in.

Track: 61 in. (front), 59.5 in. (rear)

Weight: 3,687 lbs.

 **USA** 1966

Pontiac **GTO**

Taking a huge engine and putting it into a smaller vehicle was the concept behind the GTO. Pontiac's original muscle car grew larger for 1966 but retained the essential performance ingredients that made it a winner from day one.

"...few cars are cooler."

"Even today, there are few cars as cool as the 1966 GTO. The front bucket seats may be lacking support by today's standards, but the dash is a delight and the interior tastefully restrained. Once on the road, acceleration is tremendous, and the four-speed shifter is well mated to the 389 V8. However, on damp surfaces wheelspin is almost unavoidable if you're heavy on the gas pedal. The GTO is no corner-carver and tends to oversteer if you don't take care."

A two-spoke steering wheel is standard, although a three-spoke one was available.

Milestones

1964 A new, larger and more conventional

Tempest® line arrives. The biggest news is the debut of the GTO (Gran Turismo Omologato), with a standard 389-cubic inch V8 and sporty touches. 32,450 GTOs are sold in the first year.

The GTO got a crisp restyle for 1965, that included vertical headlights.

1966 The GTO gets a larger, curvier

body, but the basic style and performance remain the same. By this stage muscle car competition is getting tougher. However, the GTO sets an all-time muscle car production record with 96,946 cars built.

In 1969 Pontiac releases The Judge™ option to strike more interest in perspective buyers.

1967 Pontiac turns its attention to

improving the car. The grill and taillights are altered, and the V8 is bored out to 400 cubic inches.

UNDER THE SKIN

Body-on-frame construction

Coil-sprung live rear axle

Wishbone front suspension

Big-block V8

Classic mid-size

The GTO became a separate model for 1966, although it was still based on the Pontiac Tempest, one of GM's mid-sized 'A'-body cars. The GTO has an all-steel body on a separate perimeter chassis with wishbone front and live axle rear coil-sprung suspension to provide a smooth ride. A front anti-roll bar and four-wheel drum brakes are standard.

THE POWER PACK

Torque monster

From 1964 until 1967, the GTO's standard engine was the 389-cubic inch V8, first seen in 1959 as an option on Pontiac's big cars. A heavy cast-iron unit, the 389 was upgraded for the GTO with a hotter camshaft and 421 High Output free-flowing cylinder heads. In 1966, the base 389 was rated at 335 bhp with a single Carter four-barrel carburetor, but the optional Tri-Power set up with three two-barrel carburetors was rated at 360 bhp. However, mid-year GM outlawed multi-carb set ups.

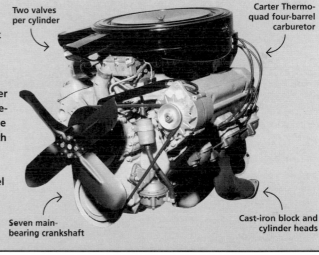

Two valves per cylinder

Carter Thermo-quad four-barrel carburetor

Seven main-bearing crankshaft

Cast-iron block and cylinder heads

Loaded Goat

Among muscle car aficionados, the 1966 GTO ranks as an all-time great. Desirable options include Rally I wheels, a four-speed transmission and Tri-Power carb set-up. Add these to a convertible body and you've got one fantastic summer cruiser.

The 1966 GTO is one of the most desirable muscle cars of all time.

Pontiac GTO

Pontiac set an all-time production record with the 1966 GTO, thanks to the car's combination of outstanding performance, eye-catching looks and attractive pricing.

Ram Air kit

The standard hood scoop was purely for decoration, but a dealer-installed Ram Air kit was also available. Quoted horsepower remained unchanged, but fresh air induction would probably add a few additional bhp.

Big-block V8

In 1966, the GTO could be ordered with the 389-cubic inch engine in two different states of tune. This car is one of 19,045 ordered with the optional Tri-Power set up, which boosted power output to 360 bhp.

Power convertible top

The GTO, if ordered in convertible form, was available with a power top.

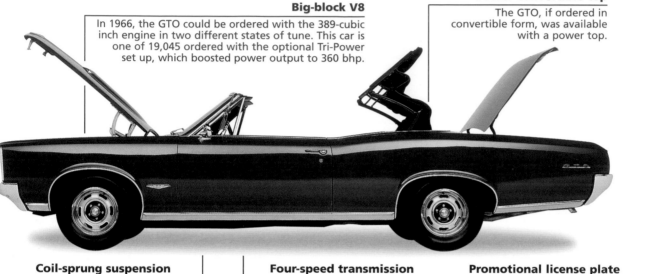

Coil-sprung suspension

Like the other General Motors 'A'-body intermediates of the time, the GTO has coil springs front and rear. This results in a much smoother ride than rival Ford and Chrysler muscle cars.

Four-speed transmission

In order to extract maximum performance from the big-block V8, a four-speed manual was the hot ticket, although a TurboHydramatic automatic was offered.

Promotional license plate

GTOs quickly became known on the streets and at the race tracks for their unbelievable performance. One of Pontiac's campaign slogans compared the car's power with that of a tiger, hence the 'growling' license plate.

Restyled body

Still Tempest-based, the GTO grew dimensionally larger for 1966 with a longer body and more flowing lines. It was offered in pillared coupe, hardtop and convertible forms. The hardtop was by far the most popular model.

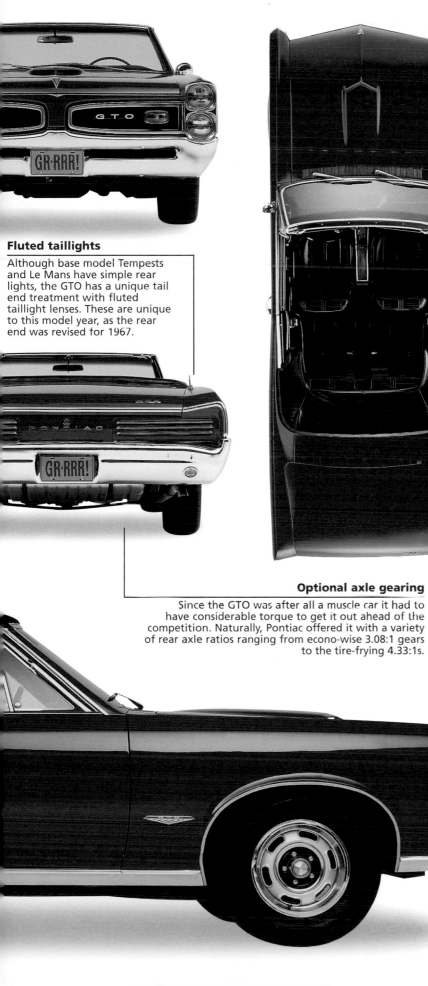

Fluted taillights

Although base model Tempests and Le Mans have simple rear lights, the GTO has a unique tail end treatment with fluted taillight lenses. These are unique to this model year, as the rear end was revised for 1967.

Optional axle gearing

Since the GTO was after all a muscle car it had to have considerable torque to get it out ahead of the competition. Naturally, Pontiac offered it with a variety of rear axle ratios ranging from econo-wise 3.08:1 gears to the tire-frying 4.33:1s.

Specifications

1966 Pontiac GTO

ENGINE

Type: V8

Construction: Cast-iron block and heads

Valve gear: Two valves per cylinder operated by a single camshaft with pushrods and rockers

Bore and stroke: 4.06 in. x 3.75 in.

Displacement: 389 c.i.

Compression ratio: 10.75:1

Induction system: Three Rochester two-barrel carburetors

Maximum power: 360 bhp at 5,200 rpm

Maximum torque: 424 lb-ft at 3,600 rpm

Top speed: 125 mph

0-60 mph: 6.2 sec.

TRANSMISSION

Muncie M21 four-speed manual

BODY/CHASSIS

Steel perimeter chassis with separate steel convertible two-door body

SPECIAL FEATURES

1966 was the last year for Tri-Power carburetion on all GM mid-size cars.

Its sinister look is attributed to the vertical headlights and split front grill.

RUNNING GEAR

Steering: Recirculating ball

Front suspension: Unequal length wishbones with coil springs, telescopic shock absorbers and anti-roll bar

Rear suspension: Live axle with coil springs and lower control arms

Brakes: Drums (front and rear)

Wheels: Steel Rally I, 14-in. dia.

Tires: Uniroyal 155/F70 14

DIMENSIONS

Length: 199.0 in.   **Width:** 79.8 in.

Height: 54.8 in.   **Wheelbase:** 116.0 in.

Track: 53.8 in. (front), 50.1 in. (rear)

Weight: 3,555 lbs.

173

Pontiac GRAND PRIX

The top-of-the-line Grand Prix was a sales sensation for Pontiac. The 1967 model year was unique because there was a convertible and a hardtop model. Stylistically, this Grand Prix also stands out because of its bold, wraparound, front-end treatment.

"...drives like a muscle car."

"Because of the sensational GTO, Pontiacs had a strong performance car image in the 1960s. The Grand Prix is certainly a big luxury car but it drives like a muscle car. Using a stout 350-bhp, 400-cubic inch engine, the GP has plenty of power. It leaps away from the lights defying its bulk for a 9.4 second 0-60 mph time. This is all easily handled by the automatic transmission. The all-coil suspension provides a supple ride and fine handling."

The combination of leather and wood in the cabin hides the GP's sporty potential.

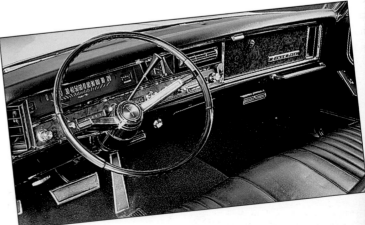

Milestones

1962 Pontiac launches the first ever Grand Prix hardtop coupe.

The X400 was the 1963 Grand Prix show car.

1965 The Grand Prix wheelbase is increased by an inch.

1967 New front-end styling marks the Grand Prix, which is offered for this year only in convertible form as well. A 400-cubic inch V8 replaces the 389. A big 428 is optional.

The 1965 Catalina™ shared some mechanicals with the Grand Prix.

1968 Styling is altered with a more pronounced grill and a revised rear bumper.

1969 An all-new, neo-classic Grand Prix series is launched. It is built off the smaller A-body intermediate chassis and was known for having one of the biggest hoods at this time.

UNDER THE SKIN

Separate chassis

line rear axle

Four-wheel self-adjusting drum brakes

Large bore V8

Conventional basis

The Grand Prix is closely based on the Pontiac Catalina, the full-size offering from Pontiac. Its suspension is typical of most 1967 GM cars with a chassis that is separate from the body. The engineering is conventional, offering A-arms and coil springs up front and a live axle and coils at the rear. It has self-adjusting drum brakes all around, although there was an option of front discs. The Grand Prix was supplied with a TH400 automatic transmission but a manual was available.

THE POWER PACK

Massive power

The 1967 Pontiac 400-cubic inch V8 engine is a bored-out version of the 389. This was a full-size engine and among the most powerful in Pontiac's 1967 lineup. Its high torque output meant that it was an ideal power plant for a street cruiser. Thanks to its semi-aggressive camshaft, the power rose from 325 bhp (as in the Bonneville™) to 350 bhp. During this era there seemed to be no limit to the size that the engines could grow. The Grand Prix could be ordered with a massive 428-cubic inch V8. This was available in two states of tune: 360 and 375 bhp.

Collectable

During the 1960s, Pontiac sold so many Grand Prix models that the car nearly became its best seller. Only one style was offered—a hardtop coupe—although the 1967 model year had a convertible option. Only 5,856 were made, and they are now collector's cars.

The convertible was only available in 1967 and has become quite collectable.

Pontiac GRAND PRIX

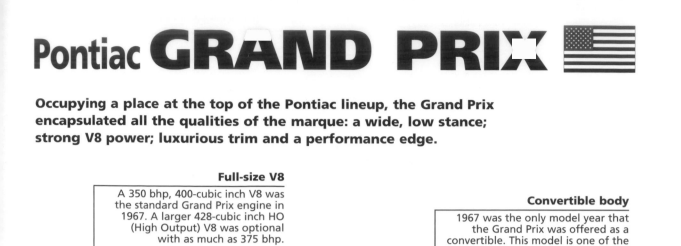

Occupying a place at the top of the Pontiac lineup, the Grand Prix encapsulated all the qualities of the marque: a wide, low stance; strong V8 power; luxurious trim and a performance edge.

Full-size V8

A 350 bhp, 400-cubic inch V8 was the standard Grand Prix engine in 1967. A larger 428-cubic inch HO (High Output) V8 was optional with as much as 375 bhp.

Convertible body

1967 was the only model year that the Grand Prix was offered as a convertible. This model is one of the more common hardtops.

Wasp-waist styling

A prominent downward-sliding body accent starts in the door and runs to the rear fender. This gives an impression of a slim midriff and chunky rear. The covers on the rear wheels are optional.

Wedge-shaped fender tips

The front fenders jut forward with a strong wedge-shaped thrust mirroring the ridge along the hood that splits the grill in two pieces. It might not be very aerodynamic but it set a style that evolved through the 1970s.

Hooded headlights

In contrast to the 1966 Pontiac lineup and the rest of the 1967 Pontiac range that feature stacked quad headlights, the 1967 Grand Prix has concealed headlights. This clean look has the parking lights hidden behind vacuum-operated headlight doors concealed in the grill.

Automatic or manual transmission

The majority of 1967 Grand Prix cars had TurboHydramatic three-speed automatic transmissions that were smooth-shifting and reliable. Fully synchronized four-speeds were offered as well, but only 760 cars were ordered with them.

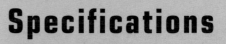

Specifications

1967 Pontiac Grand Prix

ENGINE

Type: V8

Construction: Cast-iron block and heads

Valve gear: Two valves per cylinder operated by a single camshaft with pushrods and rocker arms

Bore and stroke: 4.125 in. x 3.75 in.

Displacement: 400 c.i.

Compression ratio: 10.5:1

Induction system: Single Carter four-barrel carburetor

Maximum power: 350 bhp at 5,000 rpm

Maximum torque: 440 lb-ft at 3,200 rpm

Top speed: 110 mph

0-60 mph: 9.4 sec.

TRANSMISSION

TH400 automatic or four speed manual

BODY/CHASSIS

Separate chassis with steel two-door coupe body

SPECIAL FEATURES

The split front grill was a Pontiac trademark in the mid 1960s.

The concealed headlights make the Grand Prix instantly identifiable.

RUNNING GEAR

Steering: Recirculating ball

Front suspension: A-arms with coil springs and shock absorbers

Rear suspension: Live axle with coil springs and shock absorbers

Brakes: Drums (front and rear)

Wheels: Steel, 14-in. dia.

Tires: 8.55 x 14

DIMENSIONS

Length: 215.6 in.   **Width:** 79.4 in.

Height: 54.2 in.   **Wheelbase:** 121.0 in.

Track: 63.0 in. (front), 64.0 in. (rear)

Weight: 4,005 lbs.

Pontiac FIREBIRD

The 1968 Firebird was a huge hit among those who wanted performance. It was offered with a 175-bhp six-cylinder all the way up to the 335-bhp Ram Air® 400. Those who wanted the perfect compromise of power and economy chose the 350 H.O.

"...handles extremely well."

"The best kept secret in the 1968 Firebird had to be the 350 H.O. model. As with all first generation Firebirds, this one handled extremely well for a car with multiple rear leaf springs and unitary construction. The interior utilizes bucket seats and center console. With an ample 320 bhp, it nearly rivaled the performance of the base 330-bhp 400 V8, but was made available at much lower price. It offered a 0-60 mph time of 6.9 seconds.

Vinyl bucket seats and deep-set instruments give the cabin a sporty feel.

Milestones

1966 In September, GM introduces the Chevrolet® Camaro®. The Pontiac version is delayed.

First-generation Firebirds were heavily facelifted for 1969.

1967 The Pontiac Firebird is introduced in February. Although mechanically similar to the Camaro, it has a different nose and tail treatment.

In 1988, after 19 years, a Firebird convertible reappeared.

1969 After minor changes in 1968, there is a restyle for both the Camaro and the Firebird. The top Pontiac performance variant is the Firebird Trans Am.

1970 A second-generation Firebird makes its debut in February. It later proves to be a modern classic with the 345-bhp Ram Air IV 400 cubic-inch V8 being the pinnacle performance engine.

UNDER THE SKIN

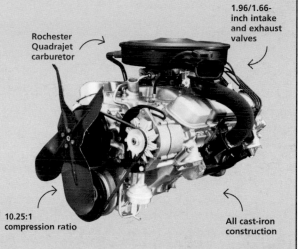

Leaf-sprung live rear axle

Optional power-assisted front disc brakes

Independent front suspension

High-output V8

Classic recipe

Firebirds follow the classic recipe for high-performance American cars. A big V8 at the front driving the rear wheels through a live axle. Base models are fitted with manual steering and brakes. However, the majority of Firebird 350 buyers requested most of the optional extras which transform the car, such as power disc brakes and power steering.

THE POWER PACK

High output

Pontiac's 350-cubic inch engine is the same mix as most big American V8s— all iron construction with the cylinder banks at a 90-degree angle to each other and with a single camshaft in the center of the engine working two valves per cylinder through pushrods and rockers. In its H.O. (High Output) role the 350 with its short-stroke, 10.25:1 compression ratio, long duration camshaft, D-port cylinder heads with 1.96/1.66-inch intake and exhaust valves was a great alternative to the 400 H.O.

Rochester Quadrajet carburetor

1.96/1.66-inch intake and exhaust valves

10.25:1 compression ratio

All cast-iron construction

350 H.O.

The 1968 Firebird offered the perfect compromise of power, handling and economy all wrapped up in an extremely sporty shell. As the more popular muscle car prices soar, the Firebird 350 remains relatively affordable and easily obtainable.

Many 1968 350 H.O. models are readily available and easily affordable.

Pontiac FIREBIRD

Even before the Trans Am® appeared, Pontiac already had a performance version of the Firebird—the 400. However, its intermediate version—the 350 H.O.—nearly rivaled its performance, but at a bargain price.

V8 engine

The biggest and most powerful engine available in early Firebirds is a Pontiac 400-cubic inch V8. It could be ordered with Ram Air to boost the power output. However this model is equipped with the intermediate 350 H.O. engine.

Convertible top

The Firebird was available in both convertible and coupe forms. In 1968, only about 15 percent of production were convertibles.

Optional disc brakes

The standard brakes on all early Firebirds are four-wheel drums, but with the immense power and torque of the 350 V8, optional front disc brakes are a wise and safe option.

Revisions from the 1967 model

For 1968, the Firebird now had wraparound front parking lights around the lower valance. In addition, small marker lights in the shape of the Pontiac Arrowhead were installed on the rear quarters. A new Astro ventilation system eliminated the vent windows.

Three-speed manual

A three-speed manual transmission was standard on 1967 Firebirds, although a four-speed manual and TurboHydramatic three-speed automatic were available as options.

Rear suspension

The factory 10-bolt rear end housing with the optional Safe-T-Track limited slip could be ordered with a variety of axle ratios from 2.56:1 to 3.23:1. Any higher ratio would require a 12-bolt unit.

Specifications

1968 Pontiac Firebird 350 H.O.

ENGINE
Type: V8
Construction: Cast-iron block and heads
Valve gear: Two valves per cylinder operated by a single V-mounted camshaft, pushrods and rockers
Bore and stroke: 3.88 in. x 3.75 in.
Displacement: 350 c.i.
Compression ratio: 10.25:1
Induction system: One four-barrel Rochester carburetor
Maximum power: 320 bhp at 5,000 rpm
Maximum torque: 380 lb-ft at 3,400 rpm
Top speed: 114 mph
0-60 mph: 6.9 sec

TRANSMISSION
Four-speed manual

BODY/CHASSIS
Steel unitary construction with two-door coupe body

SPECIAL FEATURES

Early Firebirds have dummy scoops on the rear quarter panels.

Owner-installed gauges are mounted on the center console.

RUNNING GEAR
Steering: Recirculating ball
Front suspension: Double wishbones with coil springs, telescopic shock absorbers and anti-roll bar
Rear suspension: Live axle with semi-elliptic leaf springs and telescopic shock absorbers
Brakes: Optional discs (front), drums, 11-in dia (rear)
Wheels: Steel, Rally II, 6 x 14 in.
Tires: F70 x 14

DIMENSIONS
Length: 189.2 in.   **Width:** 72.8 in.
Height: 49.3 in.   **Wheelbase:** 109.0 in.
Track: 60.0 in. (front and rear)
Weight: 3,740 lbs.

Pontiac TRANS AM

Since Pontiac only made eight Firebird® Trans Am convertibles in 1969, over the years many enthusiasts decided to build their own. The owner of this modified Trans Am drop-top decided to give it a modern touch by adding a late-model fuel injected 350-cubic inch engine and automatic transmission with overdrive.

"...an original stoplight warrior."

"This modified classic takes you back to cruising the boulevard in the summer of '69. But there's a twist—the 350 Chevy® engine puts out a serious rumble to ward off pretenders as you prepare for "The Stoplight Grand Prix." You're running fuel injection and a Positraction rear end to get all that power to the ground. Ready? Red...green...blast off! Light up the tires, and listen to the righteous sound of 250 horses slam you back in the seat and leave them all in a cloud of smoke! You're driving an original stoplight warrior."

The interior of this modified gem is perfect for cruisin'. There's lots of room to spread out and listen to old time rock 'n roll on the 8-Track.

Milestones

1967 Firebird is introduced with a range of engines; the most powerful is the 400 c.i. V8, pumping out 325 bhp.

1969 Most sought after of all the Firebirds becomes the Trans Am, named after the racing series.

1970 Shape is changed. All Firebirds now look longer, lower and sleeker. The convertible Firebird is discontinued.

1974 facelift proved popular with buyers.

1974 A facelift gives the Firebird a new lease on life.

1982 Third-generation Firebird appears. It's smaller and lighter than before, but by this stage even the Trans Am produces only 155 bhp.

Camaro IROC Z28 lent its engine to the car featured overleaf.

1989 Power rises steadily—the 350 c.i. V8 is available with 220 bhp in Camaro Z28 IROC trim. A modified version is transplanted into this 1969 Trans Am.

UNDER THE SKIN

All-steel body and chassis

Double-wishbone front suspension

Heavy duty rear axle

BFG Radial T/A tires

1989 Camaro IROC V8

Heavy duty

The first Trans Am arrived when America was making the transition from body-on-frame construction to unitary build. The car shown overleaf has discarded the original single-leaf spring per side rear end in favor of the heavy-duty Chevy Nova® axle on to which later Trans Am disc brakes have been added. Front suspension is the original double-wishbone system and the whole car is better balanced with the big Pontiac V8 replaced by the lighter Chevy V8.

THE POWER PACK

Small-block power

Chevrolet's 350-cubic inch V8 is one of the all-time greats, fitted in various forms in everything from the Blazer® to the Corvette®. In the 1989 Camaro® IROC trim, it has cast-iron block and heads, roller rockers and fuel injection. Cast-iron headers were installed as standard, but tuners would replace those with freer-flowing steel headers to increase output. There's a vast number of other tuning parts for the 350—higher lift cams with longer overlap, and reworked ports, combustion chambers and valves. It's easy to tune to 300 bhp or beyond; it's just a question of how fast you want to go.

Electronic fuel injection

Roller rockers

Cast-iron heads and block

Five-bearing crankshaft

Plush Pontiac

Pontiac's answer to the Camaro Z28 appeared a year after its in-house rival. It was made a bit plusher in keeping with Pontiac's higher status in the GM hierarchy. In Trans Am form, it uses a bigger, 400-cubic inch V8, rather than the Z28's 302 cubic inch.

First-year Trans Ams were white with blue stripes.

Pontiac TRANS AM

Why take a genuine collector's car and modify it? Why replace an immensely powerful 400-cubic inch V8 with a smaller 350? Look deeper at all the other modifications and improvements, and drive the car. Then it becomes obvious.

350 cubic inch V8

Pontiac's 400-cubic inch V8 was not one of America's greatest V8s, even though it produced plenty of power. Here it's been replaced by the superior, lighter and smaller 350 Chevrolet V8, as found in the Camaro Z28 and close to the specs found in the Corvette.

Taller wheels

The 1969 Trans Am ran on 14-inch wheels. They have been replaced by taller 15-inch wheels that fill the wheel arches to a greater extent and improve the car's overall look.

Power top

When the power convertible top was fitted to the Trans Am, all the effort was taken out of raising and lowering the top.

Positraction limited slip

The Nova axle is complemented by the Positraction limited slip differential with its 3.42:1 final drive ratio, taken from the 1979 Camaro Z28. This combination means the car can put its power down far more effectively than the original 1969 model.

Rear disc brakes

In the late-1960s, even front disc brakes were only an option on Firebirds and the rears were always drums. To help deal with the car's performance in the modern world, it's been fitted with the rear discs taken from a 1979 model Trans Am.

Hood scoops

The two hood scoops look impressive, but their function was to force air to the intake of the appropriately named Ram Air engine.

Rear spoiler

Part of the Trans Am package on the early Firebirds was the rear spoiler. It wasn't huge, but it was big enough to provide some downforce and, just as important, to make the car stand out from other Firebirds.

Chevy Nova rear end

Chevrolet produced Novas for Police Departments across the country. They have a heavy-duty rear suspension designed to cope with lots of power and sustained chases and abuse. This suspension has been incorporated into this Trans Am.

Specifications

1969 Modified Pontiac Trans Am

ENGINE

Type: Chevrolet small-block V8
Construction: Cast-iron block and heads
Valve gear: Two valves per cylinder operated by single block-mounted camshaft via pushrods, rockers and hydraulic tappets
Bore and stroke: 4 in. x 3.48 in.
Displacement: 350 c.i.
Compression ratio: 10:1
Induction system: Throttle body electronic fuel injection
Maximum power: 250 bhp at 5,000 rpm
Maximum torque: 295 lb-ft at 3,650 rpm
Top speed: 140 mph
0-60 mph: 6.8 sec

TRANSMISSION

1989 700R4 automatic transmission with overdrive

BODY/CHASSIS

Semi-unitary body/chassis with two-door convertible body

SPECIAL FEATURES

Rear disc brakes installed on this car come from a 1979 model Trans Am.

Fuel injection on IROC Z28 engine gives cleaner emissions and smoother pick-up. With a modified engine management chip, as used on this car, it also gives more horsepower.

RUNNING GEAR

Steering: Recirculating ball
Front suspension: Double wishbones with coil springs, telescopic shocks and anti-roll bar
Rear suspension: Live axle from 1979 Chevrolet Nova Police specification with semi-elliptic leaf springs and telescopic shocks
Brakes: Discs (front), with discs from a 1979 model Trans Am (rear)
Wheels: Steel 15 in. x 6 in.
Tires: BF Goodrich 235/60R15

DIMENSIONS

Length: 191,1 in.   **Width:** 173.9 in.
Height: 49.6 in.   **Wheelbase:** 108.1 in.
Track: 60 in. (front and rear)
Weight: 3,649 lbs.

Porsche 911

Unlike most premium sports car companies, instead of coming up with a whole new car every few years, Porsche kept evolving its existing platform. Today, the 911 is a very sophisticated car but this is where it began over 35 years and six generations ago.

"...a classic thoroughbred."

"The light, airy interior makes the 911 feel much younger than it really is. The gauges are spread out in front of the driver, with the tachometer occupying the prime position in the center. The flat six sounds quite rough at idle, but when the revs are up, it sounds like a classic thoroughbred. Entering a corner, the 911 starts to understeer, tightening its line with judicious application of the throttle. Don't back off, though, or the car will suddenly go into a terrifying spin."

The early 911's interior is surprisingly basic but incredibly functional.

Milestones

1959 Porsche engineers start development of a sports car to replace the aging 356.

1963 Porsche shows its new car, tagged the 901, at the Frankfurt Motor Show.

The 911 quickly proved itself as a really fine rally car.

1964 The '901' goes into full production at Porsche's factory in Zuffenhausen, Stuttgart, Germany. The name is formally changed to 911 in response to legal action from Peugeot.

Porsche experimented (unsuccessfully) with a four-seater version of the 911.

1966 A higher-powered variant, the 180-bhp 911S, is launched.

1967 The basic 911 is replaced by the 911L.

UNDER THE SKIN

Renaissance racer

The basic bodyshell is a unitary design with much of its strength coming from a stiffened floorpan, large box-section sills and a stressed roof. The front suspension consists of MacPherson struts with lower wishbones and longitudinal torsion bars. The rear suspension uses a trailing arm layout that survived, essentially, until the type 993 that was introduced in 1993.

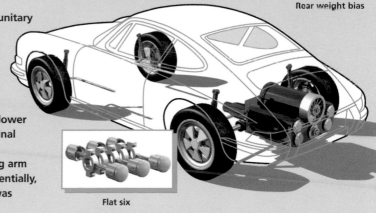

MacPherson-strut front suspension

Steel monocoque

Rear weight bias

Flat six

THE POWER PACK

Advanced technology

The first generation 911 needed an engine with the power of the existing four-cylinder, four-cam, Carrera racing engine but without the complexity. The 2.0-liter flat-six 901 engine (the engine kept the original type number until the 2.2-liter unit came along in 1969) was an innovative design. It incorporated features that were usually seen only in racing engines at the time, such as dry-sump lubrication and hemispherical combustion chambers. In original carbureted form, it produced a reliable 145 bhp.

Two valves per cylinder

Hemispherical combustion chambers

Dry-sump lubrication

Power-up

In 1966, a more powerful variant of the 2.0-liter 911 was launched. The 911S uses a higher compression ratio, free-flow exhaust system and a pair of triple-choke Weber carburetors to produce 180 bhp at 6,600 rpm, improving performance dramatically.

Engine tweaks produced the 911S. Thus its evolutionary process begins.

Porsche 911

Looking at the latest Porsche 911, it is easy to see that, even after more than 35 years, the famous German sports car builder has applied the theory of 'evolution, not revolution' to the 911.

Five-speed transmission

The five-speed transmission uses a dog-leg first gear, which was criticized in magazines, because road testers found it too easy to shift from first to fourth and completely miss second gear.

Air-cooled flat six

Porsche launched the 911 with a 2.0-liter version of its new horizontally opposed, six-cylinder engine. With two triple-choke Solex carburetors it produces 145 bhp.

Torsion-bar front suspension

The 911's MacPherson strut front suspension uses lower wishbones and is sprung by space-saving longitudinal torsion bars.

Unitary construction

The 911's monocoque gets its strength from a stiffened floorpan, large box-section sills and a stressed roof panel. Extra box sections support the engine and rear suspension, and the front is kept stiff by the assembly of sheet metal, especially the sculpted inner fenders and the crossmember supporting the gas tank.

Four-wheel discs

The original 911 uses four-wheel, solid disc brakes. To deal with the rear weight bias, the rear pair has a slightly larger diameter (11.2-inch) than at the front (11.1-inch)

Rear weight bias

The original 911 has a weight distribution of 43/57 percent front/rear. With the car's short wheelbase, this made handling tricky at high speeds.

Specifications

1965 Porsche 911

ENGINE

Type: Horizontally-opposed six-cylinder

Construction: Alloy block and heads

Valve gear: Two valves per cylinder operated by one camshaft per cylinder bank

Bore and stroke: 3.15 in. x 2.60 in.

Displacement: 1,991 cc

Compression ratio: 9.0:1

Induction system: Two triple-choke Solex carburetors

Maximum power: 145 bhp at 6,100 rpm

Maximum torque: 143 lb-ft at 4,200 rpm

Top speed: 132 mph

0-60 mph: 9.0 sec.

TRANSMISSION

Five-speed manual

BODY/CHASSIS

Unitary monocoque construction with steel two-door coupe body

SPECIAL FEATURES

The slatted front is a horn grill rather than an engine air intake.

This car has been fitted with later 4.5-inch, Fuchs alloy wheels, which were introduced in 1967.

RUNNING GEAR

Steering: Rack-and-pinion

Front suspension: MacPherson struts with lower wishbones, longitudinal torsion bars, telescopic shock absorbers and anti-roll bar

Rear suspension: Semi-trailing arms with transverse torsion bars and telescopic shock absorbers

Brakes: Discs (front and rear)

Wheels: Alloy, 4.5J x 15

Tires: Dunlop SP, 165/70 HR15

DIMENSIONS

Length: 164.5 in.   **Width:** 63.6 in.

Height: 52.0 in.   **Wheelbase:** 87.0 in.

Track: 54.1 in. (front), 51.8 in. (rear)

Weight: 2,360 lbs.

Porsche 912

The elevated price of the Porsche 911 meant many Porsche 356 buyers turned to other marques. Hence the 912: a 911 with the old 356 engine. It had all of the 911's style but not quite the performance.

"...a budget-wise 911."

"If you hadn't checked the badge on the engine cover, you'd think you were in the legendary 911. Starting the engine soon dispels this thought, however. The 912 was billed as a budget-wise 911. The flat-four rasps rather than howls like the 911's flat-six unit. It's a willing performer though, and will wind the car up to high speeds. Once on the move it's easy to maintain momentum. With less power, the handling is more forgiving than a 911's, yet responses are as sharp."

The interior is classic early 911—stark, stylish and very functional.

Milestones

1964 Porsche launches
the new 911 sports car. Replacing the 356, it looks set to become an automotive legend, with its sleek styling and lusty flat-six engine.

The 912 used the engine from the Porsche 356.

1965 In an effort to capture
sales lower in the market, Porsche launches the 912. It shares its body with the new 911 but uses the 1,582-cc flat four from the 356 Super 90. It makes 102 bhp.

The 912 shares its bodyshell with the famous 911.

1969 Production of the 912
comes to an end after 30,300 have been built. In 1975, it gets a revival as the 912E with a VW engine as used in the Porsche 914. This goes out of production in 1976 after only 2,099 have been built.

UNDER THE SKIN

Just like the 911

Just like the 911 upon which it was based, the 912 is a steel mono-coque with all-independent suspension. Up front, there are MacPherson struts with lower wishbones, longitudinal torsion bars and an anti-roll bar. At the rear are trailing arms with transverse torsion bars rather than the swing axles of the 356. This gives predictable handling and deals better with rear weight bias. Servo-assisted discs take care of braking.

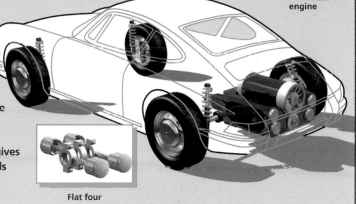

Four-wheel disc brakes

MacPherson-strut front suspension

Rear-mounted engine

Flat four

THE POWER PACK

Porsche four

The 912 uses the engine that had been fitted to the previous 356 Super 90, the most powerful 356 except for the quad-cam Carreras. The flat four has an alloy crankcase, cylinder barrels and heads. There are two valves per cylinder operated by a single camshaft, pushrods and rockers. Displacing 1,582 cc, it uses two twin-choke Solex carburetors. Power output is 102 bhp. The four-cylinder unit weighs more than 100 lbs. less than the flat six used in the 911.

Twin Solex carburetors

All-alloy construction

Two valves per cylinder

Single camshaft

Budget 911

Available in both coupe and targa body styles, the 912 is a great classic sports buy. It is far cheaper than the 911 and is almost as entertaining to drive. The cleaner styling of the 1965-1969 912 makes it more desirable than the 912E of 1975-1976.

The 912 fools most people into thinking that it is a 911.

Porsche **912**

For many, the Porsche 911 is simply too expensive. The four-cylinder 912 has always been much more affordable but has just the same street presence.

911 interior

It is difficult to tell that it's not a 911 when you're inside the 912. It has exactly the same trim as the basic 911.

356 engine

The pushrod flat-four engine taken from the 356 Super 90 is all alloy and with two twin-choke Solex carburetors it produces 102 bhp at 5,800 rpm.

Trailing arms

Whereas the 356 used swing-axle rear suspension, the 911 and 912 use triangulated semi-trailing arms to reduce much of the sudden snap oversteer of the earlier model.

Five-speed transmission

Until 1967 a five-speed transmission was optional. First and fifth gears were the same ratios as the four-speed unit but the intermediate gears were closer together.

911 styling

The classic 911 shape was penned by Ferdinand 'Butzi' Porsche, son of Dr. Ferry Porsche who had started the company with the 356 in 1948. The 912's body was exactly the same as its more expensive brother.

Front luggage compartment

With the engine in the back, the luggage compartment is located up front. Longitudinal torsion bars give more space than the transverse bars of the previous 356.

Rear-mounted engine

The flat four, being all alloy, is more than 100 lbs. lighter than the flat six fitted to the 911. This improves the strong rear weight bias.

Specifications
1967 Porsche 912

ENGINE

Type: Flat four-cylinder

Construction: Alloy block and heads

Valve gear: Two valves per cylinder operated by a single camshaft

Bore and stroke: 3.25 in. x 2.91 in.

Displacement: 1,582 cc

Compression ratio: 9.3:1

Induction system: Two twin-choke Solex carburetors

Maximum power: 102 bhp at 5,800 rpm

Maximum torque: 90 lb-ft at 3,500 rpm

Top speed: 119 mph

0-60 mph: 11.6 sec.

TRANSMISSION

Four- or five-speed manual

BODY/CHASSIS

Unitary monocoque construction with steel two-door coupe body

SPECIAL FEATURES

Apart from the 912's badge, there is little to differentiate it from the more expensive 911.

The 912 was fitted with these 15-inch chromed steel wheels as standard.

RUNNING GEAR

Steering: Rack-and-pinion

Front suspension: MacPherson struts with lower wishbones, torsion bars, telescopic shock absorbers and anti-roll bar

Rear suspension: Trailing arms with transverse torsion bars and telescopic shock absorbers

Brakes: Discs (front and rear)

Wheels: Steel 4.5 x 15 in.

Tires: Goodyear Highspeed, 165 x 15 in.

DIMENSIONS

Length: 163.9 in.   **Width:** 63.4 in.

Height: 52.0 in.   **Wheelbase:** 87.0 in.

Track: 52.6 in. (front), 51.8 in. (rear)

Weight: 2,100 lbs.

Renault **8 GORDINI**

For three years, a generation of up-and-coming French racing drivers fought each other in the Gordini Cup, driving one of the most unlikely looking racing cars—the surprisingly quick Renault 8 Gordini.

"...fantastic traction."

"Forget the looks, this is a very serious performance car. The smooth four-cylinder is designed to rev its heart out, and it really comes on cam above 3,500 rpm, sending the tachometer needle flying around. The close-ratio five-speed transmission helps maintain those rising revs, and, with fantastic traction from its rear-heavy design, the car seems to take off. The steering is quick and direct, and the car can be cornered easily at great speed without oversteer."

With a host of extra gauges, the Gordini has a much more sporty dash than other 8s.

Milestones

1962 Renault
introduces its Dauphine replacement, the R8. The styling is a bold departure, being as deliberately oblong as possible. Early cars have a 956-cc four-cylinder engine giving 48 bhp.

The Gordini made a competitive rally car in the 1960s.

1964 Amedée
Gordini transforms the 8. A new crossflow hemi-head on the 1,108-cc four-cylinder engine enables it to rev to 7,500 rpm.

For domestic national cup racing, Renault used the standard 8TS.

1966 More power is
needed to turn the R8 into a genuine rally contender, and the engine is stretched to 1,255 cc by fitting new pistons and liners. Power rises to 103 bhp.

1970 Production
ends.

UNDER THE SKIN

Strong and stiff

The basic rear-engined Renault 8 was a unitary monocoque construction with front wishbone suspension and rear swing axles. It did not need fundamental design changes to produce the fast Gordini versions, although the number of modifications was large. The structure is braced with stronger crossmembers, the suspension is lowered, and the springs are stiffer. Large disc brakes are fitted all around, along with a new instrument panel.

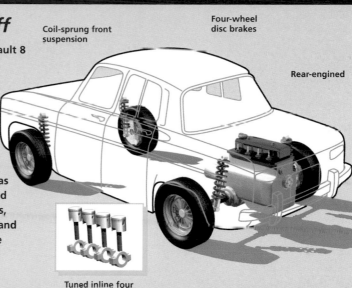

Coil-sprung front suspension

Four-wheel disc brakes

Rear-engined

Tuned inline four

THE POWER PACK

Miracle worker

Legendary engine tuner Amedée Gordini transformed small Renault engines in the 1960s. He did so by developing a new alloy head for the iron block four-cylinder with its replaceable cast-iron wet liners. The new head was a more efficient crossflow design and featured angled valves in hemispherical combustion chambers just like a twin-cam engine, but the trick was that there was still just one block-mounted camshaft working the valves via pushrods and long rockers. Combined with large carburetors and a four-branch exhaust header, great power increases became possible.

First version

Although it has a smaller engine, and less power than the 1300, the original version of the R8 Gordini is well worth considering. Its 1,108-cc engine gives an impressive 95 bhp, and because the car is lighter, performance does not suffer too much. The handling is just as good, too.

With Gordini tweaks the Renault 8 made a fine competition car.

Renault 8 GORDINI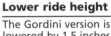

After the curves of the Dauphine, Renault wanted a contrast—a shape that would shock and get noticed by looking as box-like and deliberately unstyled as possible. The concept worked.

Tuned pushrod engine

One of Gordini's tuning tricks was to have the spark split by a forked tunnel. This has the effect of spreading the flame and improving combustion. It helps in producing 103 bhp from a pushrod 1,255-cc engine.

Lower ride height

The Gordini version is lowered by 1.5 inches all around, as well as having stiffer springs and extra rear shocks. The rear wheels have a negative camber so that even under hard cornering they will not tuck under and lose traction.

Two fuel tanks

The original Renault 8 had a small fuel tank mounted at the back, so to improve the range of the thirstier Gordini, an extra fuel tank was mounted in the front trunk. The two tanks are entirely separate, with a switch mounted on the cockpit floor to change from one to the other.

One color only

The Renault 8 Gordini came in just one color—French Racing Blue. In France, the cars also came with the distinctive white stripes as standard, although for foreign markets the stripes were made from tape which could be removed if the owner chose to do so.

Wishbone front suspension

Double pressed-steel wishbones are used at the front, with a co-axial coil spring/shock unit operating vertically between the two wishbones, plus a thick anti-roll bar.

Specifications

1967 Renault R8 Gordini

ENGINE

Type: Inline four-cylinder

Construction: Cast-iron block and alloy head

Valve gear: Two valves per cylinder operated by a single block-mounted camshaft with pushrods and rockers

Bore and stroke: 74.5 mm x 72.0 mm

Displacement: 1,255 cc

Compression ratio: 10.5:1

Induction system: Two sidedraft Weber 40 DCOE carburetors

Maximum power: 103 bhp at 6,750 rpm

Maximum torque: 86 lb-ft at 5,000 rpm

Top speed: 112 mph

0-60 mph: 10.9 sec.

TRANSMISSION

Five-speed manual

BODY/CHASSIS

Unitary monocoque construction with steel sedan body

SPECIAL FEATURES

A small fuel tank is mounted behind the engine.

The 1300 version has two extra large Halogen driving lights.

RUNNING GEAR

Steering: Rack-and-pinion

Front suspension: Double wishbones with coil springs, telescopic shock absorbers and anti-roll bar

Rear suspension: Swing axles with radius arms and coil springs/twin telescopic shock absorbers per side

Brakes: Discs, 10.30-in. dia. (front and rear)

Wheels: Pressed-steel disc, 5.3 x 15 in.

Tires: Dunlop SP radial, 135-380 mm

DIMENSIONS

Length: 157.0 in.   **Width:** 58.0 in.

Height: 53.0 in.   **Wheelbase:** 89.0 in.

Track: 49.0 in. (front), 48.0 in. (rear)

Weight: 1,885 lbs.

Rover P5B COUPE

Rover pulled off quite a coup when it bought the rights to an all-alloy Buick V8 engine. Its first use was in the aging P5 sedan, a car which became one of the most majestic cars that Rover has ever built.

"...refined good taste."

"A gentleman's carriage would be a correct description for the sophisticated P5B. The seats have the feel of luxury leather armchairs and the wood paneling suggests refined good taste. The alloy V8 engine and automatic transmission are perfectly matched. The P5B is most at home cruising on the highway. On twisty roads it really shows its age as the car rolls through the turns, however, the tires do grip confidently."

P5Bs have traditional British interiors. Sliding behind the wheel gives a feeling of confidence.

Milestones

1958 Rover first launches
its 3.0-liter model, code-named the P5. It bears similar styling to the P4, but is larger and heavier. It is also the first Rover to adopt unitary construction.

1962 A four-door coupe
bodyshell with a lower roof line joins the sedan. It proves to be a real success.

The P4 had much more restrained upright styling than the P5.

1967 The P5 range is replaced
by the P5B, which is the first model to use the Buick V8 engine, Rostyle steel wheels and front foglights.

1973 The P5B is retired
with no direct successor.

The P6 was available with four-cylinder engines as well as the V8.

UNDER THE SKIN

Unitary construction

Live rear axle

Power front disc brakes

Lightweight V8

New ground

Launched in 1958, the P5 was Rover's first unitary construction car. It still retained a separate front subframe as some link with its heritage of separate chassis: this carries the engine, transmission, steering and suspension. The result of the monocoque body/chassis unit is a welcomed weight reduction. The front suspension is quite sophisticated for the time, consisting of MacPherson struts, with a rigid rear axle and leaf springs.

THE POWER PACK

Buick V8

When Rover's managing director, William Martin Hurst, came across an aluminum V8 engine while visiting the U.S., he was curious. Hurst found out that this was a 215-cubic inch Buick unit, offered in the early 1960s Skylark compact. Rover saw it as an ideal replacement for the aging 3.0-liter engine used in the Rover P5. In 1965, Buick duly granted a license for Rover to build it. Rover changed the casting process, designed a new intake manifold and fitted twin SU carburetors. In the P5B it produces 161 bhp.

Twin SU carburetors

Rover-designed intake manifold

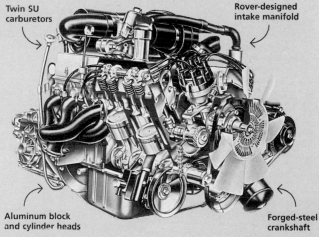

Aluminum block and cylinder heads

Forged-steel crankshaft

P5B Coupe

Two body styles were offered on the luxurious P5B: a standard sedan and the Coupe. Despite its name, the latter is also a four-door but has a lower roof line which makes it look more sporty. Enthusiasts tend to prefer the Coupe, but any P5B is a value for the money.

Today, these stately old Rovers have a loyal enthusiast following.

Rover **P5B COUPE** 🇬🇧

Installing a V8 engine into the P5 transformed it from a stuffy sedan into a powerful and refined luxury cruiser. Though still considered small, especially for a four door, it proved to be popular in many other markets.

Buick V8

The V8 engine under the P5B's hood really made the car fast. Because it was made from a light alloy, the engine weighed about the same as the Rover 2.0-liter four-cylinder engine. The U.S. engine was so effective that it powered successive generations of Rover sedans, and is still used today.

Front disc brakes

The P5B uses front disc brakes to stop its considerable weight at high speeds.

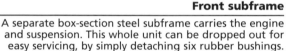

Front subframe

A separate box-section steel subframe carries the engine and suspension. This whole unit can be dropped out for easy servicing, by simply detaching six rubber bushings.

Sumptuous interior

The leather-trimmed seats in the P5B are deeply padded andvery comfortable. Cabin ambience is created by plush carpeting, extensive wood veneer trim, chrome detailing and surprisingly modern-looking instruments set right in front of the driver.

200

Coupe shape

Two inches lower than the P5B sedans, the Coupe has steeper front and rear pillars. It was originally intended to have been a pillarless design, but wind noise and torsional rigidity problems prevented this design.

Power steering

Although optional on the original P5, power steering was a standard item on the V8-engined P5B. This helps when maneuvering the hefty barge at low speeds.

Laminated torsion bars

Rover's choice of laminated torsion bars was very unusual. The advantage of using them was to save valuable space underneath.

Specifications

1968 Rover 3.5-liter P5B Coupe

ENGINE

Type: V8

Construction: Aluminum block and heads

Valve gear: Two valves per cylinder operated by a single camshaft via pushrods and rockers

Bore and stroke: 3.50 in. x 2.79 in.

Displacement: 3,528 cc

Compression ratio: 10.5:1

Induction system: Two SU carburetors

Maximum power: 161 bhp at 5,200 rpm

Maximum torque: 210 lb-ft at 2,600 rpm

Top speed: 110 mph

0-60 mph: 12.4 sec.

TRANSMISSION

Three-speed automatic

BODY/CHASSIS

Integral chassis with four-door steel coupe body

SPECIAL FEATURES

A fold-out wood veneer armrest with glass holders adds a touch of class.

Side marker lights are set in small housings at the edge of the fenders.

RUNNING GEAR

Steering: Worm-and-nut

Front suspension: Wishbones with radius links, torsion bars, telescopic shock absorbers and anti-roll bar

Rear suspension: Rigid axle with semi-elliptic leaf springs and telescopic shock absorbers

Brakes: Discs (front), drums (rear)

Wheels: Steel, 15-in. dia

Tires: 6.70 x 15

DIMENSIONS

Length: 186.5 in.   **Width:** 70.0 in.

Height: 57.3 in.   **Wheelbase:** 110.5 in.

Track: 55.3 in. (front), 56.0 in. (rear)

Weight: 3,479 lbs.

UK 1963-1977

Rover **P6**

Rover's old-fashioned image was completely swept aside by the P6 in 1963. It was so good that it won a British Car of the Year Award. It offered excellent handling, strong performance and amazing refinement.

"...relaxed drive."

"Inside, the P6 feels a lot more modern than it actually is. It is bright and airy; only the instruments and large, thin-rimmed steering wheel give its age away. On the road the ride is excellent, the supple suspension soaking up even the biggest road shocks. Although body roll is quite severe under hard cornering, the roadholding is good. The four-cylinder engines offer decent performance, but the V8 makes for a much more relaxed drive."

The delicate steering wheel gives excellent feedback when the P6 is on the move.

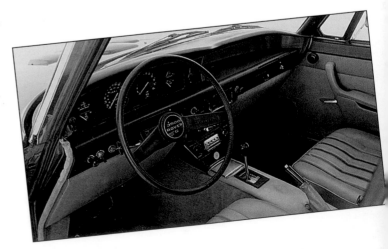

202

Milestones

1963 Rover introduces its

new sedan, the P6 2000. It is smoothly styled and has a new overhead cam four-cylinder engine as well as four-wheel disc brakes.

The P5B was the first Rover to use the ex-Buick V8.

1966 A new twin-carburetor

version, the 124-bhp 2000 TC, is launched. An automatic transmission also becomes available.

The P6 was replaced by the Rover SD1 in 1976.

1968 Rover fits the ex-Buick V8

and produces the 3500 model, available only with automatic transmission. The 3500S of 1971 has a four-speed manual transmission. In 1973, the four-cylinder is bored out to 2.2 liters, but the range is taken off the market in 1976.

UNDER THE SKIN

Bolt-on body panels

Four wheel discs

De Dion rear suspension

Alloy V8

Steel skeleton

The P6 was the first Rover to use monocoque construction. The steel unitary skeleton has bolt-on outer panels. The roof panel is load-bearing, but the fenders and rocker panels are not. The suspension was unconventional, too. At the front, the coil springs are mounted horizontally, actuated by rocker linkages. At the rear, there is a De Dion setup, also with coil springs.

THE POWER PACK

Four or eight

The P6 could be had with either an overhead-camshaft four-cylinder engine or a V8. The 2-liter four (later bored out to 2.2-liters) was advanced in having its combustion chambers set into the pistons. In twin-carb form, it produces 124 bhp. The V8, fitted from 1968, is an ex-Buick unit of 3,528 cc. It is all alloy and runs two SU carburetors. It produces 184 bhp, although a European-spec, high-compression unit was available with an output of 207 bhp.

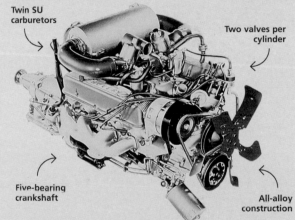

Twin SU carburetors

Two valves per cylinder

Five-bearing crankshaft

All-alloy construction

P6 Power

The V8 models are the most desirable of the range. The 3500S manual transmission model is preferred by many, but the four-speed transmission has trouble dealing with the V8's power. The automatic transmission is stronger.

The V8 models command higher prices than the four-cylinders.

Rover P6

Only 2,043 of these North American-specification 3500s were built. With its aggressive hood scoops and generous standard equipment, it is one of the most valuable variants.

All-alloy V8

Rover's all-alloy 184-bhp V8 was originally a Buick design. Rover modified it to deal with the higher speeds expected from a V8 powered 4-door.

Hood scoops

Only the North American-specification 3500 had these distinctive hood scoops. The center scoop is for ram air and the outer pair are for engine-bay cooling.

Deck lid-mounted spare wheel

On European-specification cars, the deck lid-mounted spare was an option. On cars destined for North America they came as standard equipment. It freed up a good deal of luggage space.

High equipment levels

The North American-spec 3500 has higher levels of standard equipment than European-spec models. The list includes side-impact protection beams, side marker lamps and reflectors, an ice-warning system and wrap-around bumpers.

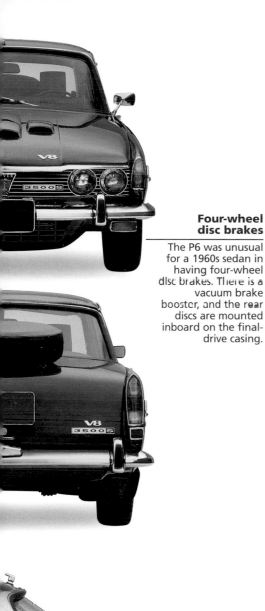

Four-wheel disc brakes

The P6 was unusual for a 1960s sedan in having four-wheel disc brakes. There is a vacuum brake booster, and the rear discs are mounted inboard on the final-drive casing.

Bolt-on panels

All the P6's body panels are bolt-on and, apart from the roof panel, unstressed. The extremely rigid steel monocoque skeleton takes all the load. Bolt-on panels reduce the cost of body repairs.

Specifications
1970 Rover 3500

ENGINE

Type: V8

Construction: Alloy block and heads

Valve gear: Two valves per cylinder operated by a single camshaft

Bore and stroke: 3.50 in. x 2.80 in.

Displacement: 3,528 cc

Compression ratio: 10.5:1

Induction system: Two SU carburetors

Maximum power: 184 bhp at 5,200 rpm

Maximum torque: 226 lb-ft at 3,000 rpm

Top speed: 108 mph

0-60 mph: 11.5 sec.

TRANSMISSION

Three-speed automatic

BODY/CHASSIS

Unitary monocoque construction with bolt-on steel panels

SPECIAL FEATURES

These distinctive wheels identify the car as the 3500S model.

The box on the grill is the Ice-alert ice warning sensor.

RUNNING GEAR

Steering: Recirculating-ball

Front suspension: Leading top links, lower wishbones, coil springs, telescopic shock absorbers and anti-roll bar

Rear suspension: De Dion sliding tube located by Watt linkage and driveshafts, coil springs and telescopic shock absorbers

Brakes: Discs (front and rear)

Wheels: Steel, 5J x 14

Tires: 165SR-14

DIMENSIONS

Length: 181.0 in.   **Width:** 66.0 in.

Height: 56.3 in.   **Wheelbase:** 103.4 in.

Track: 53.4 in. (front), 51.8 in. (rear)

Weight: 3,200 lbs.

Saab 96

Saab's third-generation, front-drive model, the two-stroke 96, gave the Swedish company a world-class rally car. Even in later four-stroke V4 form and outdated by its rivals, it remained highly competitive.

"...muffled-sounding two stroke."

"Although the excellent seats adjust to fit anyone, the position of the pedals, which are offset toward the center of the car, take some getting used to. Start the engine and it idles with the characteristic muffled sound of a two-stroke motor. For rapid progress, the revs need to be kept up using the slick column shifter. The front-wheel drive works great and has sure-gripping handling, although understeer builds toward the limit."

The simple and elegant dashboard is well stocked with gauges.

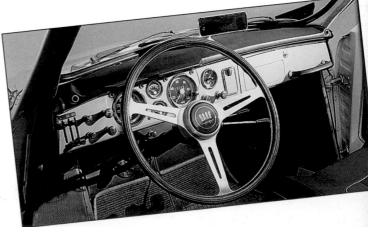

Milestones

1960 The Saab 96 hits the streets. Its biggest win this year is in the RAC Rally in the hands of Erik Carlsson.

The Saab 95 station wagon introduced the 841-cc engine.

1961 The factory cars win the Acropolis, Midnight Sun and RAC rallies.

1962 Erik Carlsson drives the 96 to win the RAC and Monte Carlo rallies.

1963 Carlsson takes another win in the Monte Carlo Rally.

The last 300 96s were all finished in metallic blue.

1966 The two-stroke 96 has its last big win in the Swedish Rally before the V4 model takes over.

1980 Production of the Saab 96 comes to an end.

UNDER THE SKIN

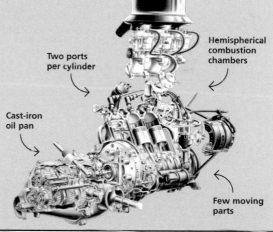

Front-wheel drive

Dead rear axle

Monocoque construction

In-line three

THE POWER PACK

Front driver

The monocoque 96 was well-known for its sturdy build and was advertised as one of the most robust sedan car bodies ever made. The front suspension is by wishbones and coil springs, with a coil-sprung beam rear axle. Initially, braking was by four-wheel drums, but front discs became standard in 1962.

Tuned two-stroke

Like the 92 before it, the 96 was launched with a two-stroke, three-cylinder engine, now enlarged to 841 cc. The water-cooled unit has hemispherical combustion chambers and produces 42 bhp in the basic 96 and up to about 80 bhp in full competition tune. In 1967, the car gained a 1.5-liter (1.7-liter in emissions form), four-stroke, V4 engine from Ford of Germany. This produces an unstressed 65 bhp in road cars but can pump out an extra 100 bhp in full rally tune.

Two ports per cylinder

Hemispherical combustion chambers

Cast-iron oil pan

Few moving parts

Triple carb

The most desirable 96 variant is the 850 GT, launched in 1962. The sportiest of the range, it has a triple-carb setup on the two-stroke engine giving 57 bhp. It also has the more characterful and rounded bullnose front-end styling.

With 57 bhp and a near 90 mph top speed, the 850 GT was a driver's dream.

Saab 96

On rallies where the tracks had loose surfaces or were covered in ice and snow, the front-wheel drive 96 could leave much more powerful competitors in its wake.

Freewheel transmission

Because conventional two-strokes give no lubrication on the overrun, the Saab has a freewheel transmission that disengages the engine from the wheels when the accelerator is released. It also allows clutchless gear shifts.

Two-stroke engine

Like the 92 and 93 before it, the 96 uses a three-cylinder, two-stroke engine. It displaces 841 cc, a size first seen in the 95 station wagon in 1959.

Disc brakes

The 850 GT's front disc brakes stop the car with ease. This is a must since the freewheel transmission gives no engine braking.

Aerodynamic body

Saab's aircraft background meant that it was one of the first manufacturers to make use of a wind tunnel in designing its cars.

Front-wheel drive

The Saab's biggest advantage in rallying was its sure-footed front-drive handling, helped by the weight of the engine over the driven wheels.

Increased luggage space

A redesigned rear fender line improved luggage space over the earlier 93 model. The spare wheel is stored underneath in a separate compartment.

U-beam rear axle

The coil-sprung rear suspension uses a shallow U-beam dead axle that helps keep the rear end from lifting under heavy braking.

Specifications

1963 Saab 850 GT

ENGINE
Type: In-line three-cylinder
Construction: Cast-iron block
Valve gear: Two-stroke, open ports and reverse-flow
Bore and stroke: 2.70 in. x 2.80 in.
Displacement: 841 cc
Compression ratio: 9.0:1
Induction system: Three Solex carburetors
Maximum power: 57 bhp at 5,000 rpm
Maximum torque: 68 lb-ft at 3,500 rpm
Top speed: 87 mph
0-60 mph: 21.2 sec.

TRANSMISSION
Four-speed manual with freewheel

BODY/CHASSIS
Unitary monocoque construction with steel two-door sedan body

SPECIAL FEATURES

A discreet vent on the C-pillar gives much-needed cabin ventilation.

The bluff front end gives the car its 'bullnose' nickname.

RUNNING GEAR
Steering: Rack-and-pinion
Front suspension: Double wishbones with coil springs and telescopic shock absorbers
Rear suspension: Beam axle with coil springs and telescopic shock absorbers
Brakes: Discs (front), drums (rear)
Wheels: Steel, 15-in. dia.
Tires: 155 x 15

DIMENSIONS
Length: 159.0 in.   **Width:** 62.0 in.
Height: 58.0 in.   **Wheelbase:** 98.0 in.
Track: 48.0 in. (front and rear)
Weight: 1,860 lbs.

Shelby MUSTANG GT500

Softer, roomier and more practical than the original stark GT350, the GT500 still boasted masses of brute strength with over 350 bhp and a gigantic 420 lb-ft of torque from its 428-cubic inch V8.

"...so much power and torque."

"With so much power and torque available, anyone can get stunning performance from the GT500, particularly with the automatic. There are two surprises in store: You expect it to be faster than a 15.6-second quarter mile suggests, but you don't expect it to handle as well as it does. Despite the huge engine making it front heavy, the power steering makes sure the GT500 goes where you want it to. The ride isn't bad for a late-'60s muscle car and the engine isn't very temperamental, although it does throw out an awful lot of heat, making the air conditioning option a must."

The dashboard has a special 140-mph speedometer and 8,000-rpm tachometer as well as plenty of extra gauges.

Milestones

1965 First Shelby GT350s appear as 1966 models, but sell slowly.

1966 Efforts to make it more of a street car lead to the specifications being toned down: The exhaust is quieter, the limited slip differential is an option and Koni shocks are left off.

1968 was the first year you could get a GT500 convertible.

1967 The last year before Ford takes over building the Shelby Mustang. The GT350 is restyled and the bigger engined GT500 is introduced.

1968 GT500 is joined by the GT500KR (King of the Road). It has a 428-cubic inch engine—the Cobra Jet rather than the Police unit.

Ford's own Mach 1 Mustang killed off the GT500.

1969 Whole Mustang range is restyled, including the GT500 to the big, flatter looking Mach 1 style.

UNDER THE SKIN

Stiffened springs

Live rear axle

Adjustable shock absorbers

Stiff anti-roll bar

Wishbone front suspension

Police-spec V8

Suspension improvements

Like all performance Mustangs, the GT500 had a straightforward front V8 engine driving a live rear axle. Shelby's improvements saw the springs stiffened and Gabriel adjustable shock absorbers added, and a stiff anti-roll bar at the front. The modification which lowered the pivot for the front upper wishbone was so good Ford adopted it on the stock Mustang.

THE POWER PACK

Simply big

Don't confuse the 428-cubic inch unit installed in the GT500 with the fierce 427 engine in Shelby's Cobras. The 428 has a different bore and stroke and, although it shares the same all-iron pushrod V8 layout, it is a less sophisticated design, and less powerful. It was designed for lower engine speeds and for long sustained use, often in the police chase cars in which it was used. Later the police-spec unit was replaced with the Cobra Jet version which was rated with an extra five bhp but no increase in torque.

Holley carburetor

Two valves per cylinder

High compression ratio

Strong bottom end

Early or open?

Although the GT500 continued until the 1970 model year, by that stage there was very little to set it apart from the rest of the Mustang range. So if you're after one of the big-engined Shelby Mustangs, it's best to go for an earlier, more subtle car or one of the rare convertibles, which are highly collectible and often faked.

The rarest of the GT500s is the factory convertible.

Shelby MUSTANG GT500

If bigger was better, the GT500 was the best of the Shelby Mustang line. There was no way you could have added a bigger engine to the car, and that made sure it was the most powerful of all.

Front heavy
That huge cast-iron V8 naturally made the GT500 front heavy, with a weight distribution of 58 percent front and 42 percent rear. It was just as well that the hood was fiberglass.

Fiberglass hood
A new fiberglass hood with functional air scoops helps to accommodate the big engine and also reduces the car's weight.

Power steering
With so much weight over the nose and with wide tires, power steering was a very good idea. In fact you had no choice—it was a standard feature, as were the power brakes and shoulder harnesses.

V8 engine
With the GT500, Shelby went for the biggest engine he could fit in the bay, the Police Interceptor type 428-cubic inch V8. It filled the engine compartment so fully you couldn't even see the spark plugs.

Wide tires
The GT500 needed to put as much rubber on the road as possible to cope with its power. Shelby opted for Goodyear Speedway E70-15s, a popular choice for muscle cars of the era that were rated at 140 mph.

Alloy wheels
Steel wheels were a standard feature, but these Shelby alloys were available as an option. They are very desirable today.

Adjustable shocks
The standard shocks were thrown out and replaced by Gabriel adjustables. However, the car left the Shelby works with what was considered the optimum settings.

Unique tail lights

The back of the car was distinguished from the standard Mustang fastback by different tail lights, two very wide ones replacing the two sets of triple lights. Above the lights, the trunk lid was another Shelby fiberglass part.

Specifications
1967 Shelby Mustang GT500

ENGINE

Type: V8

Construction: Cast-iron block and heads

Valve gear: Two valves per cylinder operated by single block-mounted camshaft via pushrods, rockers and hydraulic lifters

Bore and stroke: 4.13 in. x 3.98 in.

Displacement: 428 c.i.

Compression ratio: 10.5:1

Induction system: Two Holley four-barrel carburetors

Maximum power: 355 bhp at 5,400 rpm

Maximum torque: 420 lb-ft at 3,200 rpm

Top speed: 132 mph

0-60 mph: 7.0 sec.

TRANSMISSION

Ford Cruise-O-Matic three-speed automatic or four-speed manual

BODY/FRAME

Unitary steel with two-door coupe body

SPECIAL FEATURES

The hood scoops added by Shelby were changed with each model year. They became more prominent after these rather subtle scoops on this 1967 car.

1967 Shelby GT500s were equipped with two extra driving lights but were spread farther apart toward the end of the 1967 model year.

RUNNING GEAR

Steering: Recirculating ball

Front suspension: Double wishbones with adjustable Gabriel shock absorbers and 1-inch dia. anti-roll bar

Rear suspension: Live axle with semi-elliptic leaf springs

Brakes: Discs, 11.3 in. dia. (front), drums, 10 in. dia. (rear)

Wheels: Shelby alloy, 7 in. x 15 in.

Tires: E70-15 (front and rear)

DIMENSIONS

Length: 186.6 in.   **Width:** 70.9 in.

Height: 49 in.   **Wheelbase:** 108 in.

Track: 58 in. (front and rear)

Weight: 3,520 lbs.

Shelby GT350

The original Shelby Mustangs were fast and furious, designed for the committed driver. By 1968, the rough edges were gone and comfort had increased. As an effort to rejuvenate its power, this rare Shelby has a Paxton supercharger.

"...good weight distribution."

"Forget the virtually stock engine; the supercharged 302 is a fine V8. Performance is obviously very strong, and nearly matches the power of the much larger 428 engine. Handling is not as sharp, but having a fiberglass hood plays its part in making the front/rear weight distribution better. It reduces understeer and makes the car a bit more neutral. Bigger wheels than on the original do the trick of providing more grip."

Deep-set instruments and a bar-operated horn typify late-1960s design trends.

Milestones

1965 Carroll Shelby gets the job of transforming the Mustang into a high-performance car and he uses the Fastback bodyshell with the 289 V8 modified to give 306 bhp.

1966 The Mustang convertible gets the Shelby treatment but fewer than 10 are made.

Bigger brother to the GT 350 is the 428-engined GT 500 KR.

1967 The 1967 line-up of Shelby Mustangs is increased with the new GT 500. Built on the fastback body, it has a 427 (later 428) V8. More than 2,000 are built.

The GT 350 was facelifted in 1969 and got a new 351 V8.

1968 Ford takes control of the Shelby Mustang operation, and for 1969 model year the GT 350 gets the 351-cubic inch Ford Windsor V8.

1970 It's the end for the Shelby line.

UNDER THE SKIN

Standard Mustang floorpan

Live rear axle

Front disc brakes

Standard V8

Mustang at heart

The standard Mustang was considered good enough as the basis for the Shelby GT 350 and that meant the same floorpan and welded-on body, except for a lightweight hood which changed the weight distribution. Mechanically, there is the same A-Arm front suspension with anti-roll bar. At the rear the live axle continued to ride on semi-elliptic leaf springs without any extra location.

THE POWER PACK

Subtle revisions

To follow the performance image, there is a supercharged engine powering the GT 350: the newer 302-cubic inch (4,949 cc) V8 rather than the famous 289 found in earlier Mustangs. It follows the same basic design of cast-iron block and heads, single V-mounted cam, pushrods, rockers and hydraulic lifters, but there are differences. It has a longer stroke than the 289, although at 4.0 x 3.0 inches it is still square and has a short stroke. The valve sizes and the intake and exhaust port area and shape, as well as the valve lift and timing devices, stayed the same as on the original. However, a centrifugal supercharger is fitted.

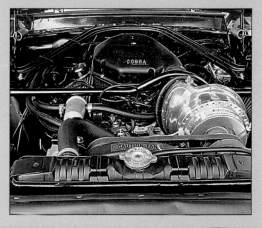

Paxton Power

In an effort to boost performance, a dealer-installed Paxton supercharger could be ordered. Because the larger displacement engine was just a few dollars more than a supercharged 302, most buyers opted for the larger engine.

Rarity and image make convertible models the most collectible today.

Shelby GT350 🇺🇸

Mechanically the GT 350 may have been softened for the 1968 version, but an imposing look was still a vital part of the car's appeal. There was a new, aggressive nose treatment, which suggested power and speed.

V8 engine
Compared with the work Shelby did on the original GT 350, the 302 V8 was left almost unaltered. An alloy high-rise intake manifold was fitted to take the four-barrel Holley rather than stock Motorcraft carburetor. The 10.5:1 compression ratio helps give 250 bhp.

Optional supercharged V8
More power was available for the GT 350 if you specified the optional supercharged engine with a Paxton blower. That made a really significant difference, taking power all the way from 250 bhp at 4,800 rpm to 335 bhp at 5,200 rpm.

Uprated suspension
Although the GT 350 rides on the same double-wishbone suspension at the front and the same live axle on semi-elliptic leaf springs as lesser 1968 Mustangs, spring and damper rates are stiffer to improve handling and roadholding.

Four-speed transmission

Standard transmission for the GT 350 was the four-speed manual with a direct 1:1 fourth gear ratio. An automatic was available for an extra $50.

Front discs

Standard Mustangs carried on with drum brakes. Those who forgot to specify the better discs option on the GT 350 missed out on large 11.4-inch front disc brakes.

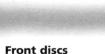

Specifications

1968 Ford Shelby Mustang GT 350

ENGINE

Type: V8

Construction: Cast-iron block and heads

Valve gear: Two valves per cylinder operated by a single V-mounted camshaft with pushrods and rockers

Bore and stroke: 4.0 in. x 3.0 in.

Displacement: 302 c.i.

Compression ratio: 10.5:1

Induction system: Single Holley four-barrel carburetor Paxton/McCulloch supercharger

Maximum power: 335 bhp at 5,200 rpm

Maximum torque: 325 lb-ft at 3,200 rpm

Top speed: 131 mph

0-60 mph: 6.2 sec.

TRANSMISSION

Four-speed manual

BODY/CHASSIS

Unitary steel construction with two-door fastback or convertible work

SPECIAL FEATURES

A pop-open gas cap is flanked by 1965 Thunderbird taillights.

Twin quick-release catches lock the hood and prevent it from getting airborne.

RUNNING GEAR

Steering: Recirculating-ball

Front suspension: A-arms with coil springs, telescopic shocks and anti-roll bar

Rear suspension: Live axle with semi-elliptic leaf springs and telescopic shocks

Brakes: Discs, 11.4-in. dia. (front), drums, 10.0-in. dia. (rear)

Wheels: 15 x 6 in.

Tires: E70 - 15

DIMENSIONS

Length: 186.8 in. **Width:** 70.9 in.

Height: 51.8 in. **Wheelbase:** 108.0 in.

Track: 58.1 in. (front and rear)

Weight: 3,340 lbs.

Singer **CHAMOIS**

In an era of badge engineering, the Singer Chamois was the luxurious flagship of the Rootes Group's Hillman Imp range. The unconventional little car was technically very advanced for its time.

"...great fun to drive."

"The Chamois is unique to drive. To begin with, it has an extraordinary engine that sounds like a racer even if it's not actually revving that fast. The controls are delightfully light, with a precise manual gearshift. There is a lot of grip and the built-in understeer counteracts the tendency of a rear-engined car to oversteer. The Chamois is great fun to drive, because it requires total concentration to get the best from it."

The walnut trimmings on the Chamois fascia and doors set it apart from standard Imps.

Milestones

1956 Independent since 1905, the Singer car company is taken over by Rootes.

1963 The Rootes Group's new small car, the Hillman Imp, is launched. It is available in sedan, coupe and station wagon form.

The Hillman Imp was the no-frills version of the Chamois.

1964 A plush Singer Chamois version joins the Imp, in sedan form only.

1966 With a twin-carb engine, the Chamois Sport becomes a real Mini Cooper rival.

The Vogue was the last car to carry the Singer name.

1967 A fastback coupe model arrives, though it lacks the twin-carb engine.

1970 Under new owners Chrysler the Singer badge is pulled in April.

UNDER THE SKIN

Adventurous

Few other small cars of the early 1960s were so adventurous in their use of technology. In addition to its alloy engine, the Chamois boasts an all-independent suspension using swing axles at the front and semi-trailing arms out back. All-synchromesh transmission and rack-and-pinion steering are other advanced features for the time. Early cars had a pneumatic throttle linkage, but this was replaced by a conventional cable. Compared to the Imp, the Chamois has wider wheels and meatier tires.

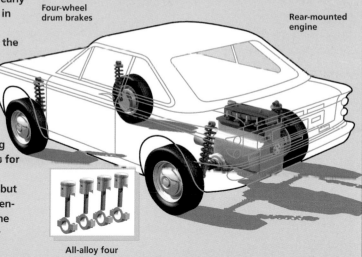

All-independent suspension

Four-wheel drum brakes

Rear-mounted engine

All-alloy four

THE POWER PACK

Climax grunt

The tiny 875-cc four-cylinder engine in the tail was a real revelation—genuine racing-car technology in a small and affordable family car. It was based on the highly successful Coventry-Climax engine that was dominating world-class racing at the time. It was the first all-aluminum engine seen in a mass-produced British car. The sedan and coupe both use a single carburetor version of the overhead camshaft engine, developing 39 bhp, but the Sport model has twin carburetors and an output of 51 bhp.

Sporty number

In an era of Rootes Group badge engineering, the basic Imp chassis was available in several forms. The base, volume production model was the Hillman Imp. The more luxurious version was known as the Singer Chamois and the sporty edition was the Sunbeam Stilleto.

The Sunbeam Stiletto is the sporty family member.

Singer CHAMOIS

No other major British car maker used a rear-engined layout, but the Singer Chamois was a triumph of engineering over a flawed layout. In the Rootes Group hierarchy, Singer was definitely the superior brand.

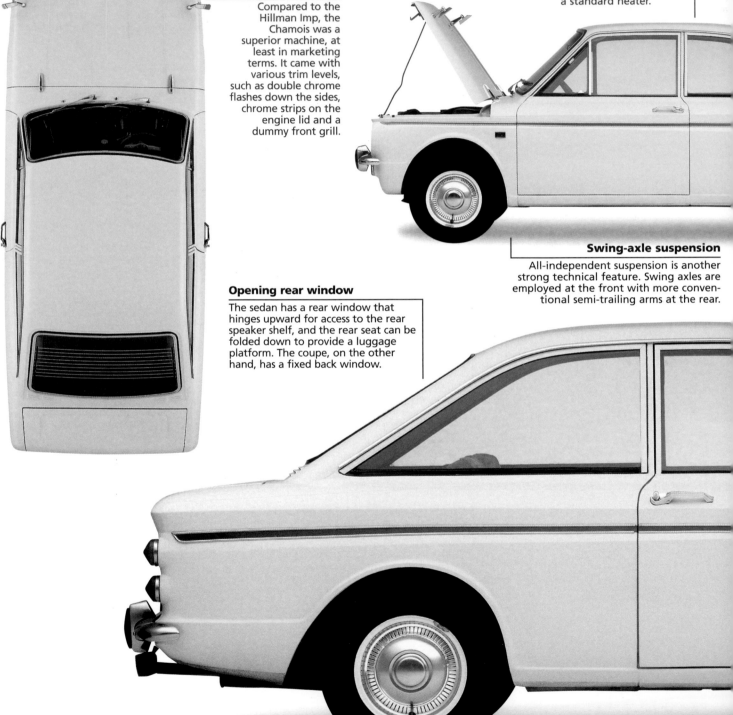

Luxury interior
The Chamois' cabin is also more luxurious than the Imp's. Superior features include extra instruments, a padded fascia, door panels and a standard heater.

Superior chrome
Compared to the Hillman Imp, the Chamois was a superior machine, at least in marketing terms. It came with various trim levels, such as double chrome flashes down the sides, chrome strips on the engine lid and a dummy front grill.

Swing-axle suspension
All-independent suspension is another strong technical feature. Swing axles are employed at the front with more conventional semi-trailing arms at the rear.

Opening rear window
The sedan has a rear window that hinges upward for access to the rear speaker shelf, and the rear seat can be folded down to provide a luggage platform. The coupe, on the other hand, has a fixed back window.

All-alloy racing engine

Although it was one of the most affordable cars on the market, the Chamois was fitted with an advanced powerplant. It was derived from a Coventry/Climax racing engine that had an overhead camshaft and aluminum construction.

1965 Singer Chamois

ENGINE

Type: Inline four-cylinder
Construction: Aluminum block and head
Valve gear: Two valves per cylinder operated by a single overhead camshaft
Bore and stroke: 2.70 in. x 2.40 in.
Displacement: 875 cc
Compression ratio: 10.0:1
Induction system: Single Solex carburetor
Maximum power: 39 bhp at 5,000 rpm
Maximum torque: 52 lb ft at 2,800 rpm
Top speed: 84 mph
0-60 mph: 22.9 sec.

TRANSMISSION

Four-speed manual

BODY/CHASSIS

Unitary monocoque construction with steel two-door sedan body

SPECIAL FEATURES

The tiny, rear-mounted, aluminum engine is surprisingly responsive.

The petite round rear lights are in keeping with the Chamois' cute looks.

RUNNING GEAR

Steering: Rack-and-pinion
Front suspension: Swing axles with coil springs and shock absorbers
Rear suspension: Semi-trailing arms with coil springs and shock absorbers
Brakes: Drums (front and rear)
Wheels: Steel, 12-in. dia.
Tires: 155 x 12

DIMENSIONS

Length: 141.0 in.   **Width:** 60.3 in.
Height: 54.5 in.   **Wheelbase:** 82.0 in.
Track: 49.1 in. (front), 47.9 in. (rear)
Weight: 1,530 lbs.

Sunbeam ALPINE

When Sunbeam revived the Alpine name after a gap of four years, the new car bore no resemblance to its namesake. Sleek and low, the new Alpine was stylish and offered excellent performance.

"...luxuriously trimmed."

"Compared to many sports cars of the period, the Alpine is quite luxuriously trimmed and it's easy to make yourself comfortable. The four-cylinder engine is very willing and pulls hard through the gears with a distinctive rasping exhaust note. The suspension gives a supple ride and predictable handling, but the live rear axle gets caught out on bumpy corners. The front disc brakes give excellent stopping ability."

A wooden and leatherette-trimmed dashboard gives the Alpine an air of luxury.

1959 The Rootes Group launches the new Sunbeam Alpine sports car. It has a 1,494-cc four-cylinder engine.

Mainly used for racing, the Alpine also competed in rallying.

1960 An improved Series II Alpine is launched with a larger 1.6-liter engine.

1963 Improved suspension and servo-assisted brakes are introduced for the Series III Alpine.

Coachbuilders Harrington fitted a fiberglass hard top.

1964 Cut-down, rounded rear fins and a new grill set the Series IV Alpine apart from its predecessors.

1965 The Series V Alpine has a 1.7-liter, five-main-bearing engine.

1968 Production ends with nearly 70,000 built.

UNDER THE SKIN

Unitary construction

Front disc brakes

Live rear axle

In-line four

Stiff structure

The Sunbeam Alpine's basic structure consists of a unitary design. Strong box sections running longitudinally and transversely, plus an extremely stiff cruciform member, maximize the shell's torsional rigidity. Suspension is by double wishbones and coil springs at the front, while at the rear there's a simple live rear axle, sprung and located by semi-elliptic leaf springs.

THE POWER PACK

Highly tuned four

The Alpine borrowed its engine from the Sunbeam Rapier sedan. Initially displacing 1,494 cc, it was highly tuned with twin carburetors, a free-flowing exhaust, and a redesigned, high-compression, cylinder head giving a gain of 10 bhp over the Rapier. The engine was enlarged to 1,592 cc for the Series II in 1960 and later to 1,725 cc for the Series V of 1965. This last engine has a stronger five-bearing crankshaft and produces 92 bhp at 5,500 rpm, with 110 lb-ft of torque at 3,700 rpm.

Two valves per cylinder

Alloy cylinder head

Cast-iron block

Three-, later five-, bearing crankshaft

Big fins

The early Series I, II and III Alpines are certainly the most striking from the British firm, with their large rear tail fins. They were designed by Kenneth Howes, who had recently returned from working in the U.S., which explains the car's modern styling.

Series I, II and III cars are recognized by their large rear fins.

Sunbeam ALPINE

The Alpine went through five incarnations during its nine-year life span. The car shown here is the last and, to many, the best, thanks to the more subtle styling and bigger, stronger five-bearing engine.

Five-bearing engine

The Series V was the only Alpine to get the five-bearing 1,725-cc version of Rootes' four-cylinder pushrod engine. With twin Stromberg carburetors and a 9.2:1 compression ratio it makes 92 bhp.

Subtle fins

The Series I, II and III Alpines had very large rear fins. These were rounded off for the Series IV to keep up with contemporary styling fashions.

Unitary construction

Unlike the separate-chassis Sunbeam Alpine of the mid-1950s, the new Alpine uses more modern unitary construction. To ensure maximum torsional rigidity, the structure is stiffened with longitudinal and transverse box sections and a very stiff cruciform member.

Soft or hard top

From the Series III model, the Alpine was available with a normal soft top. GT versions, however, had a standard hard top which made the car marginally heavier. The Series III GT actually produced less power than its soft-top counterpart due to a more restrictive but quieter cast-iron exhaust manifold.

Wishbone suspension

The Alpine uses the classic sports car setup of double-wishbone front suspension with coil springs and telescopic shock absorbers.

Overdrive transmission

The four-speed manual transmission has optional overdrive that operates in third and fourth gear.

Disc brakes

Front disc brakes were standard from the start of production and were combined with rear drum brakes.

Specifications

1967 Sunbeam Alpine Series V

ENGINE

Type: In-line four cylinder

Construction: Cast-iron block and head

Valve gear: Two valves per cylinder operated by a single camshaft via pushrods and rockers

Bore and stroke: 3.21 in. x 3.25 in.

Displacement: 1,725 cc

Compression ratio: 9.2:1

Induction system: Twin Stromberg 150CD carburetors

Maximum power: 92 bhp at 5,500 rpm

Maximum torque: 110 lb-ft at 3,700 rpm

Top speed: 100 mph

0-60 mph: 13.6 sec.

TRANSMISSION

Four-speed manual with overdrive

BODY/CHASSIS

Unitary monocoque construction with steel two-door open body

SPECIAL FEATURES

Even the later, more subtle cars are fitted with plenty of chrome.

Smart center-lock wire wheels were a popular option with buyers.

RUNNING GEAR

Steering: Recirculating ball

Front suspension: Double wishbones with coil springs, telescopic shock absorbers and anti-roll bar

Rear suspension: Live axle with semi-elliptic leaf springs and telescopic shock absorbers

Brakes: Discs (front), drums (rear)

Wheels: Wire, 4.5 x 13 in.

Tires: Dunlop RS5, 5.90-13

DIMENSIONS

Length: 156.0 in. **Width:** 60.5 in.

Height: 51.5 in. **Wheelbase:** 86.0 in.

Track: 51.8 in. (front), 48.5 in. (rear)

Weight: 2,246 lbs.

Triumph **TR4**

Triumph's first sports cars, the TR2 and TR3, were confirmed old-school roadsters, but their successor brought things right up to date with a smart Michelotti design. The TR4 remains an icon of the sports car world.

"…superb, flexible engine."

"Rugged to the point of basic, yet loads of fun is the best way of summing up the TR4. Performance is fairly strong for a car from this era, but the best way to get the most out of the TR4 is to use its superb, flexible engine. Full of torque, it can take off smoothly and vigorously in high gears and just keep on going. Cornering is good by the standards of the day, but the ride quality is poor because of the short rear suspension travel."

Although the ride is firm, the TR4 is far better appointed inside than previous TRs.

226

Milestones

1961 The public gets its first chance to see the new Michelotti-styled TR4 in September. It is well received.

1962 Thicker and wider seats are installed.

The TR3A was a big hit—most models came to the States.

1963 Carburetor choice switches from SU to Stromberg, and the front suspension geometry is revised to improve handling.

1964 The TR4 gives way to the 4A, with its new suspension, extra power, all-in-one soft top, altered grill and wooden dashboard.

The TR5 uses the TR4's body added to a straight-six engine.

1967 The TR5 takes over from the TR4A. It has the same body as its predecessor, but the TR5 is the first British production car sold in the UK to use fuel injection.

UNDER THE SKIN

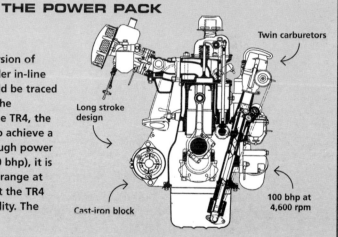

All-synchromesh transmission

Rack-and-pinion steering

Front disc brakes

In-line four

Rugged character

The chassis under the TR4's svelte body is basically the same as the TR3's channel-section chassis (which dates back to 1953), but the TR4 has rack-and-pinion steering in place of cam-and-lever. The major shortcoming of the chassis—limited rear axle movement—was not addressed until the 1965 TR4A, which has an independent rear borrowed from the 2000 sedan. American customers were offered a TR4A with leaf springs.

THE POWER PACK

Tough cookie

The TR4's engine is a newer version of Triumph's renowned four-cylinder in-line powerplant, whose origins could be traced back to a Ferguson tractor via the Standard Vanguard sedan. In the TR4, the bore is increased by .118 inch to achieve a new capacity of 2,138 cc. Although power did not go up (remaining at 100 bhp), it is developed lower down the rev range at 4,600 rpm. The best thing about the TR4 engine is its tremendous flexibility. The TR4A has an extra four bhp.

Twin carburetors

Long stroke design

Cast-iron block

100 bhp at 4,600 rpm

Independent

Choosing between the TR4 and TR4A isn't easy. The earlier TR4 is lighter and has less understeer and less body roll, but it has a harsh ride. The TR4A's independent rear end cured that at the expense of some dynamic sharpness. For daily use, the A is best.

Independent rear suspension makes the A model the most comfortable TR4.

Triumph **TR4** 🇬🇧

Triumph's sports cars always had a reputation for simplicity, ruggedness and value for the money. The TR4 continued the tradition but added a smart new body to produce a sporty classic.

Italian styling

Triumph's favorite design house, Michelotti, was called in to give the TR4 its sharp new suit of clothes. The old TR3 cut-away doors were replaced with full-length ones with proper winding windows—a TR first! The car is much wider and more practical than the TR3, too.

'Tractor' engine

The 2.1-liter four-cylinder engine's origins lie with the Ferguson agricultural tractor. It isn't a glamorous unit, but it is extremely powerful, rugged, reliable and reasonably economical.

Steel or wire wheels

The standard wheel choice for the TR4 was 15-inch perforated steel discs. As an option, you could choose classic multi-spoke wire wheels with center spinners.

Surrey top

As an alternative to the normal fold-away soft top, Triumph offered what it called a Surrey top, now known as a targa roof. This was very novel in 1961. A metal or folding fabric top was also available.

Optional overdrive

With Laycock overdrive specified as an option, there are no fewer than seven forward gears to choose from because overdrive is fitted to the top three ratios.

Traditional-style front end

The front end establishes a styling link with the popular TR3. The bug-eye headlights of the TR3 are echoed in the 4's circular front lights, shrouded by bulges in the hood.

Specifications

1962 Triumph TR4

ENGINE

Type: In-line four-cylinder

Construction: Cast-iron block and head

Valve gear: Two valves per cylinder operated by a single camshaft via pushrods and rockers

Bore and stroke: 3.38 in. x 3.62 in.

Displacement: 2,138 cc

Compression ratio: 9.0:1

Induction system: Two carburetors

Maximum power: 100 bhp at 4,600 rpm

Maximum torque: 128 lb-ft at 3,350 rpm

Top speed: 110 mph

0-60 mph: 10.7 sec.

TRANSMISSION

Four-speed manual with optional triple overdrive

BODY/CHASSIS

Separate chassis with steel two-door roadster body

SPECIAL FEATURES

The TR4 lacks the fender-mounted side marker lights of the TR4A.

The classic multi-spoke wire wheels with center spinners were offered as an option.

RUNNING GEAR

Steering: Rack-and-pinion

Front suspension: Wishbones with coil springs and shock absorbers

Rear suspension: Rigid axle with semi-elliptic leaf springs and shock absorbers

Brakes: Discs (front), drums (rear)

Wheels: Steel or wire, 15-in. dia.

Tires: 165 x 15 in.

DIMENSIONS

Length: 155.0 in.   **Width:** 57.5 in.

Height: 50.0 in.   **Wheelbase:** 88.0 in.

Track: 49.0 in. (front), 48.0 in. (rear)

Weight: 2,200 lbs.

Triumph **TR5/TR250**

By 1967, Triumph's principal sports car needed more stamina to remain competitive. It was given a larger, 150-bhp, fuel-injected engine. Naturally, more power gave the little car quicker acceleration and a higher top speed to stay ahead of its rivals.

"...all about performance."

"The six-cylinder TR has real character. Its power delivery is more than ample and its unmistakable sound lets you know that this little car is all about performance. 100 mph arrives much sooner than you'd expect. The fast-action transmission is precise, while the overdrive permits effortless top speed cruising. The chassis, however, is slightly flexible. For such a tiny car, it is brawny and aggressive, with a hard and choppy ride on all but the smoothest roads."

Triumph's trademark wooden-dash is used to particularly good effect on the TR5.

Milestones

1961 Having already modernized
the TR with Italian Michelotti styling for the TR4, Triumph makes it even more modern with the TR4A, which has independent rear suspension.

The TR5 shares its styling with the previous TR4A.

1967 It's time for more power
from the TR, and the 2.5-liter six-cylinder TR5 is born. Power output leaps from 104 bhp to 150 bhp. For the U.S. market, Triumph produces a detuned version, the TR250, with dual carburetors. It makes 111 bhp and has a 0-60 mph time of 10.6 seconds.

The Karmann-styled TR6 succeeded the TR5 in 1969.

1969 After a short
production run, the TR5 and TR250 are discontinued in favor of the new Karmann-style TR6 with the 150-bhp injected engine. Mechanically, the TR6 is identical to the TR5 and stays in production until 1976.

UNDER THE SKIN

Four-speed manual with overdrive

Rack-and-pinion steering

Box-section chassis frame

Straight six

TR evolution

Much of the TR4A was carried over to the TR5 including the box-section chassis frame, front wishbones, rear semi-trailing arms and rack-and-pinion steering. Swapping the four for a six-cylinder engine proved to be a substantial improvement. However, the car's weight distribution suffered slightly going from a perfect 50:50 with the four to 54:46 front/rear with the six.

THE POWER PACK

Room for expansion

For the TR5, Triumph took the existing Triumph 2000 straight-six engine and lengthened the stroke bringing it from 2.0 to 2.5 liters. At the same time, a new cylinder head was used. It had bigger valves and ports. It is a cast-iron engine with a single camshaft mounted in the side of the block that operates two valves per cylinder. Because of its non-crossflow design, the exhaust and intake ports were on the same side of the head. U.S. models came with twin Stromberg carbs: all other models received Lucas fuel injection.

All-iron block

Side-mounted camshaft

Two valves per cylinder

Non-crossflow design

Fuel injection connection

The TR250 has a slight power and torque advantage over the out-of-date TR4. This drastically improves the car's performance. The 150 bhp injected TR5, however, is faster than its predecessor. Both models benefit from a larger and smoother 2.5-liter straight six.

The straight six was a better all around performer than the four cylinder.

Triumph **TR5/TR250**

The very short-lived TR5 was an interim model. It continued to use the slightly antiquated style of the 1961 TR4 but with a bigger, more powerful engine. After the TR5, Triumph continued to use the big six engine in the restyled TR6, until 1976.

Six-cylinder engine

There was more involved in stretching the 2.0-liter engine to 2.5 liters than lengthening the stroke. The crankshaft was strengthened, the bearing sizes were increased and the pistons and cylinder head were updated.

Separate chassis

The TR chassis has a steel box section frame which is narrow up front to carry the engine and then it widens out to almost the full width of the car. In the center section, there are two more box-sections forming a 'backbone.'

Optional tops

Apart from the full-fabric soft-top, the TR5/250 also came with a fixed rear window with either a steel targa top or fabric 'Surrey top.'

Unfortunately, the fuel injected engine could not meet U.S. emissions regulations and came equipped with twin Strombergs.

Center fuel filler

The TR5 has a race-style, quick-release fuel filler cap mounted in the center of the body just behind the rear window. This permits the car to be refilled from either side. It is a feature first seen on the TR2 and carried over to the TR6.

Specifications

1968 Triumph TR5

ENGINE

Type: In-line six-cylinder

Construction: Cast-iron block and head

Valve gear: Two valves per cylinder operated by single block-mounted camshaft via pushrods and rockers

Bore and stroke: 2.94 in. x 3.74 in.

Displacement: 2,498 cc

Compression ratio: 9.5:1

Induction system: Lucas mechanical fuel injection

Maximum power: 150 bhp at 5,500 rpm

Maximum torque: 164 lb-ft at 3,500 rpm

Top speed: 107 mph

0-60 mph: 10.6 sec.

TRANSMISSION

Four-speed manual with overdrive

BODY/CHASSIS

Separate chassis frame with steel two-door convertible body

SPECIAL FEATURES

Front marker lights are mounted in small pods on the top of the fenders.

The smooth six-cylinder engine is what gives the TR5 its impressive reputation.

RUNNING GEAR

Steering: Rack-and-pinion

Front suspension: Double wishbones with coil springs and telescopic shock absorbers

Rear suspension: Semi-trailing arms with coil springs and lever-arm shock absorbers

Brakes: Discs, 10.9-in. dia. (front), drums, 9.0-in. dia. (rear)

Wheels: Pressed steel discs, 4.5 x 15 in.

Tires: Radial, 165 HR15

DIMENSIONS

Length: 153.6 in.   **Width:** 58.0 in.

Height: 50.0 in.   **Wheelbase:** 88.0 in.

Track: 49.8 in. (front), 49.2 in. (rear)

Weight: 2,270 lbs.

Triumph SPITFIRE

In the 1960s, Triumph needed a small sports car to rival the MG Midget. Named after a World War II fighter plane, the Spitfire was a convincing package, with sharp styling by Michelotti and enthusiastic performance.

"...agile in action."

"The Spitfire is agile in action, the four-cylinder engine works hard to produce sporty acceleration and a near-100 mph top speed. The crisp transmission invites frequent gear shifts and overdrive makes for relaxed highway driving. The steering is light and accurate, while the brakes are certainly incisive. The Spitfire's Achilles' heel, however, is its handling. The swing axle rear suspension can lead to wayward oversteer."

The Spitfire's interior is spacious compared with its rivals from MG and Austin-Healey.

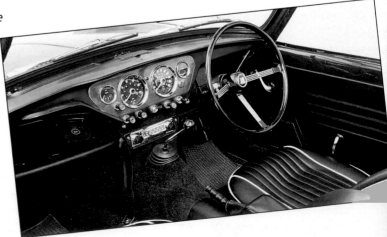

Milestones

1962 Triumph announces its new sports car—the Spitfire 4.

The GT6 was a coupe version of the Spitfire with a 2.0-liter straight-six engine.

1965 The Mk II Spitfire is launched with more power and a better cabin.

1967 Raised bumpers and a 1.3-liter engine identify the new Mk III.

1970 The Mk IV has restyled front and rear ends and revised rear suspension.

The Mk IV Spitfire was completely reskinned and was available with a 1,500-cc engine.

1973 A bigger 1,500-cc engine is fitted.

1980 Triumph retires the Spitfire—its last ever separate chassis model.

UNDER THE SKIN

Swing axle rear suspension

Front disc brakes

Separate chassis

Sedan-sourced engine

Hark the Herald

The Spitfire was based on the separate chassis of the Triumph Herald sedan to keep costs down. The Herald chassis was shortened, and as many parts as possible came from the earlier car, including the engine, steering, transmission and suspension. The swing axle rear suspension is not ideal for sports cars, and Triumph switched to revised leaf-to-pivot rear suspension for the Mk IV. Standard front disc brakes and optional overdrive were available from 1963.

THE POWER PACK

Twin-carb four

The Spitfire's powerplant dates back to the 1953 Standard Eight sedan. The original Spitfire 4 was fitted with a 1,147-cc version of this four cylinder engine, producing 63 bhp. In Mk II form power rose to 67 bhp. The Mk III, with its 1,296-cc engine, had an output of 75 bhp. Power then began to fall as a result of emission regulations: 63 bhp for the Mk IV and just 48-58 bhp in the U.S. Even the larger 1,500-cc engine did not make much impact, registering a mere 52.5-57 bhp in U.S. specification.

Two valves per cylinder

Twin carburetors

All cast-iron construction

Single camshaft

Best 'Spit'

The model preferred by collectors is the Mk III. Its 75-bhp, 1,296-cc engine makes it the fastest of all the Spitfires. It also retains more of the original styling than the later Mk IV, and has raised bumpers that were fitted to satisfy U.S. safety regulations.

The Mk III combines the sharpest styling and peppiest performance.

Triumph SPITFIRE

Compared to the cramped MG Midget, the Triumph Spitfire heralded a new beginning for sports car drivers. Nimble and agile, yet willing and exciting to drive, it became one of the best-selling sports cars of all time.

Swing-forward front end

All Spitfires feature a one-piece front end, encompassing the hood and front fenders. It swings forward for easy access to the engine and front suspension.

Improved soft-top

The Spitfire was conceived as a traditional-style British sports car with an open roof. The first Spitfires had a completely removable top. However, a much more practical soft-top arrived in 1967 on the Mk III. A detachable steel hardtop was optional.

Rack-and-pinion steering

The very light and direct steering derived from the Herald was remarkable for the tightness of its turning circle. At 23 feet, it was the tightest of any production car.

Overdrive option

No other small sports car offered optional overdrive. This Laycock device, operating on third and fourth gears, made highway cruising much more relaxed.

Michelotti styling

One of the main advantages of the Spitfire over the slab-sided MG Midget was its Italian styling by Michelotti. Michelotti was used again in 1970 to restyle the front and rear ends, notably adding a cut-off 'Kamm' tail.

Backbone chassis

The separate chassis is essentially that of a Herald but with the wheelbase shortened by 8 inches. It is a double-backbone channel-section, with outriggers to support the bodywork on each side.

Specifications

1967 Triumph Spitfire Mk III

ENGINE

Type: In-line four-cylinder

Construction: Cast-iron block and head

Valve gear: Two valves per cylinder operated by a single camshaft via pushrods and rockers

Bore and stroke: 2.90 in. x 2.99 in.

Displacement: 1,296 cc

Compression ratio: 8.0:1

Induction system: Twin carburetors

Maximum power: 75 bhp at 6,000 rpm

Maximum torque: 75 lb-ft at 4,000 rpm

Top speed: 97 mph

0-60 mph: 13.6 sec.

TRANSMISSION

Four-speed manual with optional overdrive

BODY/CHASSIS

Separate chassis with two-door open steel body

SPECIAL FEATURES

The Spitfire's wishbone suspension comes from the Herald sedan.

The bumper was raised on Mk III models to comply with U.S. safety legislation.

RUNNING GEAR

Steering: Rack-and-pinion

Front suspension: Wishbones with coil springs, shock absorbers and anti-roll bar

Rear suspension: Swing axles with transverse leaf springs and shock absorbers

Brakes: Discs (front), drums (rear)

Wheels: Spoked wires, 4.5 x 13 in.

Tires: 155/70 SR13

DIMENSIONS

Length: 149.0 in.   **Width:** 58.6 in.

Height: 44.3 in.   **Wheelbase:** 83.0 in.

Track: 49.0 in. (front), 50.0 in. (rear)

Weight: 1,680 lbs.

Triumph VITESSE

This British sports sedan and convertible was given one of the smallest six-cylinder engines ever. The Vitesse's sharp Italian styling and keen performance soon brought it universal popularity, and surprisingly low prices helped.

"…classy six-cylinder power."

"No question, the best thing about the Vitesse is its engine. Firing it up produces a satisfying rumble in front matched by a purposeful sounding exhaust note. And then there's the performance, which is more impressive than many contemporary sports cars. The handling, however, demands some care. Because of the swing-axle rear suspension, hard cornering produces severe tuck-in, which can be very scary."

The Vitesse combines a classic interior and a great engine. Early cars had twitchy handling.

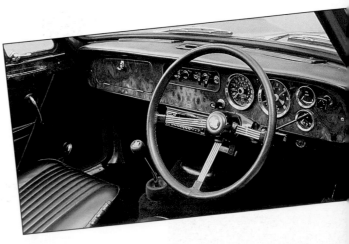

Milestones

1959 Triumph launches its new Herald small sedan, which is powered by a four-cylinder 948-cc engine.

The Michelotti-designed Herald range included a coupe version.

1962 The Vitesse is launched as a beefed-up, six-cylinder version of the Herald with a quad headlight nose.

1965 The addition of twin Stromberg carburetors boosts the power output of the 1.6-liter engine.

1966 The 2.0-liter model supercedes the 1600.

Triumph's Spitfire was the Vitesse's contemporary small sports car.

1968 Following criticisms of the handling, the MkII is fitted with rear wishbones and has an extra 9 bhp.

1971 While the Vitesse-engined Spitfire-derived GT6 continues in production, the Vitesse and Herald are axed.

UNDER THE SKIN

'Dow-tie' chassis

Bolt-on bodywork

Front disc brakes

In-line six-cylinder

A kit of parts

It is not too far from the truth to describe the Vitesse as a kit car, for all the major bodywork components are simply bolted on. Underneath lies a chassis of two curved backbone sections, splaying out toward the front and rear. The transmission is derived from the Standard Eight via the Herald, although with the option of overdrive, Wishbone/coil spring front suspension allows a tight turning circle.

THE POWER PACK

Six-cylinder punch

The peppy little in-line unit fitted to the first Vitesse was just 1,596 cc, thanks to a tiny bore of only 2.63 inches and a stroke of 2.99 inches. It was a tight squeeze to get the engine under the hood but it was a gem, outperforming other 1.6-liter engines by a mile. In 1966 the launch of the 2.0-liter version really got the Vitesse going. The 1,998 cc unit had a bigger bore that made it nearly 'square' and produced 95 bhp at 4,700 rpm. In its ultimate MkII guise, from 1968, the engine developed 104 bhp at 5,300 rpm.

Two valves per cylinder

Solex carbs later replaced by Strombergs

Cast-iron block

'Square' cylinder dimensions

MkII convertible

By 1968 the Vitesse had become a mature compact sports sedan, with its powerful 104-bhp MkII engine and proper wishbone rear suspension that transformed its handling. Of the two body styles built, the convertible is certainly the more appealing.

Late versions cured handling horrors and offered optimum performance.

Triumph VITESSE

'Vitesse' means speed in French—an apt name for Triumph's stylish compact sports sedan and convertible. No other British car could match its combination of good looks, low price and punchy pace.

Six-cylinder engine

In the early 1960s, six cylinders had never been heard of in a British compact family car. As a result, the Vitesse became an icon in much the same way that BMW's six cylinders did in Germany at this time.

Michelotti styling

Giovanni Michelotti, head of the Michelotti styling house in Italy, was responsible for designing the sharp lines of the Herald and Vitesse. He and Triumph's chief of design, Harry Webster, collaborated as early as 1957, creating the legendary tail fins.

Forward-hinging hood

The whole front section was designed to hinge forward in one piece. All you have to do is unclasp the rear base of the fenders on each side and tip the whole thing back. This opens up an unrivaled view of the engine bay, providing superb access.

Four seats

True to its economy sedan origins, the Vitesse was a proper family car, with space for four (although the convertible was more restricted). That led Triumph to use the ad line 'The Two-Seater Beater'—suggesting that their four-seater car was faster than sports car rivals.

Separate chassis

Unusually for a European car conceived in the 1960s, the Vitesse has a separate chassis. This was really due to logistics—there was no supplier able to produce a unitary body for Triumph at the time. The 'bow-tie' chassis is ultra-simple and acts as a jig to make sure the body fits correctly.

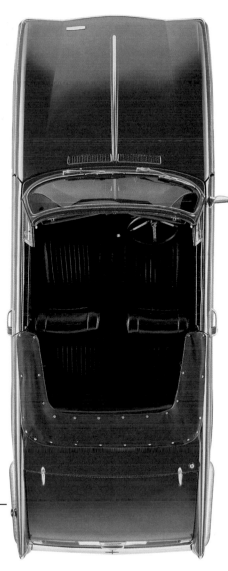

Bolt-on body

All the main body panels on the Vitesse, including the valances and roof, are just bolted on, making restoration and maintenance easy.

Specifications
1969 Triumph Vitesse 2.0-liter MkII

ENGINE
Type: In-line six-cylinder
Construction: Cast-iron block and head
Valve gear: Two valves per cylinder operated by a single camshaft via pushrods and rockers
Bore and stroke: 2.63 in. x 2.99 in.
Displacement: 1,998 cc
Compression ratio: 9.2:1
Induction system: Twin carburetors
Maximum power: 104 bhp at 5,300 rpm
Maximum torque: 117 lb-ft at 3,000 rpm
Top speed: 102 mph
0-60 mph: 11.9 sec.

TRANSMISSION
Four-speed manual with optional overdrive

BODY/CHASSIS
Separate chassis with steel two-door sedan or convertible body

SPECIAL FEATURES
The sporty look of the sloping quad headlight nose was unique to the Vitesse.

The front quarter windows betray the period when this car was first designed.

RUNNING GEAR
Steering: Rack-and-pinion
Front suspension: Wishbones with coil springs, shock absorbers and anti-roll bar
Rear suspension: Swing axles with lower wishbones, transverse leaf spring, and shock absorbers
Brakes: Discs (front), drums (rear)
Wheels: Steel, 13-in. dia.
Tires: 155 x 13

DIMENSIONS
Length: 153.0 in.   **Width:** 60.0 in.
Height: 52.5 in.   **Wheelbase:** 91.5 in.
Track: 49.0 in. (front), 48.5 in. (rear)
Weight: 2,170 lbs.

SWEDEN 1960-1971

Volvo **P1800**

Volvo is best known for its tough and boxy sedans, but it has always had a sporty side to its character. The P1800 was Volvo's first sports coupe and is a stylish-looking 2+2 with typical Swedish values of safety, quality, and reliability.

"...a smooth grand tourer."

"The P1800 is more of a smooth grand touring machine than a sports car. It is quite heavy, and performance from the five-bearing, pushrod overhead-valve 1.8-liter engine is adequate rather than exciting. Around corners the Volvo handles pretty well, with a tendency to understeer as well as plenty of roll because of its soft suspension. Perhaps the P1800's biggest drawback is its steering, which is very heavy."

The Volvo's stark cabin may not have every creature comfort, but it's quite functional and all of the gauges are easy to see.

Milestones

1960 Volvo first
shows the P1800 at the Brussels and New York Motor Shows.

1961 Production of the P1800 begins, in
Sweden, but is later switched to the Jensen factory in West Bromwich, England.

Volvo began its sporty tradition with the PV544 Sport.

1964 When Volvo switches production
back to Sweden, the model is renamed the 1800S and power is increased slightly. Roger Moore is seen driving one in the TV series *The Saint*.

Many components of the P1800 were borrowed from the Amazon.

1969 A new B20
118-bhp, 2.0-liter engine becomes standard.

1970 Bosch fuel
injection is installed, plus four-wheel disc brakes, and the model is renamed the 1800E; it survives until 1971.

UNDER THE SKIN

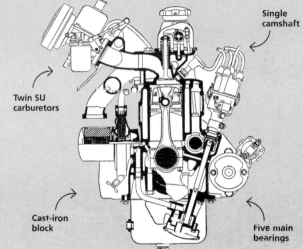

Monocoque structure

Live rear axle

Independent front suspension

Sturdy in-line four

Swedish sturdiness

The P1800 has a similar structure to the tough 120 Amazon, and uses a shortened version of its floorpan. The steel bodywork was originally made in Scotland and sent to Jensen in England for assembly. However, due to quality problems, production returned to Sweden.

THE POWER PACK

Volvo resilience

When the P1800 was announced in 1960 it was the first Volvo to be powered by the company's brand-new B18 five-bearing engine. In the P1800, the 1,780-cc, four-cylinder unit was used with twin SU carburetors and a standard oil cooler, giving it a healthy 100-bhp output. Later, the engine grew to 2.0 liters and received Bosch fuel injection for the 1969 1800E. By this stage power output was up to 130 bhp and it had more of a sporty edge.

Single camshaft

Twin SU carburetors

Cast-iron block

Five main bearings

Injection

The Volvo's final power boost came with the introduction of the P1800E in 1969. It uses a 1,986-cc engine with fuel injection to produce 130 bhp. It also has alloy wheels and a modern interior to take the 10-year-old car into the 1970s.

Bosch fuel injection boosts the power of the P1800E to 130 bhp.

243

Volvo **P1800**

Style, sporty manners, and rugged reliability make the Volvo P1800 a durable and practical sports car. With no true rivals, the P1800 is very unique.

Safety features
Volvo prides itself on high safety standards. Naturally, the P1800's standard padded dashboard was rare in the early 1960s.

English body styling
Simple body styling gives away where the P1800s were built. This car was built in England since its side body moldings turn up to the door handle and the front bumper splits in the middle. The cover car was built in Sweden.

Twin-carb engine
Volvo's tradition for powerful engines is upheld in the P1800, the first with the 1.8 liter, five-bearing B18 engine.

All-synchromesh transmission
Synchromesh on all four gears was unusual in 1961. The P1800 could also be ordered with optional overdrive, which became standard from 1963.

Galvanized bodywork
Volvo used high-quality, galvanized steel on most of the P1800's body, and applied widespread underseal. The bodies last far longer than those of other cars from the same period, and Volvo used this fact to market its cars.

Specifications

1961 Volvo P1800

ENGINE

Type: In-line four-cylinder

Construction: Cast-iron cylinder block and head

Valve gear: Two overhead valves per cylinder operated by pushrods

Bore and stroke: 3.31 in. x 3.14 in.

Displacement: 1,780 cc

Compression ratio: 9.5:1

Induction system: Two SU carburetors

Maximum power: 100 bhp at 5,500 rpm

Maximum torque: 108 lb-ft at 4,000 rpm

Top speed: 105 mph

0-60 mph: 14.0 sec.

TRANSMISSION

Four-speed manual with optional overdrive

BODY/CHASSIS

Steel monocoque with two-door coupe body

SPECIAL FEATURES

Distinctive features of the early P1800 are the cowhorn front bumpers underneath an egg-crate oval grill.

In keeping with its era, the P1800 has small chrome-tipped tail fins and attractive circular tail lights.

RUNNING GEAR

Steering: Cam-and-roller

Front suspension: Independent with wishbones, coil springs, shocks and anti-roll bar

Rear suspension: Live axle with torque arms, Panhard rod, coil springs and shocks

Brakes: Discs (front), drums (rear)

Wheels: Steel, 15-in. dia.

Tires: 165 SR15

DIMENSIONS

Length: 173 in.   **Width:** 66.9 in.

Height: 51 in.   **Wheelbase:** 96.5 in.

Track: 51.6 in. (front and rear)

Weight: 2,404 lbs.

Italian-Swedish styling

The P1800 shape was penned by the Italian studio Frua, although a Swedish designer, Pelle Petterson, carried out the initial studies.

Hydraulic front disc brakes

The sporty prowess of the P1800 is boosted by the standard Girling hydraulically-operated front disc brakes.

Volvo 120 SERIES

After the dated-looking PV cars, the 120 series (Amazon in its home market) was a breath of fresh air. It not only looked good but helped Volvo gain its reputation for producing cars with amazing reliability and strength.

"...overwhelming solidity."

"The first thing that strikes you when you get into the Volvo is its very basic interior. It's comfortable though, with supportive seats and an air of overwhelming solidity. The dash includes a horizontal speedometer, and the long shifter looks like it belongs in a truck. The four-cylinder engine isn't very smooth but it pulls strong and will cruise at 90 mph with overdrive. There is a fair amount of body roll through turns, but its roadholding is good."

The interior of the Amazon is spacious and surprisingly comfortable.

Milestones

1956 Volvo shows
its new car in September. Public response is excellent and many orders are placed. Volvo announces that the first Amazon will reach buyers at the beginning of 1957.

The Amazon was sold alongside the PV544 until 1965.

1958 An 85-bhp
Sport model is introduced. A four-speed transmission becomes available.

1959 Front safety
belts become standard equipment—an industry first.

The 140 series was introduced in 1967 to replace the Amazon.

1961 The Amazon
gains a more powerful 1.8-liter engine.

1968 A 2.0-liter
engine is also available as are dual-circuit brakes. Production finally comes to an end in 1970.

UNDER THE SKIN

Monocoque construction

Live rear axle with trailing arms

Cam-and-roller steering

Pushrod in-line four

Solid as a rock

Like the PV444 before it, the Amazon uses a rugged steel monocoque construction. It has an independent front suspension with wishbones and coil springs. At the rear there is a live axle, also suspended on coils, located by hefty trailing arms. Early examples used four-wheel drum brakes, but front disc brakes arrived in 1964. The transmission is a three- or four-speed manual. A three-speed automatic became an option in 1963.

THE POWER PACK

Strong four

The first engine used in the Amazon was the all-iron, pushrod 1.6-liter B16 unit with 60 bhp. A 1.8-liter version arrived in 1961. This engine has a stronger, five-bearing crankshaft than the older, three-bearing unit. With twin SU carburetors, power is increased to 115 bhp on the sporty 123GT. The 2.0-liter version became available in 1968. It produces up to 118 bhp and 123 lb-ft. In five-bearing form, it's a famously strong engine and is easily capable of exceeding 200,000 miles.

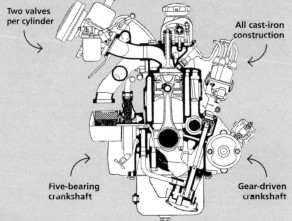

Two valves per cylinder

All cast-iron construction

Five-bearing crankshaft

Gear-driven crankshaft

Swift Swede

The most collectable of the 120-series range is the sporty 123GT. Its 1.8 liter engine with a higher compression ratio and twin carburetors gives 115 bhp—enough to propel it to around 110 mph. About 2,500 were built between 1966 and 1968.

The 123GT is the most desirable Amazon, but few were made.

247

Volvo 120 SERIES

With handsome, full-width styling by Jan Wilsgaard, and continuing Volvo's astounding reputation for reliability, the 120-series was the car that really saw Volvo's sales take off here in the U.S.

Strong engine

Volvo gained a reputation for reliability with its pushrod four-cylinder engines. This car has the 1.8-liter B18 engine with five main bearings. Twin SU carburetors take power to 90 bhp.

High build quality

High standards in the Volvo factory and the use of high-quality steel have ensured that most Amazons have stood the ravages of time remarkably well. Many unrestored cars are still in daily use.

All-coil springing

Unlike many sedans of its era, the Amazon is suspended with coil springs and telescopic shock absorbers.

Three body styles

Volvo offered the Amazon in three body styles. There were two- or four-door sedans and a five-door station wagon. Also, there was a handful of convertibles made by various coachbuilders.

Overdrive transmission

The four-speed manual transmission is supplemented by an optional Laycock de Normanville overdrive unit. Operating only in top gear, it is activated by a column-mounted shifter. Overdrive makes high-speed cruising more relaxed. An automatic transmission was optional from 1963.

Live rear axle

Like the PV series, the Volvo Amazon uses a live rear axle. It is extremely well located with large torque arms and a hefty Panhard rod.

Specifications

1965 Volvo 122S

ENGINE

Type: In-line four-cylinder

Construction: Cast-iron block and head

Valve gear: Two valves per cylinder operated by a gear-driven camshaft

Bore and stroke: 3.31 in. x 3.15 in.

Displacement: 1,778 cc

Compression ratio: 8.5:1

Induction system: Two SU carburetors

Maximum power: 90 bhp at 5,000 rpm

Maximum torque: 105 lb-ft at 3,500 rpm

Top speed: 100 mph

0-60 mph: 14.9 sec.

TRANSMISSION

Four-speed manual; optional overdrive

BODY/CHASSIS

Unitary monocoque construction with steel four-door sedan body

SPECIAL FEATURES

The 1955 Chrysler Imperial influenced the styling, especially the grill.

The parking brake is mounted between the door and the seat.

RUNNING GEAR

Steering: Cam-and-roller

Front suspension: Independent with wishbones, coil springs, telescopic shock absorbers and anti-roll bar

Rear suspension: Live axle with coil springs, torque arms, Panhard rod and telescopic shock absorbers

Brakes: Discs (front), drums (rear)

Wheels: Steel, 6 x 15 in.

Tires: Radials, 5.9 x 15 in.

DIMENSIONS

Length: 175.2 in. **Width:** 64.0 in.

Height: 59.3 in **Wheelbase:** 102.5 in.

Track: 51.5 in. (front and rear)

Weight: 2,380 lbs.

Volkswagen **KARMANN GHIA**

Although it owed much to the pedestrian Beetle, the Karmann Ghia was an altogether different proposition having unmatched style and charisma. It was a huge success, particularly in the U.S., and later inspired other manufacturers to build sporty coupes based on the standard sedan chassis.

"...responsive steering."

"With a lower body and the addition of a front anti-roll bar, the Karmann Ghia handles slightly better than the lighter Beetle. The extra weight helps prevent the car from jacking up in hard cornering and also gives a smoother ride. With its swing axle rear suspension, handling in the wet can be tricky, but the responsive steering allows for easy correction. The Karmann may not be outstandingly fast, but it is still a delight to drive."

A woodgrain dashboard was first seen in 1967 on the 1500 model.

Milestones

1955 Based on a Ghia-styled
prototype and using stock Beetle components, the first Karmann Ghia appears.

1957 A convertible is added
to the range and the Karmann Ghia gets a facelift.

The Type 3 Karmann Ghia lasted until 1969.

1962 A Karmann Ghia version
of Volkswagen's new sedan is introduced in coupe form only. It has far more aggressive styling than the original Type 1 Ghia.

The Beetle provided engines and running gear for the Type 1.

1965 A 1.3-liter
engine is standardized.

1966 Disc brakes
and a 1.5-liter engine become standard.

1973 Production ends
after 445,300 Karmann Ghias have been built.

UNDER THE SKIN

Beetle-derived

Apart from the body, the Karmann Ghia is virtually identical to the VW Beetle, with simple rear swing-axle torsion-bar suspension. The major differences are the wider floorpan and the fact that the Ghia is considerably heavier. As with the Beetle, the engine hangs out beyond the rear axle line with the four-speed manual transmission ahead of it, but is housed in a far larger engine compartment.

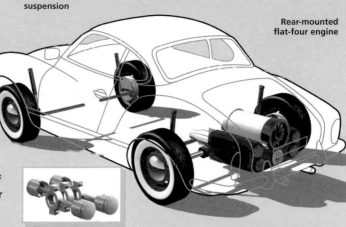

Torsion-bar suspension

Steel backbone chassis

Rear-mounted flat-four engine

Detuned flat-four

THE POWER PACK

Low compression ratio

Single one-barrel Solex carburetor

Cast-alloy block with integral crankcase

Finned alloy cylinder heads

Venerable flat four

In the early 1960s, VW's famous flat-four engine was already well over two decades old but had only reached 1,192 cc with a 34-bhp output. It was all-alloy with separate cylinder barrels and cast-iron liners under an alloy head each side. It was always deliberately detuned with a low compression ratio and mild valve timing. That was so it would last as long as possible and also run safely at full throttle for extended periods.

Cabrio

Like the Beetle, later Karmann Ghia models are easier to live with and make great daily drivers. However, collectors tend to prefer the pre-1958 cars, with the early convertible versions being the most popular choice.

The early models are the most desirable Karmann Ghia Cabrios.

Volkswagen KARMANN GHIA

The Ghia's styling showed just what could be done with the standard Volkswagen Beetle. With a minimum of mechanical changes a new body transformed the car and it stayed in production for almost 20 years.

Flat-four engine

Although the Karmann Ghia started off with the 34-bhp, 1,190-cc version of the flat-four Beetle engine, many different versions were used over the years. The final iteration was the 1,584-cc Super Beetle unit, fitted from 1970 onward.

Rear-end heavy

Despite having a rear-mounted engine and 41:59 front/rear weight distribution, the Karmann Ghia handles quite nicely, especially once drivers have learned to master it.

Four-speed manual

The Beetle's four-speed manual was the only transmission choice until 1967, when a semi-automatic became available as an option.

Convertibles and coupes

The most popular version of the Karmann Ghia is the two-door coupe, with more than 360,000 being built by 1973. The convertible looks as attractive, although the top does not fold completely out of sight; only just over 80,000 were made, however.

Front fuel tank

Like the Beetle, the Karmann Ghia has a front-mounted gas tank behind the luggage compartment. Total capacity is 11 gallons with a 1.3-gallon reserve, which could be switched through by moving a lever in the footwell.

Supercharged option

In the 1960s, the Judson Research and Manufacturing Co. of Conshohocken, Pennsylvania, offered a bolt-on supercharger for the engine, increasing power to 57 bhp.

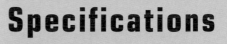

Specifications

1961 Volkswagen Karmann Ghia

ENGINE

Type: Flat four

Construction: Alloy block and heads with separate finned cylinder barrels

Valve gear: Two valves per cylinder operated by a single block-mounted camshaft via pushrods and rockers

Bore and stroke: 3.03 in. x 2.52 in.

Displacement: 1,192 cc

Compression ratio: 7.0:1

Induction system: Single one barrel carburetor

Maximum power: 40 bhp at 3,900 rpm

Maximum torque: 64 lb-ft at 2,400 rpm

Top speed: 78 mph

0-60 mph: 26.4 sec.

TRANSMISSION

Four-speed manual

BODY/CHASSIS

Modified VW Beetle floorpan with Karmann Ghia two-seater coupe or convertible body

SPECIAL FEATURES

This 1967 1500 model has been uprated with an open aircleaner.

Post-1958 cars are distinguished by their larger vents in the front panel.

RUNNING GEAR

Steering: Rack-and-pinion

Front suspension: Trailing arms with transverse torsion bars, telescopic shock absorbers and anti-roll bar

Rear suspension: Swing axles with torsion bars and telescopic shock absorbers

Brakes: Drums, 9.1-in. dia. (front and rear)

Wheels: Pressed steel discs, 5 x 15 in.

Tires: Bias-ply, 5.60 x 15 in.

DIMENSIONS

Length: 163.0 in. **Width:** 64.2 in.

Height: 59.2 in. **Wheelbase:** 94.5 in.

Track: 51.4 in. (front), 50.7 in. (rear)

Weight: 1,753 lbs.

Index